The Animal Catalyst

The Animal Catalyst

Towards Ahuman Theory

EDITED BY
PATRICIA MACCORMACK

B L O O M S B U R Y
LONDON · NEW DELHI · NEW YORK · SYDNEY

Bloomsbury Academic
An imprint of Bloomsbury Publishing Plc

50 Bedford Square	1385 Broadway
London	New York
WC1B 3DP	NY 10018
UK	USA

www.bloomsbury.com

Bloomsbury is a registered trade mark of Bloomsbury Publishing Plc

First published 2014

© Patricia MacCormack and Contributors, 2014

Patricia MacCormack and Contributors have asserted their right under
the Copyright, Designs and Patents Act, 1988, to be identified as
Authors of this work.

British Library Cataloguing-in-Publication Data
A catalogue record for this book is available from the British Library.

ISBN: HB: 978-1-4725-2684-7
PB: 978-1-4725-3444-6
ePDF: 978-1-4725-2927-5
ePub: 978-1-4725-2775-2

Library of Congress Cataloging-in-Publication Data
A catalog record for this book is available from the Library of Congress.

Typeset by Integra Software Services Pvt. Ltd
Printed and bound in India

For Steve Cain and Maria Desposito

CONTENTS

NOTES ON CONTRIBUTORS

Carol J. Adams is an American writer, feminist and animal rights advocate. She is the author of several books, including *The Sexual Politics of Meat* (now in its 20th anniversary edition) and *The Pornography of Meat* (2004). Adams has published more than 100 articles or entries in journals, books, magazines and encyclopaedias on vegetarianism, animal rights, domestic violence and sexual abuse. She is internationally recognized as one of the most influential writers on animal activism, anti-speciesism and feminism, and her work continues to influence in these areas.

Charlie Blake is an executive editor of *Angelaki: Journal of the Theoretical Humanities* and was until recently Head of the Department of Film, Media and Communications at the Liverpool Hope University. He has recently co-edited studies on *Sadism, Masochism and Philosophy*, on *Animality, Posthumanity and Transhumanism*, and has published on *Bataille and Divine Dissipation, Sonic Spectrality, the Politics of Apiasophy* and *Pornotheology*. He is currently working on studies of *Immanence and Speculative Materialism* and *Deleuze and Affect*.

Claire Colebrook is Edwin Erle Sparks Professor of English at the Penn State University. Her most recent books include *Theory and the Disappearing Future* (2012), co-authored with Tom Cohen and J. Hillis Miller, and *Death of the Posthuman* (2013).

Colin Gardner is Professor of Critical Theory and Integrative Studies at the University of California, Santa Barbara, where he teaches in the departments of Art, Film & Media Studies, Comparative Literature, the History of Art & Architecture as well as the College of Creative Studies. He is the author of *Joseph Losey* (2004); *Karel Reisz* (UP 2006); and a new critical study of Samuel Beckett's film and television work entitled *Beckett, Deleuze and the Televisual Event: Peephole Art* (2012).

Patricia MacCormack is Professor of Continental Philosophy in English, Communication, Film and Media at Anglia Ruskin University, Cambridge.

She has published extensively on Guattari, Blanchot, Serres, Irigaray, queer theory, teratology, body modification, posthuman theory, animal rights and horror film. Her work includes 'Inhuman Ecstasy' (*Angelaki*), 'Becoming-Vulva' (*New Formations*), 'The Great Ephemeral Tattooed Skin' (*Body and Society*), 'Necrosexuality' (*Queering the Non/Human*) 'Unnatural Alliances' (*Deleuze and Queer Theory*), 'Vitalistic FeminEthics' (*Deleuze and Law*) and 'Cinemasochism: Time, Space and Submission' (*The Afterimage of Gilles Deleuze's Film Philosophy*). She is the author of *Cinesexuality* and the co-editor of *The Schizoanalysis of Cinema*. Her most recent book is *Posthuman Ethics*.

John T. Maher is an attorney, author and adjunct professor of Animal Law at Touro Law Center. John studied at Harvard and Columbia Universities and is a graduate of the University of Pennsylvania, where he majored in economics. He received his J.D. from New York Law School and encourages corporate responsibility for more humane treatment of animals by his clients. John has served as counsel for the Best Friends Animal Society, Companion Animal Protection Society and various other animal organizations. He regularly speaks from a post-humanist perspective on animal issues in the areas of legal personhood for animals, synthetic biology and the effect of anthropocentric environmental change and globalization on animals. His direct interventions on the part of animals have included humans, wolves, bears, hawks, dogs, cats, rats, pigeons, deer, camels, cows, horses, raccoons, frogs and turtles.

Ruth McPhee was awarded her PhD in Film Studies from King's College, London, in 2009 and lectures in the department of English, Communication Film and Media at Anglia Ruskin University, Cambridge. She has published on feminist theory and the cinema of Catherine Breillat, and has an article (with Patricia MacCormack) forthcoming on non-reproductive semen in *InterAlia*. Her book *Female Sexuality in Contemporary Western Cinema: Masochism, Ethics and Aesthetics* is forthcoming.

Chrysanthi Nigianni is an independent researcher teaching in the sociology and psycho-social program at the University of East London. She is the editor of *Deleuze and Queer Theory* (EUP, 2009), *Deleuzian Politics* (*New Formations*, Issue 68) and *Undutiful Daughters* (Palgrave, 2012). She is currently completing a monograph on film philosophy and the notion of the exhausted.

Danielle Sands is Fellow at the Forum for European Philosophy and Visiting Lecturer at the Queen Mary, University of London, where she teaches literary theory, feminism and aesthetics. Her work has been published in *Textual Practice*, *Times Higher Education*, *Parrhesia*, *The Journal of Theoretical and Philosophical Psychology* and *The Encyclopaedia of Literary and Cultural Theory*.

Charles J. Stivale is Distinguished Professor of Classical and Modern Languages, Literatures and Cultures at Wayne State University, Detroit. He is the author of numerous books and journal articles, which include *Gilles Deleuze: Image and Text* (co-edited with Eugene W. Holland and Daniel W. Smith), *The Two-Fold Thought of Deleuze and Guattari, Intersections and Animations, The Art of Rupture, Narrative Desire and Duplicity in the Tales of Guy de Maupassant, Gilles Deleuze's ABC's, The Folds of Friendship,* and the translation of *Félix Guattari: Thought, Friendship, and Visionary Cartography, by Franco Berardi (Bifo).* He was the editor of *Gilles Deleuze: Key Concepts* and *Modern French Literary Studies in the Classroom: Pedagogical Strategies.*

Jason J. Wallin is Associate Professor of Media and Youth Culture in Curriculum in the Faculty of Education at the University of Alberta, Canada, where he teaches courses in visual art, media studies and cultural curriculum theory. He is the author of *A Deleuzian Approach to Curriculum: Essays on a Pedagogical Life*, co-author of *Arts-Based Research: A Critique and Proposal* (with jan jagodzinski), and co-editor of *Deleuze, Guattari, Politics and Education* (with Matt Carlin). Jason is Assistant Editor for the *Journal of Curriculum and Pedagogy* and reviews editor for *Deleuze Studies*. Jason was raised by wolves.

ACKNOWLEDGEMENTS

Editing this book is an inspiring reminder that there is hope for nonhuman life, and for this reason thanks go to every act of grace and compassion towards all animals exerted by humans, in whatever stage of ahumanity they may find themselves. Thanks to the marvellous and creative contributors for their patience and imaginative innovations of the topics addressed, to Carol Adams for remaining an inspiration of activism and for allowing the reprinting of her chapter, to John Maher for precision and patience, to Danielle Sands for clarity and velocity, to Charles Stivale for letting me voraciously pounce on his paper in San Francisco and claim it for this volume, to Colin Gardner, who not only contributed an incandescent piece but tirelessly proofed the final version during my Leverhulme visit to Santa Barbara, to Charlie Blake, who rightly invoked Lovecraft in our shared Necronomic dreaming, to Chrysanthi Nigianni for a last-minute addition that mesmerizes, to Claire Colebrook, another victim of my pounce, who allowed me to take her Tate paper for this volume, to Jason Wallin, who, at a moment's notice, produced a paradigm-changing work, to Ruth McPhee, my friend and many times saviour during philosophical crises who also helped complete this volume. Thanks to my editors at Bloomsbury, Liza Thompson and Rachel Eisenhauer, to Neil Jordan at Ashgate for permission to reprint, in distorted form, some of my *Posthuman Ethics*. Thanks also to Fitzy Fitzpatrick, Phil Hine, Jacinta MacCormack, Tony Moleta, Leon Tencer, activists, vegans and abolitionists everywhere, and most of all, my effulgent Watcher James Campbell Fowler and the miraculous nonhuman who allows me to share her life, Jane.

Chapter 1 reprinted with kind permission from Carol J Adams. Originally published in *The Feminist Care Tradition in Animal Ethics: A Reader*, eds. Josephine Donovan and Carol J. Adams, Columbia University Press, Copyright © 2007.

Chapter 11 adapted from 'Epilogue' and sections of the introduction adapted from Chapters 1 and 4 of *Posthuman Ethics*, by Patricia MacCormack, by kind permission of the publishers Ashgate: Farnham, Copyright © 2012.

INTRODUCTION

Patricia MacCormack

The persistently metamorphic contortions of all grammatical varieties of the word 'animal' fascinate contemporary thought in a unique way. For many connected reasons, including the most basic two – the horrified sympathy elicited via bearing witness to humanity's accursed excess of power, and the fetishization of inaccessible alterity in the face of posthumanism's existential mid-life crisis – this simultaneously meaningful and meaningless word has become a catalyst for trajectories of thought in contest with each other, epistemically and philosophically, ethically and creatively. The animal conundrum begins with the 'we' that we are as human animals – so like nonhuman animals but so unlike, depending on which rhetoric benefits humans at any given time. Shared animality laments our organic fate while it emphasizes our very capacity to define through what is a 'non' human animal. The word is insipid, seductive, dangerously useful and perhaps the ripest frontier for delivering life from the pestilence of the only true parasite – the human. This collection reconfigures the conundrum at turns, acknowledging that there are no easy solutions, but there is most definitely a need to get away entirely from this shared species of human, from which so much life, human and nonhuman, is extricated. No longer seeking inclusion, no longer validating the phantasized attractiveness of majoritarian concerns, emphasizing interconnected affectivity, *The Animal Catalyst* understands the word 'animal' as nothing more than organic life, which is shared between myriad organisms, their expressions and affects, and nothing less than an absolute refusal of the word in all its incarnations (too often incantations): 'human'. Animal does not replace human. The ethical and creative inspirations catalysed by stepping outside of human-ness engender connectivities which may foster new openings for the liberty of nonhuman life, while simultaneously producing incomprehensible emergences of formerly human life lived singularly and differently, based on the very premise of connectivity and multiplicity of the unlike or unnatural (because for the human all non-parasitic nonhuman connections are unnatural). If *'affects are the becoming inhuman of man'* (Deleuze & Guattari 1994: 169), then man must pass through inhumanity towards ethics. This book suggests as a term for encountering the outside of human the word 'ahuman', inspired by Guattari's statement: 'In the last resort what will be determinant in the political and aesthetic plane is not the words and the content of ideas but essentially a-signifying messages that escape dominant ideologies' (Guattari 1996: 154). Ahuman verges on a nothing that includes everything. It utilizes our animalness in a non-speciesist way to remind us there are escape routes from humanism which may encourage ethical relations, not by knowing, fetishizing or making an idea of an animal, but because when there is no human there is no deferral to human signifying systems. Just as this book is premised on an absolute abolitionist stance on all interaction with – conceptually and actually – any nonhuman, the concept term 'ahuman' is an absolute abolitionist refusal of the human.

Then what of this word 'animal' which endless things have in common? Deleuze explicates Spinozan ethics through the concept of common notions:

> In short a common notion is the representation of a composition between two or more bodies, and a unity of this composition…For when we encounter a body that agrees with ours we experience an affect or feeling of joy-passion, although we do not adequately know what it has in common with us…(1988: 55, 56)

Crucial to Deleuze's definition of ethics borne of common notions is that each element or entity does not come to the relation already fixed in their qualities, which will therefore either be or not be clearly commensurable with the other. Deleuze emphasizes that a defining element of the experiencing of affects of joy comes from an encounter even when we do not (or cannot) know the commonality from which the affects arise. This requires that we think carefully what is meant by 'commonality'. Refining this ethic, commonality can be interpreted not as resemblance but by the openness of each element to experiencing the other as self and thus self as other. 'Now rejecting this way of defining by kind and specific difference', explains Deleuze,

> Spinoza suggests a completely different way, linked to common notions; being will be defined by their *capacity for being affected*, by the affections of which they are capable, the excitations to which they react, those by which they are unaffected, and those which exceed their capacity and make them ill or cause them to die. In this way one will obtain a classification of beings by their power. (1988: 45)

Defining, signifying, classifying and placing into a hierarchy certain kinds of life is an act which is based not on the quality or essence of an entity but on the powers which constitute the capacity to define. In this exertion to detrimental effect, the human exceeds par excellence. Enriching ethical encounters are also expressions of power. From a Spinozan perspective power as 'potestas', as imposing structure 'Power', operates via a ubiquitous territory pre-established by the dominant but never exhaustively or externally known (in this sense man making himself God). Gracious ethical expressions acknowledge all affects are the result of power, but power as 'potentia', deterritorializing force in the world 'power' – not oppositional or conflicting but the communion of difference itself and the self which expresses as a coalescence of the forces which in turn have produced it. Affective expressions which elicit joy and novel passions emerge through each entity's capacity to act and be affective not as what they are but *that* they are. This book offers novel interactions. By virtue of openness to the alterity of the other, commonality is reduced to the majestic but simple notion of openness itself. Encounters are not conditionally based on pre-conceived definitions of the other to which one comes. This would mean the other is experienced before the event of experience and thus the other as a singularity is denied their specificity. An encounter with the pre-conceived is no encounter, but a reification of self through confirmation of opposition or commonality based on structures that by their very definition cannot locate two entities without one subsuming the other through exertions of the power to define. Insipid claims to these resolutions offering some nonhuman species their freedom define freedom – both human and nonhuman – in a flawed way. Lyotard's exploration of freedom inflects with Spinoza's definition of will and appetite as that which allows the other to flourish in their capacity to express and be affected in a way which benefits their living and their own appetites and will. Spinoza's concept of the activity to express is through a tactical, always impossible but still sought expectation of expanding the other's capacity to express through the self's affects. Lyotard offers *You are able to*, 'a partial silence, as a feeling, as respect' (1988: 121). This silence comes both through opening to the expressive potential of the other and as the silence inherent in seeking to create liberating affects in the other but acknowledging there is no guarantee or dividend. *You are able to* should always be an *I am able to so you are able to*. This ensures obligation remains with the 'I'. 'You' is diminished as a comprehensible addressee to a life with will and appetite unknown but to which we are obliged without demanding obligation or reciprocity.

> The entity harbouring this spontaneous causality [which is neither principle nor demand] cannot be the addressee. The latter receives the announcement of spontaneity in the form of [quoting Kant] 'dependence', 'constraint' or 'coercion'. The addressee is not the one who is able to. The addressor is the one who is able to, who is the power. (Lyotard 1988: 121)

If the addressor makes ability a compulsory obligation, he or she returns to the *you ought to*. At this time the reification of the empowered 'I' – the human – also returns. The 'I' that asks what it is able to do without legitimating edict is the ahuman ethical 'I'. When we are able to give the nonhuman animal their *you are able to*, which we must do without condition or expectation, we give freedom to both ourselves and the other. The word gift is the ethical spontaneity, for which a better word is conceptually preferable but within a posthuman abolitionist vocabulary, perhaps not yet available. Grace comes from the ethical turn to the 'I am able to' which acknowledges the most beneficial, most liberating ability is to leave be, to turn away from the addressee where turning away opens to the addressee being something unto itself other than an addressee. Grace turns away from the addressee to open to the world without addressor or addressee, obligation without object or subject, freedom without the free. 'What is invoked in the phrase of freedom is not a power in the sense of an eventuality, but one in the sense of an ability to act, that is, an ability to be a first cause from the cosmological point of view' (Lyotard 1988: 121). Our obligation to leave the nonhuman life alone from an activism perspective still obliges us to turn towards the other human, to make demands not of *you ought* but *you are able to* because speciesist humans think they are either unable to live without animal slavery, torture and murder, which is fallacious, or in the overwhelming face of animal (ab)use in all facets of human life they think they are unable to do anything because they really seek to tell the other human *you ought to*. Command and response evince a lack of freedom, of will, of appetite. But the submission most humans give to the *you ought to* shows that ability takes efforts of corporeality and imagination, while succumbing to command fosters the luxuries of apathy, many of which masquerade as a demand of the 'I' for the 'right' to (ab)use. The right to dominance claimed by humans is the individual's exploitation of the perception of the *you ought to* as being *you must* but is actually *you are able to but choose not to*. The dominating structures of capital which perpetuate torture, slavery and murder of nonhumans also perpetuate human belief in the incapacity to be able to not to do so. But humans are able to, and most ethically, are able to through not – not enslaving, not cannibalizing, not torturing. Ethics never mistakes the *I can* for the *I must* or becomes involved in the question tennis which oscillates endlessly between the *why* and the *why not*. Ahuman philosophy begins towards the nonhuman with the *I will not* which creates the *I am not all* thus *I am not, so the other may be*.

Ethical encounters are jubilant, joyous encounters of both affectivity and liberty. Anxiety is also present in ethics: these two passions are the wonders of ethics in its non-dismembered consistency. A number of constellations initialize this emergence. There is anxiety in forsaking privileged positions and annexations to reliable significations but there is also anxiety in jubilance, trepidation in liberty, while in the cliché of fear of the unknown the fear is as exhilarating and creative as the jubilance is frightening by facilitating an encounter with a beyond. Jubilant may sound idealistic and redemptive, anxiety a kind of capital hysteria. The passions and affects of ethics are extensive – rather than leap to overcome them we reel in that we thought we should avoid, because, especially for the oppressed other, all too often the less-than-human minoritarian, and most especially the nonhuman animal, there is no luxurious avoidance of diminishing affects. The aim is aimless, the act matters and is the matter of the ethics.

Serres states:

> The declaration of the rights of man had the merit of saying 'every man' and the weakness of thinking 'only men' or 'men alone' ... objects themselves are legal subjects and no longer mere material for appropriation ... law tries to limit abusive parasitism among men but does not speak of this same action among things. (2002: 37)

Refusing man as deserving of rights comes from refusing rights defined by man, a self-perpetuating mode of perception. Human apprehension and comprehension cannot limit nonhumans within an ethical relation. Radical animal rights is increasingly becoming fed up with 'thinking' the animal, even through antispeciesist philosophy, as it elucidates the luxuriant arguments in which humans indulge in the name of the rights of 'them' and 'us' based on qualities of each or critiquing the qualities ascribed to each, yet remaining within a realm that speaks *of*, thus speaks *for*, and ultimately speaks with human language. Maintaining speech within the limits that human language compels is the crux of all argument. It implies a shared language. Further from the repudiation of animal rights based on equivalence which antispeciesism has foregrounded, in order to create an ethics of the inevitable shared living with nonhumans, only the human can and needs to be deconstructed and the human's trajectories towards ahumanism have nothing to do with other life. If this were the technique of ahumanism, it would simply constitute a reverse of dragging nonhumans up to human level to be viable and resemble the revolting fetishization of animals in human becomings through continued 'use', conceptually and actually.

> The tree and cow told us that man never returned or recognised the gifts of flora and fauna. He uses and abuses them but does not exchange with them. He gives food to the animals you say. Yes sir he gives the flora to the fauna, fauna to the fauna ... what does he give of himself? Does he give himself to be eaten? The one who does so will utter a timeless word. One word, *host*. (Serres 2007: 82)

Any configurative thinking of nonhuman entities in posthuman and to an extent transhuman theory (a clear trend in current posthuman publications) fails the very premise of its ambition, no matter how amorphous or experimental. Thinking the nonhuman ethically should, indeed can, only concern itself with the human and its decentred and delimited futures, in order to create hope in reference to inevitable, perhaps unfortunate (not for humans, often for nonhumans) encounters with nonhumans. This may sound nihilistic and certain responses are presumed that come from a variety of fields of interaction, from Haraway and Derrida (and his cat) to art which uses animals, poststructural philosophies which colonize non-mammalian species structures, sci-fi film and literature and modern primitivism – 'of course animals enjoy interactions with humans' or 'we can help as much as hurt', 'animal systems can teach us how to be posthuman', or the most basic question: 'we need to think differently about animals'. No. We need to think about the undoing of us, whatever that means. From the irrefutably important work done by animal rights philosophers and activists, unfortunate in its necessity, seeking equality, thinking needs to go further enough to accept thought itself as inherently unethical in reference to the nonhuman. The simplest premise of this book's perhaps dubiously ambitious argument on the human's ahuman future vis-à-vis the nonhuman comes from Serres's devastatingly hopeful and demanding concept of grace –

> whoever is nothing, whoever has nothing, passes and steps aside. From a bit of force, from any force, from anything, from any decision, from any determination ... Grace is nothing, it is nothing but stepping aside. Not to touch the ground with one's force, not to leave any trace of one's weight, to leave no mark, to leave nothing, to yield, to step aside ... to dance is only to make room, to think is only to step aside and make room, give up one's place. (1995: 47)

Non-parasitic recognition is the turning away with grace, making no demands of the addressee's face; exchange comes from disanchoring the parasitic human and reciprocity is human absence. Serres, discussing dance as philosophy and philosophy as a dance, elaborates that dance negotiates nakedness, the unwritten tablet, the absent man. We can then speak of philosophy's liberation from situatedness (no matter how multiple or mobile) to dance, where seeking nothingness is antithetical to nihilistic nothingness, rather a means by which we can become capable of anything, and that very capacity results in the freedom of real responsibility, far from the freedom to do what we can as dominant humans, to allow the nonhuman to be.

While interactions with nonhumans must be creative, pleasurable and confounding, the contract precedes and constitutes the elements, making the categories of nonhuman and ahuman tactical. 'The object here is a quasi-object insofar as it remains a quasi-us. It is more a contract than a thing ... not a quasi-subject but a bond' (Serres 1995: 88). Gracious ahuman-nonhuman/animal contracts attempt to make the bond its most flexible, seeking a catalyst with which the interaction is made that comes from no human source, unheard of matter in a singular emergence and connecting in ways for which human vocabulary has no verbs or nouns. The nonhuman only remains such tactically, the ahuman experimentally. The nonhuman animal subject is still a different kind of quasi-object. It is independent from the ahuman quasi-object that the human is becoming. Humans do not find ethical animal encounters in the faux simpering claim that 'humans are just/ also animals'. To say so would erode the histories of violence for which we must be accountable, in whatever ways we negotiate the positive affects of the challenges of bearing witness and responsibility. In a perverse turn, where discussing animal rights is unethical because it uses the animal as currency within human rhetoric, accountability and bearing witness is, after all, for and between humans. Nonhuman animals are not benefitted by such human discourse, even though it is apologetic and seeks to make amends. Amending the history of the excesses of indescribable violence perpetrated on nonhumans comes as a step towards ahuman becomings, elucidating the detrimental effects of human discourse and thus the urgent need to forsake it and the powers which it affords. It is perhaps the why that catalyses ahumanism without concretizing genealogy or origin that predicts future or finitude. Both the nonhuman animal and the ahuman, through the ethical bond, become nothing, but nothings of different orders. The nonhuman animal is nothing as it is unthinkable, and nothing because it should be avoided in order to prevent human intervention in nonhuman worlds, even if they overlap. It is however everything and sufficient to itself and must be treated thus. The ahuman is nothing as it is also unthinkable, but involves thinking multiply and otherwise. Against all claims we need to rethink animals, the only gracious ethics of nonhuman relation is to absolutely cease all thought which includes animals and rethink the humanity that constitute thought itself. 'The teaching corps, like the dancing corps and the thinking subject, is forever evoking, forever invoking, calling, another focus than itself. So naked, so blank, so empty, so absent that it brings forth a presence' (Serres 1995: 45).

What catalyses ahumanity? 'Nameless words. Verbs without nouns…. rhythm is a fluctuation of the rhesis, the surge … to speak of these transports as positive, negative, is mere naïve anthropomorphism. The multiple moves, that is all' (Serres 1995: 101, 69, 101). This book is an experiment in movement, aware of the fatality of its own compulsion to speak, but attempting nonetheless through the multiple voices of the experimenters (though not authors) to see with a cosmic eye new cosmogenic territories which are incommensurable with the human as it is understood in its dominant mode.

We are thus in the presence of two polar modalities of consciousness: that of pseudo-territorialities of resonance and that of an irrevocable deterritorialization; that of tranquilising (and reassuring) faces and significations and that of anxiety without object, or rather, an anxiety which aims at the *reality* of nothingness … It is a question of neutralising, by reducing them, the '*n*' animal, vegetal and cosmic eye of the rhizomatic possible which could subsist within residual territorialized assemblages … the media install a vanishing point behind every glance. (Guattari 2011: 82–3)

The first section of *The Animal Catalyst* initiates new interpretations of a variety of usual suspects – rights, law, equivalences with human suffering and the dominant authorial voices in these fields. Carol Adams elucidates the perils of making equivalencies with genocide by pointing out precisely that the idealized figure of the human was never a victim of genocide and this allowed such atrocity to begin with, so that 'after the fact' raising of subjects to positions of humanity from where they can be mourned perpetuates the oppression of the nonhuman in its anthropomorphic minoritarian guise and its not-human-species incarnations. She makes a plea for compassion itself, invoking the crucial need for a paradigm shift in perception as an ethical expressivity in order to apprehend life and its worthiness to be without qualification, a feminist initially but ahuman ultimately project, in that structuration of subjects is the enemy of compassion. John Maher shows the ways in which the human compulsion to structuration of subjectivity continues to plague abolitionist animal theory by perpetuating rights as equivalence ideologies in a variety of legal situations. Through a series of fascinating case studies and analyses of the laws of various countries, Maher offers frontline material examples of the aggressive and detrimental ways in which discourse not only shapes reality but perpetuates violence through an obsession with a return to the human as the template for both constitution and comprehension of anything outside of itself. Taking up the most frequently addressed theorists of the animal in contemporary thought, Danielle Sands navigates how, with the best of intentions animal theory via writers such as Haraway, Derrida and others remain within a dialectic logic of alterity that is essentially bordering on a narcissistic mirror where the animal's absolute otherness compels the human towards either assimilation or self-reflection, rather than grace. Sands's sympathetic critical reading brings together some of the more compelling new models of animal thought and her insightful, elegant criticism offers an indispensable overview of the status of the animal now and why these theories remain atrophied in their own fatally human significations.

The second section of *The Animal Catalyst* offers a series of dances with entities and movements which may or may not be animal but which are defiantly exemplary of becomings-inhuman (as far as that which cannot operate as an exemplar can express nonetheless). As Derrida and Haraway maintain a certain camp in animal studies, Charles Stivale introduces the importance of philosophers such as Deleuze and Guattari in thinking the animal as a concept without thinking an animal as a fetishization via human perception. Stivale's amusing and scathing deconstruction of Haraway's equally vitriolic misreading of Deleuze and Guattari's becoming-animal shows that becoming-animal is only, and always, about humans repudiating humanity, not about co-opting animals for human postmodern experiments in subjectivity. This absolutely central trope of becoming-animal has too often been misunderstood or turned into a variety of trite experiments which continue to make animals metaphors for human identities, no matter how experimental. Stivale shows the inherent ahuman philosophy behind becomings-animal and a certain troubling pre-established human compulsion in those who choose interaction over grace in their concern for nonhuman life, no matter how benevolent this may seem. Colin Gardner then transfers philosophy and becomings into the Paris underground and introduces the first of the art catalysts of the book, the cinematic ahuman incarnations in Raymond Queneau and Louis Malle's *Zazie dans le Métro*. Via transformed regimes of perception which privilege movement over form, and where intensities are enhanced while subjects diminish, Gardner's writing infects the reader to extend the ways in which cinema's despotic elements infect the spectator through shared rhythms and fluxes of screen catalysts of animality and ahumanity. This creates a theatre of connectivity, a new plane that does not demarcate representation from action and affect, and that incites imagination through the inevitable becomings that the alternate and varying intensities within the film and between screen and spectator incite through relinquishing traditional signifying practices. In an enigmatically pseudo-autobiographical piece which includes apocryphal ficto-criticism, Charlie Blake is at once multiple authors traversing and therefore showing up the myth of metaphor versus real, fiction versus analysis, creative versus reflective, in his enigmatic essay of werewolves, non-Euclidean fractal zones and found arcane literature documenting one academic's ahuman Lovecraftian journey. This is a thoroughly ahuman journey in that there is neither genesis nor destination, the experiences as fragmentary as the found testament, the genus or species of animalities belonging to a cosmic, too ancient or too futuristic to be apprehended, genealogy. Blake's writing is its own form of ahuman episteme, an orphaned hybrid philosophical aberration which does not merely explore catalysts but reads like a chapter from an ahuman necronomicon and is sure to itself catalyse unheard of becomings. Chysanthi Nigianni brings the reader to literature and an almost delirious ecstasy of ahumanity informed as much by woman's status as never-was-human-thus-already-is-ahuman as the ways in which abject animals when liberated from fetishization and ownership through human perception can lead thought along paths of libidinality which collapse desire, sex, art and death. Introducing the theme of death as effervescent – not the death of the human as finitude but rather the opening out of existence towards new modes of being through the materiality of words as flesh and ideas as lovers – Nigianni romances Clarice Lispector *The Passion According to G.H.* with French feminism to affirm that the mention of animals need not subsume, but can catalyse other-wordly ahumanities within the human without detriment, and with love – of the other and of multiples within the self.

The third section of *The Animal Catalyst* takes as its premise the over-valuation of human life as it is understood and asks what alternatives occur when actual human materiality is harmed, reconfigured and ultimately ended. Unique to this project, however, ideas such as harm, destruction and extinction, as they are being applied to the human rather than the more common fact of the human afflicting nonhuman lives with these phenomena, are not detrimental, but are given as nuanced, ethical but irrefutably radical, suggestions. Claire Colebrook, like Nigianni, emphasizes the materiality of art beyond representation or metaphor. Extending this, Colebrook suggests art can only occur in the nonhumanity of humans, that is, the human must cease to exist, commit a suicide of knowledge and subjectivity, in order to create and encounter art. Arguing ferociously against the philosophies of animality from Aristotle to Derrida as *a priori* hierarchical, Colebrook at once urges means to end nonhuman suffering and catalyses an imperative to artistic creativity via rethinking what suicide means. Post-structuralism as the 'death of…' everything is turned around, as Colebrook illustrates, via the art and poetry of William Blake, so that only through stripping away both humanism and definitions of human life qualified against animal others can art come into being, showing that we can never know life, animal or subject. This never knowing makes thought itself possible. Jason Wallin connects the importance of relinquishing human knowledge for the opening of thought to the material reality of contemporary pedagogy, the classroom, and the techniques of training that enflesh both speciesism, humanism, real life suffering of nonhuman animals and the stripping away of possibilities of ahumanity in schoolchildren through the infliction of human paradigms which close thought. In a much needed and timely essay, Wallin draws together issues of disability, biotechnology, torture and murder of animals for teaching and medieval wolf-children and monsters of mud. Ultimately proposing a dark pedagogy, Wallin beautifully shows that ahuman activism and philosophy are co-emergent and need not return to reified strategies but can continually transform to the extent that the human itself lets its compulsion to repetition of its own model dissipate towards ahuman ethical pedagogy facilitated by different cartographies of animal ahumanity. Ruth McPhee picks up a key component for the exhausted harm arguments of rights ideologies and turns them in upon the human who by selecting, through an ahuman mode of agency, a reconceptualization of harm, autonomy and the over-valuation of human biophysiological regimes of signification such as skin, 'harms' in order to experience existence otherwise. Self-harm, bound and suffocated by epistemes which exert ownership upon bodies by telling them who they are, is a schizoaffective experimental expressivity which McPhee shows, is limitless in both its incarnations and also the nature of what the body can experience before it is 'harmed'. This evinces that human signification sees material harm primarily through harming the concept of the integrated sanctity of the human. Self-harm can only be defined thus when the self being harmed is a concept owned and operated by the human majoritarian observer. Without unnecessary vindication or celebration, but with an indulgence in the magnificence of the potentials of flesh to offer infinite intensities that escape binaries of good/bad, pain/pleasure, normal/pathological, McPhee gives a unique critical rewriting of self-harm. In the final chapter, I posit human extinction as a vitalistic, ethical, joyous opportunity to both live the life immanent to us and prevent the detrimental expressions and affects of any further human lives to come. Far from nihilistic, extinction in my chapter validates what this life we have is. Should it wither, life immanently lived is one of unique intensities and qualities, not extended indefinitely for the sake of being a living being, but rather life as an opportunity to care and fix whatever damage we can, while assuring a new world delivered from the human. Ultimately for any who seek the creation of a new world, I argue that this is the only way a truly ahuman existence can be guaranteed, where the nonhuman is the whole world and the human need not reflect any longer, but is simply absent. It is abolitionism taken to its only valid conclusion. Contentious but simple, finite yet affirmatively celebratory, an ahuman world can value the lives lived without lamenting those that never will be. There is no murder or suffering here, only a cessation of reproduction of the human conceptually and actually, and a slowing of the velocity of generations so this world comes to be cared for. The life lived now is enriched manifold when it is lived in immanence and with creative potentializations determining its nature rather than a necrophilosophical drive for eternity through extension, be it via extension of one's own life or through reproduction. The right to breed humans is nothing compared to the ahuman grace of not doing so. Deleuze and Guattari point out that leaving being human is the only way to exist ethically as a cosmogenic part of the universe:

> Goodbye, I am leaving, I won't look back at infinity, these refrains must rejoin the songs of the molecules, the newborn wailings of the fundamental elements … they cease to be terrestrial, becoming cosmic … [a] molecular pantheistic cosmos. (1987, 327)

Only through gracious departure can connective life be present.

The Animal Catalyst belongs to no single discourse. It is a collection of unbelongings which are designed to be a humble intervention into the wondrously difficult project of our own extrication from the value of belonging to this constructed concept of the human species. While that concept has never been stable, even within the strictures of transcendental humanism, but especially in the age of post-, trans- and biotechno-humanism, there comes a time where the term itself acts as a ligature which needs to be cut rather than contorted. The unspoken acknowledgement in contemporary animal texts that we never were and are already beyond human may be a philosophical given, but our power inclinations, our operations of desire, no matter how 'post-' we get, remain stubbornly driven by a particular collective of intensities of desire that are more human than ever – that is, more excessive in their exertions of majoritarian power and the maintenance of particular strata of dominance where humans operate, discursively and affectively, the world and its many variations of lives, rather than being within a cosmogenic connective tissue describable as this world. Terms such as 'species' – any species, ours or otherwise – maintain relations based on extrication, order and dominance. Ahumanity in its destruction of the human kills off nothing; it redistributes without a map and opens life to itself: living things become viable in each exquisite singularity. Humanism, in its monomaniacal excavation towards absolute knowledge of what we are, was already a necrophilosophy even before posthumanism's death of man, history, truth and subjectivity. Ahumanity's not-knowing is relationality operated through grace.

> We maintain relations with things without relation ... if we are alive, it is because we know, because we hope that the unforeseeable will happen, that it will be unconnected to what is already there or already assembled ... If history took its orders from one or a few laws, we would be reduced to *what we think the brute animals are* ... You are afraid of your anguish, you rush to exchange it for your money, so it will be comparable with and measurable by the general equivalent ... The most precious thing we have, the most precious thing about us, are those shifts that shred us to bits. (Serres 1995: 134, emphasis added)

Serres majestically exhibits that our human understanding of how animality is constituted is only ever driven by the inherent limits and strictures of human knowledge itself. Animality is the unknowable and unknown (and never to be known). Thus far, most work on animals ultimately comes down to working on ideas which are essentially human symptoms. Nonhumans don't care. We must learn not to be like 'them' because 'they' are only ever an expression of what we are limited to perceive based on human laws of apprehension. But we can become unlike ourselves in order that a grace towards other lives creates relations of unknowing ethical expressivity and affect. By shredding ourselves to bits, dying to human-ness, we encounter life itself as the adventurous event and open the world to the ambitious hope of lives beyond and without the human being able to flourish in their own imperceptible ways.

New Abolitionist Approaches

PART ONE

New Abolitionist
Approaches

CHAPTER ONE

The War on Compassion

Carol J. Adams

In our lifetime, what was not supposed to happen 'ever again' – genocide – has instead happened again and again. As Samantha Power shows in *A Problem from Hell* (2002), her study of genocide in the twentieth century, the perception of genocide is all in the framing. Governments acting against a minority want the violence to be perceived as civil war or tribal strife, as quelling unrest and restoring order, as a private matter that does not spill over into the international community. Other governments weigh their own national interests against the needs of those being killed. After watching the movie *Hotel Rwanda* and as I began reading *A Problem from Hell*, among the many disturbing questions that surfaced for me, besides the obvious one – 'How could we have let this happen?' – was the question, How can we get people to care about animals when they do not even care when people are being killed? But as this question came to mind, I realized that it was the wrong one because it accepts a hierarchy of caring that assumes that people first have to care about other people before they care about animals and that these caring acts are hostile to each other. In fact, violence against people and that against animals is interdependent. Caring about both is required. While I could not read about genocide without thinking about the other animals and what humans do to them, I am sophisticated enough to know that this thought is experienced as an offense to the victims of genocide. However, I am motivated enough to want to ask more about the associations I was thinking about and sensing because human and animal are definitions that exist in tandem, each drawing its power from the other in a drama of circumscribing: the animal defining the human, the human defining the animal. As long as the definitions exist through negation (human is this, animal is not this, human is not that, animal is that – although what is defined as human or animal changes), the inscription of human on something, or the movement to be seen as human (for example, Feminism is the radical notion that women are human), assumes that there is something fixed about humanness that 'humans' possess and, importantly, that animals do not possess. Without animals showing us otherwise, how do we know ourselves to be human?

Despite all the efforts to demarcate the human, the word 'animal' encompasses human beings. We are human animals; they, those we view as not-us, are non-human animals. Discrimination based on colour of skin that occurs against those above the human–animal boundary is called racism; when it becomes unspeakably murderous, it is called genocide. Discrimination by humans that occurs against those below the human–animal boundary is called speciesism; when it becomes murderous, it is called meat eating and hunting, among other things. The latter is normalized violence. Is it possible that speciesism subsumes racism and genocide in the same way that the word 'animal' includes humans? Is there not much to learn from the way normalized violence disowns compassion? When the first response to animal advocacy is, 'How can we care about animals when humans are suffering?', we encounter an argument that is self-enclosing: it re-erects the species barrier and places a boundary on compassion while enforcing a conservative economy of compassion; it splits caring at the human–animal border, presuming that there is not enough to go around. Ironically, it plays into the construction of the world that enables genocide by perpetuating the idea that what happens to human animals is unrelated to what happens to non-human animals. It also fosters a fallacy: that caring actually works this way. Many of the arguments that separate caring into deserving/undeserving or now/later or first those like us/then those unlike us constitute a politics of the dismissive. Being dismissive is inattention with an alibi. It asserts that 'this does not require my attention' or 'this offends my sensibility' (that is, 'We are so different from animals, how can you introduce them into the discussion?'). Genocide, itself, benefits from the politics of the dismissive. The difficulty that we face when trying to awaken our culture to care about the suffering of a group that is not acknowledged as having a suffering that matters is the same one that a meditation such as this faces: 'How do we make those whose suffering does not matter, matter?'

False mass terms

All of us are fated to die. We share this fate with animals, but the finitude of domesticated animals is determined by us, by human beings. We know when they will die because we demand it. Their fate, to be eaten when dead, is the filter by which we experience their becoming 'terminal animals'. The most efficient way to ensure that humans do not care about the lives of animals is to transform non-human subjects into non-human objects. This is what I have called the structure of the absent referent (Adams 2000: 51). Behind every meal of meat is an absence: the death of the non-human animal whose place the meat takes. The absent referent is that which separates the meat eater from the other animal and that animal from the end product. Humans do not regard meat eating as contact with another animal because it has been renamed as contact with food. Who is suffering? No one.

In our culture, meat functions as a mass term (Quine 1960; Adams 1994: 27), defining entire species of non-humans. Mass terms refer to things like water or colours; no matter how much of it there is or what type of container it is in, water is still water. A bucket of water can be added to a pool of water without changing it. Objects referred to by mass terms have no individuality, no uniqueness, no specificity, no particularity. When humans turn a non-human into 'meat', someone who has a very particular, situated life, a unique being, is converted into something that has no individuality, no uniqueness, no specificity. When five pounds of meatballs are added to a plate of meatballs, it is more of the same thing; nothing is changed. But taking a living cow, then killing and butchering that cow, and finally grinding up her flesh does not add a mass term to a mass term and result in more of the same. It destroys an individual. What is on the plate in front of us is not devoid of specificity. It is the dead flesh of what was once a living, feeling being. The crucial point here is that humans transform a unique being, and therefore not the appropriate referent of a mass term, into something that is the appropriate referent of a mass term. False mass terms function as shorthand. They are not like us. Our compassion need not go there – to their situation, their experience – or, if it does, it may be diluted. Their 'massification' allows our release from empathy. We cannot imagine ourselves in a situation where our 'I-ness' counts for nothing. We cannot imagine the 'not-I' of life as a mass term.

To kill a large number of people efficiently, the killers succeed when they have made the people they are targeting into a mass term. Philip Gourevitch, writing of the genocide in Rwanda, explains: 'What distinguishes genocide from murder, and even from acts of political murder that claim as many victims, is the intent. The crime is wanting to make a people extinct. The idea is the crime. No wonder it's so difficult to picture. To do so you must accept the principle of the exterminator, and see not people, but a people' (1998: 202).

Gourevitch says that 'the idea is the crime'. The victims are seen as a mass term by their oppressors: 'not people, but a people'. When a group is regarded as a people, not as being composed of individual people, certain conventions of thought and stereotypes take over. The claim is made that the people can be defined as a group, through racial, ethnic or species characteristics: in Germany in the 1930s and 1940s, what Jews are like and what Jews do; in Rwanda in the 1950s and forward, what Tutsis are like and what Tutsis do. These characteristics heighten the idea of their existence as being a threat to others or as being dirty. Then the false characteristics become fixed through their existence as a metaphor.

The presumptions and mistakes of racial biology reiterate similar presumptions and mistakes in 'species' biology. Humans think they can know 'cows' or 'birds' and use adjectives drawn from this assumption: cowlike, birdbrain. Susanne Kappeler observes that

> Western theories of racism attained proper 'scientific' status in the nineteenth and twentieth centuries in the guise of medicine, psychiatry, eugenics, anthropology, demography, and so forth. They stand in direct continuity with the theories that categorize non-human animals in species, and living beings into humans, animals, and plants – categories modelled on the paradigms of the natural sciences. These included attempts to established classifications of 'kinds' of people based on 'typical' data – be it measurements of bodies and body parts, genetic data, or behavioral features. (1995: 327)

Gourevitch (1998) writes, 'The idea is the crime', seeing a people, not people. One explanation for the appalling indifference of those of us who live in the United States, Europe, Great Britain, Australia and New Zealand to mass killings is that we, like their oppressors, may see the targeted victims as a mass term. When people are not experienced in their individuality, their deaths may not feel immediate. During the genocide in Rwanda, one American officer explained the calculations they were doing: 'one American casualty is worth about 85,000 Rwandan dead' (quoted in Power 2002: 381). The 'massification' of beings permits the dilution, the diminution of our attention. The more of a mass term they become, the less concern they need provoke. It is like an hourglass: the sands of our compassion drain into the bottom. How do we flip the hourglass? How do we revive or awaken compassion?

Mass terms are linked to subjects being diminished. In their diminishment, as I pointed out in *The Sexual Politics of Meat* (2000), all that is left for them is to become metaphors for others. According to Robert Pogue Harrison, in *The Dominion of the Dead*, what we do with our dead is what supposedly demarcates us as humans. We bury them. The dead influence us through the laws they bequeathed to us and the cultural and physical institutions we inherit from them. Everywhere we turn, we experience 'the foundational authority of the predecessor' (2005: ix). For the moment, I will not argue with Harrison's presumption that humans are necrocratic and non-humans are not. (Elephants' grieving processes are elaborate.) But, after genocides or fratricides like the Civil War, the survivors dig up the bodies buried in mass graves, as in Rwanda or Gettysburg, and try to reassert through separate burials each one's individuality against the annihilation of the mass term. We cannot undo the act of genocide – the dead are dead – but we can undo part of the idea that allows genocide, the use of mass terms, by asserting the individual and maintaining our ties to the dead as individuals. And this is a basic difference; meat eaters bury animals in their own bodies. When non-human living beings are converted conceptually into false mass terms to enable their conversion into products, we come to believe that their deaths do not matter to themselves. Animals are killed because they are false mass terms, but they die as individuals – as a cow, not as beef; as a pig, not as pork. Each suffers his or her own death, and this death matters a great deal to the one who is dying.

Treated like animals

In the face of the knowledge that genocide has happened in our lifetime – not only once, but repeatedly – and that countries such as the United States and institutions such as the United Nations failed to respond – with Rwanda, the United States was reduced to parsing the difference between 'acts of genocide' and genocide – the questions arise: 'Why didn't we respond? Why didn't we care?' Several forms of explanation have been offered, which Power details in *A Problem from Hell*. One important reason Power notes for peoples' apparent indifference, especially during the Holocaust, is disbelief: 'The notion of getting attacked for being (rather than for doing) was too discomfiting and too foreign to process readily' (2002: 36). Animals are killed daily for being rather than for doing; they may be killed because they are 'just animals'. Humans are not supposed to be killed because they are 'a people'. Moreover, it is humans who do the 'doing' to animals. Human beings may be killed for doing (doing wrong, presumably, but not for doing wrong to animals). When humans are killed for being rather than for doing, the 'beingness' attributed to them is often animal-like. Many favourable descriptions of human beings emphasize doing rather than being. Humans use their intelligence; non-humans are instinctive. Humans love; non-humans mate. Humans cultivate friendships; non-humans exhibit 'affiliative behaviour'. Humans are humane, cultivated, and refined; non-humans are beasts and brutal (Dunayer 2001). When someone says, 'I was treated like an animal', he or she means, 'I was treated as though I had no feelings, as though I were not alive.' We have created institutions that reinforce the contention that animals are, not that animals do. Karen Davis observes that 'seeing animals in industrialized settings such as factory farms encourages the view that animals are inherently passive objects whose only role in life is to serve the human enterprise' (2005: 31). When someone says, 'I was treated like an animal', he or she means, 'I was reduced to literal existence. I could not do; I was done to'. How are people made less human? Two of the most predictable ways are to define them as false mass terms and to view them as animals. Acts of violence that include animalizing language transform people into false mass terms, since animals already exist in that linguistic no-man's-land of lacking a recognizable individuality. When someone says, 'I was treated like an animal', he or she means, 'I was treated as though I were not an individual.' Conditions for violence flourish when the world is structured hierarchically, in a false Darwinian progression that places humans at the top:

Humans

Subhumans

Animals

Insects

'Material' nature; Earth, 'dirt'

The farther down the great chain of being a creature is placed, the lower the barriers to violence. When someone says, 'I was treated like an animal', he or she means, 'I was made vulnerable to violence by being moved down on the species ladder.' This is reflected in the epigraph, a quote from Adolf Hitler, to the first book of Art Spiegelman's *Maus: A Survivor's Tale* (1986): 'The Jews are undoubtedly a race, but they are not human' (quoted in De Angelis 2005). Leo Kuper writes in *Genocide*: 'The animal world has been a particularly fertile source of metaphors of dehumanization.' People designated as animals 'have often been hunted down like animals' (1983: 88), or exterminated like insects.

When a group is deemed not human, oppressors have several options for establishing just who they see the group members as. For the hierarchy that places humans at the top is more complicated than the one I presented earlier:

Humans

Subhumans

The devil (a human–animal being) walks upright, has the facial characteristics of a human, but has horns, hoofs and a tail).

Primates other than humans

Mammals other than primates

Predators

Top carnivores (The top carnivores are those that eat carnivores – for example, birds of prey, tigers and white sharks.)

Carnivores

Prey (herbivores: four-legged, two-legged)

'Vermin' (rats, mice)

Reptiles (snakes)

Insects ('pests')

Spiders

Cockroaches

Ants

'Material' nature; Earth, 'dirt'

Using propaganda campaigns, genocidal governments reinforce the idea of being, rather than of doing: Hitler considered the Jews to be subhuman and vermin; the Hutus in control in Rwanda regarded the Tutsis as cockroaches (*inyenzi*) or the devil. When genocidal governments rename humans as animals, they reinforce the ladder of human superiority by pushing some people off it. So, when someone says, 'I was treated like an animal', he or she is standing on the human ladder and looking down to those who have never been on the top rung.

The original oppression

Human society takes from the oppression of animals its structures and treatment of people. Although we often fail to see the literal origins of human institutions, as Keith Thomas (1983) and Jim Mason (1997), among others, established decades ago, all forms of oppression can be traced to the treatment of animals by humans. Domestication became the pattern for social subordination; predation, the pattern for killing and extermination. It is the nature of the burnt offering (the literal meaning of the word 'holocaust') of animals to disappear – whether consumed by fire or by human beings. The literal disappeared, but it became the form and function of an unequal human society's treatment of people.

When Theodor Adorno states, 'Auschwitz begins wherever someone looks at a slaughterhouse and thinks: they're only animals' (quoted in Patterson 2002: 53), he is saying that the structure of human inequality begins in the abattoir. But some claim that there is a difference: domesticated/enslaved animals have been brought into existence by humans and have life so humans can take it, whereas people threatened by genocide already exist, and the genocidal impulse is to completely eliminate them. Non-existence for human beings is their elimination as a specific group, ethnicity or race; non-existence for animals, according to this reasoning, is never being born in the first place. But the genocidal impulse, when considered, helps us see that this distinction is a fallacy. It assumes that speciesism is not an aspect of genocide and that racism is not a form of speciesism. At least one writer believes that 'the breeding of animals first produced the concepts of "race" and of "pure blood"' (Jean-Pierre Digard, quoted in Sax 2000: 83). Speciesism has always been a tool of colonialism, creating a hierarchy of skin colour and group characteristics. Kappeler observes that politics is zoology by another name: 'the very point of categorization is to create discriminating identities, "types" of people allegedly sharing the same (typical) feature(s), thus to justify their social and political roles … and invalidate their rights as individuals' (1995: 330).

The category 'human being' is stratified:

European colonizers evaluated indigenous peoples according to their relationship with animals and the land. They assumed that those who controlled and killed animals were more advanced than those who tilled fields. One of the demarcations of the evolutionary status of a culture was whether it was dependent on animal protein. Thus a hierarchy descends from Western meat eaters to pretechnological hunters to gatherers. Consider how the Belgians imposed a hierarchy in Rwanda. Gourevitch notes that whether Hutus and Tutsis were descended from different peoples, they 'spoke the same language, followed the same religion, intermarried and lived intermingled, without territorial distinctions, on the same hills, sharing the same social and political culture in small chiefdoms' (1998: 47–48). But still there was a distinction. Tutsis were herders, and Hutus were cultivators: 'This was the original inequality: cattle are a more valuable asset than produce, and although some Hutus owned cows while some Tutsis tilled the soil, the word Tutsi became synonymous with a political and economic elite' (48).

Racism recapitulates speciesism:

The category 'human being' is stratified by speciesism; the hierarchy imposed by colonialism mirrors that of speciesism. The race continuum not only recapitulates the species continuum, but draws its strength in categorization from it. Immigrants are also regarded, derogatorily, as animals. In an analysis of language used to discuss Latinos in newspapers, animal metaphors were found to be the predominant imagery. Researchers found metaphors of immigrants as animals that were lured, pitted, or baited; animals that can be attacked and hunted; animals that can be eaten; pack animals; and rabbits, needing to be ferreted out (Santa Ana 2002: 82–94). For example, American citizens give birth, but immigrants 'drop their babies'. Santa Ana writes, 'The ontology of IMMIGRANT AS ANIMAL can be stated concisely: Immigrants correspond to citizens as animals correspond to humans' (86, original emphasis). Thus another hierarchy can be posed:

    Human Not human
        Member of human society Outsider or other
        Citizen Immigrant

According to Kappeler:

> Classification is neither neutral, being put to political use only 'thereafter,' nor is it objective: it is itself an act of social and political discrimination and thus the expression of the subjectivity of power. What is said to be a quality of the object is in fact a difference construed in relation to an implicit norm constituted in the classifying subject. Racism and sexism as political practices construct another race and another sex, a race of 'others' and a sex of 'others.' (1995: 338)

The concept of 'other' requires a normative someone or someones who are not other; who are the measure by which otherness is established; to whom otherness might move closer or farther away, but who do not themselves depart from the normative nature of their beingness. This 'otherness' ratifies the primacy of those against whom otherness is defined.

Activist and scholar Karen Davis reminds us that from a chicken's experience, the human hand is the cruellest thing she will know (2005: 47). With Davis's insight in mind, consider this formative conversation in the history of genocide in the twentieth century: when Raphael Lemkin, who coined the word 'genocide', was studying linguistics, he asked his professor why Mehmed Talaat, the person responsible for 'the killing by firing squad, bayoneting, bludgeoning, and starvation of nearly 1 million Armenians' (Power 2002: 1), was not prosecuted for what he had done. His professor told Lemkin that there was no law under which Talaat could be arrested. The professor explained, '"Consider the case of a farmer who owns a flock of chickens," he said, "He kills them and this is his business. If you interfere, you are trespassing"' (Power 2002: 17). Perhaps one reason we did not respond to the genocides of the twentieth century is that we had learned to tolerate a hierarchical world in which killing is accepted.

I recently heard from a feminist animal rights scholar, who wrote:

I live 6 miles up the road from one of the largest slaughterhouses in the nation. Nobody in this little town blinks an eye as each day semi-trailer after semi-trailer crammed full of living entities streams down Main Street carrying cows to their brutal executions. Got behind one of these horrors the other day. The stench was overpowering, but what really got me was the bumper sticker: EAT BEEF: The West Wasn't Won on Salad.

The triumphalism of such contemporary declarations should remind us that when anxiety asserts itself about the place of animals in our hierarchical world, it is never asserting itself only about animals.

Why don't we care?

Jacques Derrida's 'The Animal that Therefore I Am' identifies the most egregious actions humans have taken against other animals (including subsuming them all under the category 'animal'): 'Everybody knows what terrifying and intolerable pictures a realist painting could give to the industrial, mechanical, chemical, hormonal, and genetic violence to which man has been submitting animal life for the past two centuries' (2002: 395). He assumes that such a description may be 'pathetic' – that is, evoking sympathy. Derrida argues that for the past few centuries, we have waged a campaign against compassion that allows factory farms and other horrors to continue. He calls it the 'war on pity'. Such a campaign instantiates objectification: both the objectification of the animals who become mass terms and the objectification of feelings, so they fail to be heeded in making decisions about the fate of terminal animals. If genocide requires the turning of humans into animals, the war on pity provides the institutional framework for not caring about what happens to someone labelled 'animal'.

Derrida says that

> no one can deny the unprecedented proportions of this subjection of the animal.... No one can deny seriously, or for very long, that men do all they can in order to dissimulate this cruelty or to hide it from themselves, in order to organize on a global scale the forgetting or misunderstanding of this violence that some would compare to the worst cases of genocide (there are also animal genocides: the number of species endangered because of man takes one's breath away). (2002: 394)

There, even he says it: what is happening to animals some 'would compare to the worse cases of genocide'. He adds,

> One should neither abuse the figure of genocide nor consider it explained away. For it gets more complicated here: the annihilation of certain species is indeed in process, but it is occurring through the organization and exploitation of an artificial, infernal, virtually interminable survival, in conditions that previous generations would have judged monstrous, outside of every supposed norm of a life proper to animals that are thus exterminated by means of their continued existence or even their overpopulation. (2002: 394)

Samantha Power (2002) offers several explanations to begin the discussion of why apathy prevails over caring: we lack the imagination needed to reckon with evil, and it is hard to even imagine evil. It is assumed that people act rationally. American policy makers discovered that 'rational people' can be gratuitously violent (with Derrida I might add, such a discovery was made by animal activists centuries ago). The failure to protest is interpreted as indifference, and those who do care do not have the political strength to change policy. The killing is reinterpreted, deflecting attention from the culprits. The national interest, or so it is thought, prevents intervention. Being attacked for being rather than doing seems unbelievable. But now we can add to Power's list. The ability to objectify feelings, so they are placed outside the political realm, is another reason people have not cared. Submission to authority requires such objectification – indeed, rewards it. Not only do people learn that feelings do not matter, but even the awareness of feelings is lost within the objectifying mind-set. As a result, people may become afraid to care, which requires that they have the courage to break from the normalizing ideological screen that has posited that 'it's okay if it's an x, but not a y'.

The war on compassion has resulted in a desire to move away from many feelings, especially uncomfortable ones. As a result, fear, which is an understandable response to a new experience – say, that of encountering a snake or a spider – becomes the justification for killing a snake or a spider. If feelings were not objectified, we might have developed the ability to interact with the fear, to respect it and the being who is causing it, rather than try to destroy both the feeling and the being. The war on compassion has caused many people to think that it is futile to care. They are unable, imaginatively, to see how their caring will change anything. They experience a passivity inculcated by current political situations as well as by the media. They lack the imagination not to believe that something terrible might be done, but that the something terrible that is happening can be undone. The war on compassion, further, has caused people to fear that beginning to care about what happens to animals will destroy them because the knowledge is so overwhelming. They prefer not to care rather than to face the fragility, at the least, or the annihilation of the caring self, at the most extreme, that they suspect arises from caring. But caring does not make people more fragile or annihilate them. In fact, through caring, individuals not only acquire new experiences and skills that accompany these experiences, but also discover that they are part of a network that can sustain them even when caring evolves into grief for what is happening. Finally, the war on compassion has caused people to believe that they have to help humans first. As long as we treat animals as animals, as long as we accept that there is the category 'animals', both the treatment and the concept will legitimize the treatment of humans like animals. Derrida (2002) hypothesized that the 'war on pity' was passing through a critical phase. It may have begun when animal activists proclaimed that 'if it's not okay for a y, it's not okay for an x', and in that proclamation began the process of overcoming the divisions between not only the x's (animals) and the y's (humans), but also compassion and the political realm.

Acknowledgements

I thank the O'Neill Lecture Committee and the O'Neill family for inviting me to present new work under the auspices of the lectureship. I thank Josephine Donovan for her editing of the original lecture.

CHAPTER TWO

Legal Technology Confronts Speciesism, or
We Have Met the Enemy and He Is Us[1]

John T. Maher

If there is anything unique about the human animal, it is that it has the ability to grow knowledge at an accelerating rate while being chronically incapable of learning from experience.

– GRAY, JOHN, THE SILENCE OF ANIMALS

Introduction

Human identity has historically and legally distinguished itself by othering animals[2] through what may be called speciesism. In jurisprudence, speciesism takes the form of ordered ontological systems based upon the hierarchal exclusion of animals as subjects, or moral beings[3] also known as legal 'persons'. Those possessed of legal personhood may or may not be included in the *polis* but have standing to argue in court for the enforcement of rights. This chapter concerns itself with the forms of legal technology used to confront speciesism as law. Humans are *a priori* speciesist because they are aware that the condition of human life harms all other life, if only at the level of microorganisms.[4] Since speciesism is not apart from the condition of the human,[5] humans have created an enabling mythology of an exceptionalist hierarchy of being to justify this harm. Kant famously wrote, 'Humanity itself is a dignity … by which he raises himself above all other beings in the world that are not human beings' (Kant 1996: 209). Thus

Kant, and his Stoic predecessors, theorized the line dividing the human and the animal which justified a speciesist oppression to which the social order expressed as law is still in thrall.

Animal Law scholar Taimie Bryant notes that speciesism is a construct of the human, paraphrasing the observation of psychiatrist Thomas Szasz, who wrote, '[i]n the animal kingdom, the rule is, eat or be eaten; in the human kingdom, define or be defined' (Szasz, 1973; Bryant 2006: 1). Alternately, Media Studies scholar Dominic Pettman, referencing Nietzsche's observation that 'error has made animals into men' (Nietzsche 1980: bk4: 324) as a point of departure, postulates that human identity is essentially a case of mistaken identity reinforced by a narcissistic technology (Pettman 2011: *passim*).

Human laws exist for the benefit of humans '*Hominem cause omne jus conentium*', as legal scholar Steven Wise[6] notes, invoking Thomas Kuhn for the proposition that a paradigm shift in thinking is necessary (Kuhn 1962: 168) to confront speciesism (Wise 2000: 71–78). This means that confronting speciesism by using legal technology as a catalyst is met with resistance. In a similar vein, Kyle Ash writes, 'speciesism reflects the backwardness of law in that it has not adequately integrated modern qualities of science, namely to be evolutive, to exhaustively refer to empirically-deduced collective knowledge, and to be interdisciplinary' (Ash 2005: 213). Materialist considerations such as animals as property, a legal term, entrench speciesism. Writer and agility training enthusiast Donna Haraway, who never once uses the term 'speciesism', favours challenges to the existing ontological order but ultimately advocates reconsideration of what the possibility of justice (Derrida 1992: 24–26) might mean for the human animal relationship. Like Derrida (1991: 112), she accepts the position that humans should endeavour to reconsider the *sacrificable* status of animals, made possible by social hierarchies of power and dominance. Like Carey Wolfe, Haraway refuses to deny the attendant 'complexities and situated histories' indicted in confronting speciesism (DeKoven & Lundblad, 2012: 5) while placing the human and the animal within the same plane of ethical consideration. Haraway also rejects simply changing the rules of sacrifice to make animals *unkillable* (Haraway 2008: 80). She reasons that killing, the 'god-trick' (Haraway 2008: 80–81, 296), is a condition of life and, following Derrida (Derrida 1991: *passim*), must therefore be undertaken with proactive responsibility as to the conditions of life and death and in a manner consistent with the human capacity to respond[7] to the complexities of the interspecies relationship (Haraway 2008: 80). Haraway's material semiosis should not be confused with hoary interspecies social contract theories updating John Locke's *Second Treatise on Civil Government*. Haraway, who is well known for writing about animal instrumentality and her reflections upon a roast feral pig (Haraway 2008: 299), restates this reordering as '*Thou Shalt Not Make Killable*' (Haraway 2008: 299). Here she means confronting speciesism by resituating where the line is drawn, rather than relying upon any ill-fitting deontological scheme to protect animals because '[t]the law cannot be counted on' (Haraway 2008: 268). For many, Haraway's work falls far short of a desired, if not completely possible, rejection of speciesism in both theory and the material world – in effect, a failure of theory to confront speciesism. In doing so, she asks us to confront how justice may possibly be approached and the conditions of instrumental use determined in a world where speciesism is reconsidered, if not eliminated.

On a parallel track, Bryant writes on the use of legal technology to confront certain aspects of speciesism. She adopts the underlying Derridian question of who is sacrificable and asks legal technology to reclassify certain animals as *unkillable*. Here she intervenes on behalf of animals who have been directed to die by application of such means as a testamentary provision to kill pets or a prohibition on release[8] from an animal shelter (Bryant 2007a: 301–314, 315–323). Following the 'animal turn' of decentring the human in theory, others have focused on changing or modifying the legally sacrificial status of animals by reclassifying animals as non-things through the vehicle of legal personhood. It is the possibility of a confrontation of speciesism through the law that we wish to interrogate by means of investigating legal technologies, such as the extension of legal personhood to animals. Ultimately all are doomed in the sense that they cannot actualize an awareness of animal alterity which fits into an anthropocentric construct such as a legal framework.

Animals as hybrid property

Traditional legal scholars, such as David Favre, view it as morally acceptable that humans own animals as property, while simultaneously acknowledging that animals have interests independent of being owned (Favre 2010a: 1022). Such interests are expressed indirectly by laws restricting instrumentality (Favre 2010a: 1022). Favre proposes a legal technology that resituates legal ontology to classify animals 'living property', previously referred to as a form of 'equitable self-ownership', in which humans recognized that animals have interests and the desire to assert rights to protect those interests. In effect, this splits legal and equitable title to an owned animal (Favre 2004a: 203). Under both incarnations of his theory, Favre justifies a favoured status[9] for companion animals by observing that humans place a premium on the value they accord to their pets over their market value as commodities which is reflected in current legal decisions.[10] In contrast, Favre advocates legal personhood for 'wild animals' in order that they may assert such limited rights as the law will allow (Favre 2010b: 1063–1067).

While Favre's views are rooted in benign paternalistic care, they clearly follow along existing speciesist lines and do not represent a radical reordering of the human–animal relationship. Indeed, Favre sees the legal concept of property as an adaptable mechanism which can be changed through grants of limited rights to animals as *living property* which will better insure their interests are met. (Favre 2010a; 2010b: *passim*). Favre does not reject speciesism, but instead argues

> legal rights for animals will move forward if legislation is adopted which simply states that any person may file a petition with a court of equitable jurisdiction for permission to represent a specific animal (a domestic animal or companion animal) for the filing of a complaint for violation of any state laws for which equitable relief might be used to eliminate an ongoing violation.[11]

Favre is essentially arguing for an adaptation of legal technology to grant humans legal standing on behalf of certain animals without a concurrent grant of subjectivity, thus conferring only limited protections to animals.

Limited versions of Favre's concept arguably exist in the context of federal[12] and North Carolina's *qui tam* statutes,[13] which have used legal technology to confer standing on humans to bring lawsuits to enforce laws which either directly or indirectly benefit animals. Favre must therefore be situated as a reformer seeking the best that the law, as gradually (re)constructed through legal technology within the existing framework, has to offer (Favre 2004b: 95–96). A version of his approach might sit well with Donna Haraway, who writes of mutual interspecies ownership, which might also split legal and equitable title for both humans and animals. Favre's work has possibly the greatest potential for enactment as law of any of the legal technologies considered. However, in terms of directly confronting speciesism, one must look elsewhere.

The abolition of property status

Professor Gary Francione, in an ethically concise technology which he terms the *Abolitionist Approach*, owing much to Marxism and antebellum anti-slavery abolitionists, views the property status of animals as the basis of speciesism and the value of animals as the sum of their instrumental uses. He writes that 'animal-welfare laws do not provide any significant protection to nonhuman animals because nonhumans are the property of humans' (Francione 2007: 9–13). The legal technology he advocates is the complete elimination of such property status coupled with a right of animals to be left alone and the converse duty of humans to leave animals alone (Francione 1996; 2008). Bryant observes,

> To date, no one has successfully refuted Professor Francione's argument that the property status of animals accounts for that extreme gap between widespread, commonsense recognition of animals as sentient beings and

the grossly inadequate legal means of protecting animals from even the most extreme types of human inflicted suffering. (2007a: 255)

While Francione's argument may be reductionist, it forces the law to radically confront many, but not all, forms of speciesism.

Francione criticizes welfarist measures as enabling speciesism. 'A right to "humane" treatment and to be free from "unnecessary" suffering is no "right" at all in that it prohibits only those actions that do not benefit humans and would, in any event, not be committed by rational property owners' (Francione 2009: 36). Extending this thought, Francione aptly notes that anticruelty statutes contain subordination clauses (Ridler 2013: 103) that criminalize acts designated *unnecessary* (Francione 2000; 2007: 142–143 n. 2) cruelty or suffering, which presumes that there exists a social presumption of a *necessary* level of which society will tolerate, thus enabling a speciesist ontology in law. Instead, what Francione offers is an approach to confronting most forms of speciesism.

Obviously few are willing to relinquish property rights over animals and their resultant instrumental uses. For example, if Francione's views became law humans would all be vegans and all vivisection would cease. Francione's personal solution is adopting the Jain precept of *Ahimsa* (Dundas 2002: 160), which entails causing no deliberate or careless harm to animals. Thus while Francione may advocate a radical legal technology, it is not absolute. In fact, Francione's work has been termed 'new-speciesist' by Joan Dunayer, author of the seminal book *Speciesism* (Dunayer 2004). His argument essentially consists of moving the line of speciesism from a point of no *unnecessary* harm to its furthest extremity of no deliberate or careless harm. While this view takes responsibility for direct actions which harm animals, Dunayer points out that it fails to consider consequential and indirect harms and in that sense relegates animal interests beneath those of the human (Dunayer 2007: 41–43).

Where Dunayer's criticism may be most valid concerns the speciesism indicted by, say, building a house and thus causing resultant harm to field mice or other animals living on that patch of land (Dunayer 2007: 41–43). An ecosophical worldview of humanity is willing to consider this cost in light of the disruptive anthropocentric effect on climate and human survivability, but rarely speciesism. While Dunayer is correct as far as maintaining consistent theory goes, in praxis Francione envisions a reordering based upon change in property status which pushes the speciesist line as far as possible while still indulging a material human existence. Echoing Haraway, even personal human choices constitute environmental interventions that kill, such as the choice to use antibiotics or washing one's hands, both of which kill. In effect, Francione answers James Rachel's question which asks: at what level do we draw the speciesist line? (Rachels 2004: 162–164). The limits of Francione's work implicate the failure of theory to confront all incarnations of speciesism and thus asks if humans are not inherently speciesist. While this legal technology may have great appeal among philosophers, it has no immediate application as a viable legal technology with which to confront speciesism because the human is unwilling to surrender the concept of animals as 'property'.

Constitutional, legislative and administrative means

The most direct means of rejecting speciesism in a human culture ruled by law are constitutional and legislative means which (re)consider the exclusion of the animal as a legal subject. The known exemplars to date have been concerned with either personhood or by limited and welfarist grants of rights. Selected examples focusing on a change in legal status of the *polis* through technical means are considered.

Germany

In 2002, Germany, which had a comprehensive set of national animal protection laws dating from the period from 1933 to 1938 (Sax 2002: 101–138, 175–80), amended its Basic Laws[14] to enact a limited guarantee of rights to animals. Art. 20a stated '[t]he State…also protects the natural living conditions *and the animals*'.[15] However, Art. 20a was not accompanied by a specific enforcement mechanism (Wagman & Liebman 2011: 267) and was welfarist in nature. Germany also has a comprehensive set of animal welfare laws, the *Tierschutzgesetz* (Kelch 2011: 273) and the German Civil Code[16] (BG) contains additional animal welfare provisions. (Kelch 2012: 273–275), notably BG §90a, which states '[a]nimals are not things. They are protected by special laws' (Kelch 2012: 273–275). This constitutes enlightened statutory speciesism because, while it excludes animals as subjects, it pretends to offer legal protections while reserving instrumental uses to humans.

Analysis of these laws reveals that Germans epitomize the 'moral schizophrenia' Francione describes concerning favouring some animals and disfavouring others (Francione 2000: 1–30). It is disturbing that §90a's declaration that *animals are not things* does not have a corresponding declaration that animals are *subjects*, which renders it a useless phrase as far as confronting speciesism. This omission evidences that Germany is committed to retaining the property status of animals but will observe a Kantian refrain from only the most shocking abuse. Such was evidenced by the *Slaughter Decision* (Nattrass 2004; Kelch 2011: 275–280), a 1980s case where a butcher appealed the denial of an operating permit because he refused to stun animals prior to ritual slaughter. The court ultimately ruled in favour of ritual slaughter because it did not wish to prohibit a human religious practice, essentially resituating the dispute away from the animal. In this sense the *Slaughter Decision* concerned only the means of ritual slaughter and never called into question the Derrida/Haraway/Bryant line of a rejection of sacrifice itself. A resultant public outcry forced the constitutional amendment to Art. 20a adding the words '*and the animals*', which essentially changed nothing. Thus, the German use of legislation and litigation as their legal technology of choice to reject some of the worst expressions of speciesism and instrumental use through welfarism has failed.

Switzerland and the Czech Republic

Switzerland granted limited rights to great apes in 1992 and amended its constitution in 2009 to recognize animals as *beings* and not *things*. In 1999, the Swiss Constitution was completely rewritten to require protection and regulation[17] of animals but not to guarantee any legal rights (Kelch 2011: 284). In 2002, the Swiss Civil Code was amended by referendum to include a provision stating, as in Germany that, 'animals are not things'. However, this provision was limited by a nonsensical phrase stating 'that provision that previously applied to animals as things now [still] apply to animals even though they are not now things'. This is classic doublespeak because it negated clear language meant to undercut the worst extremes of speciesism and declined to confer subjectivity.

Switzerland also held a referendum in 2010 on whether to grant legal standing to domestic animals which stated 'domestic creatures [have] the constitutional right to be represented by human lawyers in court' (Kelch 2011: 285). Although the referendum was applicable only to 'domestic creatures', probably based upon a preferred status conveyed by a relationship to humans, it was defeated. Notably, the referendum was not applicable to those animals with the highest cognitive abilities according to human standards and measurements, such as chimpanzees or cetaceans, but favoured an entangled kinship with companion species in a manner Haraway and Favre might favour and Francione might condemn. Kelch optimistically writes that that the animal-centric provisions of the German and Swiss constitutions 'can be seen as a foundation…a catalyst for attempts to change the human-animal relationship' (2011: 285) and further that constitutional referendums may provide the basis for further change in how society views the human–animal relationship. In contrast, one may view Switzerland as an exemplar of inherent structural resistance to the use of legal technology to confront speciesism by rejecting any meaningful legislation designed to transform the law. A similar measure declaring that under the law animals are not 'objects', Czech Civil Code §494, will go into effect in the Czech Republic in 2014 but the practical effect is expected to be merely welfarist in nature (Müllerová 2012).

New Zealand

New Zealand granted basic legal rights, but not subjectivity, to great apes in 1999, exempting them from instrumental use under most, but not all, circumstances. Critically, almost no primate research was ever conducted in New Zealand so few property interests were indicted. Wagman and Liebman point out that §85 of the New Zealand Animal Welfare Act retains a provision for instrumental uses (Wagman & Liebman 2011: 21), thus rendering all animal protection measures short of subjectivity as conditional. There seems to be a visceral reluctance of humans to surrender total control over animals, in Derridean terms to make them 'unsacrificable', which is the major reason why legal technologies proposing even a limited rejection of speciesism have no immediate prospects of gaining acceptance.

Balearic Islands

In February 2007, the Balearic Islands, an autonomous maritime region of Spain, passed a preliminary proposition or 'No de Ley', akin to a non-binding resolution, to support the legal recognition of certain basic rights for great apes, which fell short of actually changing their legal status. The proposal had been submitted in May 2006 by the Green Party as a science-based (genetic and cognitive similarity) proposal backed by the Great Ape Project (GAP) and represents an aspirational articulation of essentially welfarist goals. Utilitarian and GAP founder Peter Singer stated, 'We didn't think it was a great leap to ask for great-ape rights'.[18] As in New Zealand and San Marino, where great ape research has also been banned, there was no actual great ape research in the Balearics to confront. Likewise, a welfarist ban on great ape research was enacted in the United Kingdom 1997 and is almost completely banned in the United States as of this writing – both instances occurring only after scientists had exhausted most possibilities for such research. Therefore, the No de Lay was a pyrrhic victory against speciesism, 'full of sound and fury, signifying nothing',[19] which still allows research on other primates and animals.

Spain

On 27 April 2006 Francisco Garrido[20] submitted a science-based bill to the Cortes Generales (Spanish Parliament) which, if enacted, would have required Spain to endorse and promote the goals of the GAP and pass specific welfarist legislation.[21] Although GAP endorsed legal personhood in general, it did not seek to confront speciesism concerning other animals. The original Spanish bill fell short of granting personhood for great apes[22] and the Spanish Minister for the Environment denied that great apes 'will be granted human rights'.[23] In June 2008, the bill was approved by an Environmental Committee of Parliament but was never passed by the full Parliament because it was opposed by the Socialist Party, pharmaceutical interests, Amnesty International, and the Catholic Church. There were additional concerns within the government about promoting disharmony with the laws of the European Union. These events can be seen as another science-based attempt to confront speciesism regarding selected species which failed when the debate was dislocated from genetic similarity to the interests of humans benefiting from the existing speciesist ontology. Thus, the legal technology of legislation failed because interests in maintaining an exceptionalist ontology of being(s) and their resultant instrumental uses which disinvest humans from the possibility of using the law as a catalyst to effect transformation reflecting changing consciousness with regard to animals.

India

On 17 May 2013, Member Secretary B. S. Bonal of India's Ministry of Environment & Forests, Central Zoo Authority, issued an administrative circular denying an application for the construction of dolphinariums.[24] This circular included a recital clause stating that because scientists had determined that dolphins were possessed of 'unusual high intelligence' this means that 'dolphin[s] should be seen as "non-human persons" with "their own specific rights"' and that it was 'morally unacceptable to keep them captive for entertainment purpose[s]'. The circular, which recommended against approving permits that involved captured dolphins, fell short of granting legal personhood to dolphins on a nationwide level. However, it does represent an innovative use of the legal technology of administrative rulemaking in transforming animal personhood, and thus a part of speciesism, based upon a perceived alterity, rooted in the catalyst of scientific similarity to the human, and expressed in moral terms. The problem inherent in the circular is its root in perceived scientific similarity to humans, which itself reinforces the speciesist hierarchy as Francione and others have noted.[25] The fact that the application was prospective, and likely issued in the absence of existing property interests (as in the *Somerset* case[26] below) in dolphins and dolphinariums in India, seems an unspoken factor in the circular. On 13 August 2013, B. S. Bonal amended the circular to include a directive to reject all proposals relating to the captivity of marine mammals in India.[27]

The struggle for personhood in the courts

Legal personhood is the prerequisite to standing, or the ability to maintain a claim in a court in order to seek the protections of relevant laws (Wise, 2011: 2–3). Personhood is not limited to humans (Stone 2010: 4–43). Corporations, ships and political parties all have legal personhood but the law does not allow animals direct standing to assert their rights although some American courts have nominally allowed animals to file suit in their own name without reaching the issue of personhood[28] and some governments such as New Zealand have recognized limited standing for a river.[29] Personhood is an intriguing legal technology but one which is imprecise and speciesist because it attempts to fit animals within a human legal framework.

An emerging area of legal technology seeks to reject the paradigm of animals as things through litigation and obtain legal standing for animals to maintain lawsuits asserting their own direct legal interests through human representatives. Cary Wolfe, commenting on the legal status of animals in the biopolitical present, summarized this point in a concise manner

> [t]he underlying problem is clear. Animals are things and not persons under United States law – things that may or may not have legal status depending on whether or not they have a property relationship to an entity designated as a 'person', who thus has a legal interest in, and standing to argue on behalf of, the animal in question. (Wolfe 2013: 12)

Wise envisions personhood as extending, at least initially, to only certain classes of nonhumans such as apes and orcas, based on genetic, cognitive and experiential ability, which is to say similarity to humans (Wise 2003) and presumably perceived as such by humans. Wise states concerning this technology,

> [o]nce a court recognizes this possibility, the next legal question will appropriately shift from the irrational, biased, and overly simplistic question, 'What species is the plaintiff?', to the rational, nuanced, value-laden, and policy-enriched question, 'What qualities does the plaintiff possess that are relevant to the issue of whether she is entitled to the legal right she claims?'.[30]

It can be argued that personhood is a legal technology which is not a radical rejection of all speciesism. Instead it reinforces speciesist chains through an artificial science-based relocation of a speciesist legal ontology by expanding the class of subjects in relation to the human.

The nonhuman rights project

Wise founded the Nonhuman Rights Project (NhRP)[31] in order to litigate common law cases in American courts which seek to obtain legal personhood for certain animals and their release from confinement (Wise 2010, *passim*). Wise seeks to use litigation to push back a speciesist line rendering animals as *things* (Wise 1995; 2000) instead of *persons* or subjects, which is short of waging an overarching battle rejecting speciesism. Wise describes the problem of thinghood as 'They are legal things. Their most basic and fundamental interests – their pains, their lives, their freedoms – are intentionally ignored, often maliciously trampled, and routinely abused...Although philosophy and science have long since recanted, the law has not' (Wise 2000: 4). Again this presents a speciesist model of human primacy in terms of a type of intelligence situated in relation to the human (Bryant 2007b). In contrast, Wise maintains that he is focused solely on jurisprudence. He wants to present the most compelling argument that a court will be most receptive to, based upon cognitive similarity to humans, supported by empirical data.

The first test case to be filed under a writ of *habeas corpus* by the NhRP in December 2013[32] in New York State on behalf of chimpanzees which Wise maintains have the greatest claim on legal personhood based upon cognitive similarities to humans (Wise, 1998: 823–824; Wise, 2011: 6; Wise 2003: 231–240). The initial goals of the NhRP are concerned with pragmatic jurisprudence and are not as expansive as the set of rights demanded by the GAP (Cavalieri & Singer 1993) but go further than the *Kinshasa Declaration on Great Apes*[33] and the *Cambridge Declaration on Consciousness*,[34] which make no legal demands.

The precedent Wise relies upon is the ability of the common law to transform itself and declare, in the absence of adverse precedent, what the law should be. He seeks transformation based upon application of such cases, at the state law level, where the common law ruled that othered individuals possessed personhood and therefore standing, such as in the *Somerset* case (2006a: *passim*). In *Somerset*, British abolitionists used the technology of creating and transforming common law by first obtaining a writ of *habeas corpus* as an entrée to demanding that the slavers show cause why one James Somerset, a slave outside of Britain, should be held against his will within Britain. Because slavery had never existed in Britain *per se*, the court ruled that it was 'incapable of being introduced on any reason, moral or political, but only by positive law' (Wise 2000: 50). Unlike the ruling in *Somerset*, the American *Dred Scott*[35] decision held that black slaves were not possessed of citizenship, and therefore had no legal standing to maintain a lawsuit challenging their status as property on a federal level. The freeing of American slaves and grant of subjecthood occurred not as the result of legal technology in the form of judicial ruling as in *Somerset*, but as calculated wartime and reconstruction measures, in other words by excluding slave-owning interests. The parallel to speciesism and animal instrumentality is that even when consciousness advances, society is reluctant to change its laws where entrenched property interests are at stake.

This gradualist approach (Wise 2004: 19–41) falls short of a radical confrontation with speciesism based upon ethics possessed of a politicized alterity which attempts to compensate for its anthropocentric bias. Further, the courts are reluctant to engage in judicial activism and regularly pronounce themselves prisoners of *stare decisis* in an effort to control legal indeterminacy. Wise is keenly aware of the difficulty involved in transforming a common law that presumes that animals are property and emphasizes that he is seeking out the mutable aspect of the common law for which state law decisions granting standing serve as a catalyst. He notes that the power to transform the common law allows for legal adaptation: 'Judges who understand that changing morality or scientific findings might one day justify their [hypothetical] unmaking the legal personhood for nonhuman animals that they made will be more willing to experiment with it in the first place' (Wise 2004: 118).

The legal technology Wise will use are the writs of *habeas corpus*, as in *Somerset*, and *de homine replegiando* (Wise 2006b: *passim*), which have been employed to safeguard individual freedom through the mechanism of an independent judiciary. In a *habeas corpus* application the court orders the state to explain and justify the legal basis for its detention of a person (Halliday 2010: 35–65). In seeking such relief, Wise intends to argue under state common law decisions extending legal personhood to different classes of humans, such as slaves, mentally incapacitated persons, and minors (Wise, 2006b: *passim*; Wise 2010: *passim*). The ultimate goal of legal personhood for animals is a release from conditions of judicial confinement as a *thing* into conditions as close to a natural environment as possible, while still assuring the safety of the animal *person* in question. Some speciesist paternalism is inherent in this proposition, but so is an ethos of interspecies care and responsibility in what might be called the best of the humanist tradition. Wise's work is the only American effort to confront speciesism in praxis. If challenges such as Wise envisions succeed in even a limited redrawing of the line, such a victory will no doubt raise consciousness concerning speciesism among jurists and public alike, opening the door to legal challenges by other species.

Kama the Dolphin

Have these efforts met any success in using the law to transform the human–animal relationship along speciesist lines? In 1991 Wise filed a case in federal court which inspired his life's work, by asking a court to grant legal recourse directly to a dolphin. Kama the dolphin had been illegally transferred from New England to a naval base in Hawaii. Wise argued that the Navy violated the federal Marine Mammal Protection Act (MMPA)[36] concerning capturing live dolphins[37] (Doyle 1996: *passim*). Kama was named as the plaintiff but the court dismissed the suit, critically stating that although Kama was an individual, Kama lacked the capacity to sue because he could not properly allege legal standing under the MMPA in the absence of legal personhood.[38] The federal court refused to allow this innovative use of legal technology by avoiding a substantive ruling on the legal standard for personhood. In jurisprudence, legal standing presupposes legal personhood, which forms the foundation of the pyramid of rights (Wise 2011: 5–9) that Wise later developed which outlines the legal infrastructure necessary for obtaining and extending personhood and switched his focus to state courts where favourable precedents sometimes existed extending standing to slaves, women, children and the disabled.

United States: TILIKUM[39] v. Sea World

In 2011 lawyers for the People for the Ethical Treatment of Animals (PETA) brought suit in the name of five captive orcas at the Sea World marine park in Florida.[40] The lawsuit claimed the orcas' confinement violated the 13th Amendment of the U.S. Constitution,[41] which legally ended slavery in the United States – and critically did not first argue for personhood in state court along the lines proposed by Wise. The trial held rejected PETA's attempt to use legal technology to expand standing in federal claims to animals, ruling that the plaintiff orcas possessed no federal Art. III[42] standing, requiring the court to dismiss the suit for lack of subject-matter jurisdiction. Citing the *Slaughter-House Cases*,[43] the court explicitly rejected a federal argument that the orcas were held as slaves in violation of the 13th Amendment. The court ruled that the 13th Amendment refers exclusively to human slavery and cannot be applied to 'changing conditions and evolving norms of our society' because '"slavery" and "involuntary servitude" are "uniquely human activities"'. Continuing 'the clear language and historical context reveal that 'only human beings, or persons, are afforded the protection of the 13th Amendment,… [which] does not afford Plaintiffs any relief as non-humans'.[44] Critically, the court did not reach the issue of legal personhood, partially through the intervention of Wise and the NhRP's parent organization, which argued for dismissal of the case in order to prevent the ruling.[45]

Austria

In Austria in 2007 the courts were presented with an argument for legal personhood on behalf of a chimpanzee called Matthew Pan, aka 'Hiasl', and dismissed it on technical grounds in order to avoid a substantive resolution of the issue. An animal protection organization had filed a petition with the court in Modling, Austria, for legal guardianship of Hiasl in order to access a trust fund set up to pay for Hiasl's care (Balluch & Faber 2007: *passim*). Critically, a decision on the merits would have required a determination of whether the speciesist line should be moved. At issue were inconsistent sections of the Austrian Civil Code (AbGB). §285 stated 'According to the law, everything that differs from personhood, or is utilized to serve personhood, is named a "thing", ' which means that animals have the legal status of a thing (id.) while §285-a explicitly stated, 'Animals are not "things", and they are protected by special laws. Furthermore, by law, the terminology "thing" only pertains to animals inasmuch there are no deviations from standard lawful guidelines'.

The prospective guardians[46] also sought to show that Hiasl was a legal person under AbGB §16, which states '[e]very person has innate human rights, and as such is recognized and validated by law. Slavery or servitude, and the power to exercise control and power over an individual are not permitted, therefore, unduly in this state', for whom a guardian under §273 should be appointed. Because humans filed the application as prospective guardians for Hiasl, the issue of legal standing itself was not implicated. The guardians attempted to prove personhood by presenting evidence in the form of cognition tests showing that Hiasl possessed 'qualities and abilities' and a 'theory of mind' similar to humans and 'sees himself as human' (Bevilaqua 2013: 77, 81, 83). If the guardians could show that Hiasl had status as a *non-thing* under §285-a, then they would be able to claim the rights associated with personhood, including the right to appointment of a guardian. However, the actual claim advanced was broader and stated that *all* chimpanzees, including Hiasl, possess biological qualities which qualify them for personhood under §16 (Bevilaqua 2013: 76–77), which meant they too could ask for guardians and sue their captors (Balluch & Faber 2007: *passim*).

The trial court insisted that the applicants first produce documents proving Hiasl's identity, ironically a question philosophically richer than all the issues at bar. Then the court dismissed the case under §273, ruling that Hiasl did not meet the standard for appointment of a legal guardian, thus avoiding the scientific arguments put forth based upon similarity to humans and a ruling on personhood. Legal scholar C. B. Bevilaqua observes, 'The Austrian courts ... (re)located the discussion onto strictly legal [technical] terrain, thus making it more difficult for the applicants to return to the biologizing rhetoric of the initial petition as the case made its way through the higher courts' (Bevilaqua 2013: 78).

Appeals followed but the Austrian Supreme Court declined to hear the matter, ruling that, '§285-a notwithstanding, non-human animals are still things and have no value in themselves' (Balluch & Faber 2007: *passim*), which reads as a judicial nullification of a clear legislative entitlement. Thereafter, an appeal was made with the European Court of Human Rights (ECHR), on the grounds that the Austrian courts had refused to hear the scientific evidence and decide the substantive personhood, instead dismissing on technicalities (Bevilaqua 2013: 79). In 2010, the ECHR also declined to hear the matter.[47]

Bevilaqua observes that the Austrian courts essentially 'decided not to decide' and 'systematically avoided the fundamental question raised by the applicants: namely who are the living beings that can be considered subjects of rights and why?' (Bevilaqua 2013: 79). When the applicants claimed that Hiasl 'sees himself as human', Bevilaqua points out 'it is precisely his nonhumanity that the statement brings to the fore' (Bevilaqua 2013: 79). The 'crucial effect', he writes, 'of avoiding any decisions is precisely to reassert the legal (and ontological) difference between humans and non-humans, in spite of the applicants' efforts to convert 'otherness' into 'sameness' throughout the proceedings' (Bevilaqua 2013: 77). In other words: theory, science and the law be damned, likes will not be treated alike (Diamond 2004: 93–97), and the existing order will be maintained by refusing to reach the substantive issue. Thus, the court avoided an innovative attempt to use legal technology designed to move the speciesist line by invoking §285-a and §16 under their own language in order to maintain a *status quo* of the legal ontology.

Hiasl's case is not about seeking judicial imprimatur of becoming-human on the part of Hiasl in Deleuzian terms – as in Franz Kafka's *Report to an Academy* (Kafka: 1952) – or a case of (reverse) mistaken identity as Dominic Pettman might put it, but closer to an interspecies legal case of material semiosis within Haraway's contact zone (Haraway 2008: 19), which was rebuffed by the courts. Bevilaqua seemingly refers to this disconnect in terms proposing the legal technology of an agency standard for asserting legal rights. He notes both problematically and prophetically that while only human agency seems to be recognized in law

> [t]his uncomfortable status (of 'non-thing') foregrounds the need to conceptually fabricate another difference (a difference that is other) ... and the more difficult it is to make sense of these others as subjects, of these subjects that are others. Bringing non-human forms of agency into (legal) existence seems to depend not only on acknowledging animals as non-things, as European legal systems are gradually doing, but also as non-persons, in the sense of being something other than the person defined according to the model of human agency. (Bevilaqua 2013: 85)

Bevilaqua argues for change in the law so personhood is determined by the ability to exercise agency. This seems invested in an undefined biosemiotic principle of generalized symmetry between the law and animals such as in Latour and Callon's Actor Network Theory (Latour 2005), or in animals as biosemitic agents (Deeley 2005: 60), or possibly as '*object-agents*' (Vekavarra 2002: 293–310). Even more radically, such agency may arise in systems theory, which allows for the possibility of an alterity of non-human animals because, as was written in the environmental context, 'Society contains its absence in the form of external reference to everything that it itself is not' (Philippopoulos-Mihalopoulos 2009: 48–49). However, Bevilaqua does not articulate a comprehensive theory for such a transformation while observing that jurists are entrenched in their arbitrary desire to maintain *status quo* of the legal forum and its system of ordered dominance. This would be cause for despair except, as Wolfe argues, this very exclusionary and arbitrariness paradoxically forces jurists to define human boundaries and thus consider the possibility of animal alterity (Wolfe 2012: 88–92; Ledingham 2013) which may be where the spatial boundaries of the lawscape are forced, like opposing pressures defining a membrane, to reconsider the 'unjust violence of such a categorization' (Philippopoulos-Mihalopoulos 2012: 124; Ledingham 2013) once alterity and inherent animal agency converge in jurisprudence. Thus, transformation of the law might entail jurists coming to terms with epistemological uncertainty, in science and law, concerning consciousness and a reordering of the legal ontology of personhood. In effect, transformation would ask jurists to reject the arbitrary and heuristic to embrace the possibility of both animal agency and the law's role in obstructing the possibility of justice by denying considerations of alterity and its inherent acknowledgement of agency in human/animal/technological connections and interactions (Philippopoulos-Mihalopoulos 2012: 126).We see that the courts are reluctant to apply legal technology as a transformational agent for a paradigm shift in the human–animal relationship away from a traditional Kantian view in order to confront speciesism through even a limited redrawing of the speciesist lines. Likewise, Hiasl's advocates, who claimed he 'thought he was human', are equally wrong. Hiasl was certain he was a *person* within that shared space but lacked receptive jurists willing to consider and accommodate arguments based upon either science or theory. Application of Beviquila's agency standard or Latour's work would allow Hiasl to participate in an interspecies process which appreciated both the phylogenic differences and shared similarities existing in a relationship between himself and the human. As Hiasl's experience demonstrates, it is difficult to envision the courts considering interspecies space, identity and agency when they are willing to constrain and contort themselves to enforce an outmoded speciesist line.

Brazil

Several constitutional challenges seeking an extension of legal personhood to chimpanzees through the use of *habeas corpus* petitions have been brought in Brazil, with uncertain results. A *habeas corpus* application was filed on the behalf of a chimpanzee named Suiça[48] because the conditions of her confinement at the Salvador zoo were unsuitable as they restricted her ability to engage in locomotion in a natural manner (Gordilho 2010: 2–4). The petition sought Suiça's release and transfer to a primate sanctuary in Sorocaba where she would be able to socialize and interact with others of her species in a more suitable environment, but was dismissed as moot when Suiça was found dead in her cage. In his opinion, Judge Edmundo Lucio da Cruz stated, 'The topic will not die with this [W]rit, it will continue to remain controversial. Thus, can a primate be compared to a human being? Can an animal be released from its cage by means of a *Habeas Corpus*?' Judge da Cruz was prescient in his anticipation of further challenges.

Commenting on the legacy of the *Suiça* case, Professor Heron Santana Gordilho wrote, '[i]t is important to emphasize that the process...cannot be considered invalid, since...the judge made it clear that the Writ fulfilled all the conditions of action, which means that the judicial protection claim was susceptible to assessment, the parties were legitimate and the *Habeas Corpus* was a necessary and appropriate' (Gordilho 2010: 2–4). The fact that the court was even willing to consider the possibility that Suiça might be a legal person is encouraging.

This issue arose again in 2007 when a Brazilian judge revoked an environmental permit which was necessary to keep two chimpanzees, Lili and Megh, from their human owner. The court declared Lili and Megh 'wild fauna' who must be released 'back into nature' (Bevilaqua 2013: 73). Their owner filed a petition for a writ of *habeas corpus* on behalf of Lilli and Megh, with the Superior Court objecting to this classification, the threshold issue being whether Lili and Megh were legally able to maintain standing for the *habeas corpus* petition. Bevilaqua observes that the petition asserted that 'it is not argued that the two chimpanzees are human but that their existence is indissociable from the human world to which they belong' (Bevilaqua 2013: 76). Sensing the court would not accept this argument, Lili and Megh's advocates advanced an alternate argument claiming that they were property. Counsel argued that the judicial order classifying Lili and Megh as *wild fauna* failed to grasp that Lili and Megh had become differentiated, through property status and shared interaction with humans, from wild chimpanzees, would harm them, and was made in derogation of the owner's property rights (Bevilaqua 2013: 83). This alternate argument, reminiscent of Favre's theory of limited self-ownership for animals and a more modest claim than Hiasl's, differentiated Lili and Megh on an intra-species basis from other chimpanzees based upon a shared social space with humans in which Haraway might well feel comfortable. The court ultimately denied the application[49] on procedural grounds stating '*Habeas corpus* shall be granted...whenever anyone suffers or is in danger of suffering violence or coercion against the freedom of locomotion, on account of illegal actions or abuse of power'. This status however, did not apply to Lili and Megh, who were not anyone (i.e. human) in such danger (Bevilaqua 2013: 80). Bevilaqua notes similarity between the cases involving Hiasl and Lili and Megh and focuses on the heart of the matter:

> [t]he most radical advocates of animals as subjects of rights do not posit that all non-human beings should hold all the rights guaranteed to humans. Similarly, the most innovative legal codes do not venture beyond the statement that 'animals are not things.' Legally (but also ontologically) defined as 'non-things', the same beings are contextually subjected either to a specific protective regime (which, by definition, ignores the question of whether animals can be legal subjects), or to the general dispositions concerning things. (2013: 85)

For Lilli and Megh, however, the result was the same as for Hiasl: legal technology was ineffective in persuading an evolution of judicial thought. A similar outcome occurred in 2010 where the Brazilian courts denied a *habeas corpus* petition brought by GAP on behalf of an artistic chimp named Jimmy.[50]

Finally, in a 2010 class action case in Bahia, Brazil, involving the treatment of travelling circus animals owned by the *Circo Portugal*, the court ruled that 'The Federal Constitution and the Civil Code have two legal views about animals, leaving us no doubt that the Federal Constitution came to raise the animals as subjects of fundamental rights such as life, liberty, the physical and psychological integrity' and '[a]ccording to the constitutional provision, regardless of any other rule, animals are subjects of rights' (relief in the form granted, ironically, was not even sought by the plaintiffs). The *Circo Portugal* ruling is very different from those of Suiça, Lili and Megh, and Jimmy because it says that in Brazil animals are not things but are legal subjects, albeit without an explicit grant of personhood.[51] Whether this ruling is an aberration remains to be seen as nothing appears to have changed in its wake. Professor Gordilho advises that the Brazilian legal system does not operate in terms of strict *stare decisis*[52] or adherence to precedent because legal doctrines outweigh the decisions made by individual judges[53] and therefore view legal confrontations with speciesism sceptically.

Rejection of legal technology

We have seen the power structure controlling the law act to thwart legal technologies seeking to confront speciesism and maintain property interests and instrumental uses. Lawyers necessarily operate within a bounded universe of rules, as in the *Amistad* case,[54] which showed the power of rhetoric is limited by the audience's sense of what is plausible, not what is a contingent possibility, and can mean that unjust intransigence and entrenched property interests set the limits of discourse (Roberts-Miller 2002: 5). This is evident in judicial resistance to change. At the other end of the spectrum, frustration with the failure of legal technology to confront speciesism is evident in philosopher Steve Best's observation, 'Fuck the law. When the law is wrong, the right thing to do is break it' (Best 2013),[55] which invokes an expanded view of civil disobedience and a meditation upon violence which may succeed 'where legal tactics would fail'.[56]

Because of this failure, acts of resistance involving illegal or quasi-legal actions by, *inter alia*, Animal Liberation Front, Stop Huntington Life Sciences (SHAC), the Italian Greenhill activists,[57] and Chinese activists who intervene on behalf of dogs and cats intended as food, all proliferate despite government efforts to label proponents as criminals or terrorists. It is axiomatic that for animals the oppression of speciesism is a universally violent condition and resistance is either violent or passive. Jason Hribal points out that captive animals sometimes display agency and resilience in escaping confinement or attacking their tormenters (Hribal 2010). Property damage and violence are the legal technologies of the outsider, the abject, the excluded – and this rejection of theory and conventional legal technology in favour of direct action may prove the most enduring legacy of judicial resistance to speciesism. As Best writes, 'moral progress has occurred not through civilizing the elites who then voluntarily relinquish or broaden their power but rather through one kind of force or another – protests, demonstrations, boycotts, property destruction, and, physical violence and armed struggle'.[58] Transposed to speciesism, this is a realization that Max Planck's observation that new scientific truths become accepted because 'its opponents eventually die, and a new generation grows up that is familiar with it' (Planck 1950: 33) may become accelerated if legal recourse remains unobtainable.

Sociologists such as Humphrey and Stears and D'Arcy argue that direct action, such as liberating animals from vivisectors, serves a beneficial social purpose by engaging citizens who would otherwise be excluded or at a disadvantage in presenting an exposition of their views and thus participating in attendant political debate (Humphrey & Stears 2006: 415–422; D'Arcy 2007: 5–10). They argue that direct action tactics must be tolerated in order to level the political playing field by opening a debate on animal issues and grabbing the attention of otherwise indifferent or intransigent policy makers, thereby legitimizing the political process by making it more 'inclusive'. Indeed, speech advocating property destruction and violence is mostly allowable as long as it is not reasonably calculated to lead to actual violence,[59] although such protections have been eroded in prosecutions under various statutes directed at marginalizing environmental and animal activists as 'terrorists'.[60] Alternately, those structures grudgingly tolerate others who advocate a need for direct action and violent resistance to hierarchies of power such as Derrick Jensen, who is concerned with the meta-effect of civilization on species preservation (Jensen 2006: 322–325). The problem is that violent rhetoric and actions, however justified, rarely confront speciesism directly, but only its most extreme and symbolic forms.

Conclusion

Law is the ultimate deontological manifestation of the misrepresentation and unattainability of social justice. The possibility of an inclusive justice for animals[61] is an illusion as long as humans define species-based ontologies and decide what justice might mean for all species. Legal scholar Edward Mussawir writes of a refusal to grant subjectivity to animals and how misplaced animals would be within an anthropocentric system of judicial constraints:

it is not after all from a lack of rights in this sense that animals suffer in contemporary society. There is little use that an animal could make of these legal rights when one first of all can barely ascribe it a lawful condition, a capacity or a meaning in jurisprudence. (Mussawir 2013: 99)

Because there is no tsunami of public consciousness concerning speciesism, jurists themselves are disinclined to view speciesism as an issue and be receptive to the legal technologies described. Instead jurists focus on welfarist measures instead of the structural change needed for approximating animal liberation (Senatori & Frash 2010: 209–236).

The only material efforts to confront speciesism by any incremental degree are the lawsuits Wise and the Brazilians are pursuing. Although limited in scope, lawsuits challenging legal personhood within the judicial systems force a consideration of (re)defining and (re)ordering the ontologies and means of othering animals in a way alternatives do not. Humans are not willing to embrace Francione's abolitionism and Favre's work retains a speciesist framework unacceptable to those seeking radical change. European legislative initiatives have essentially failed. The recent development in India is promising but has not been litigated. Any reconsideration of speciesism must start by presupposing the failure of theory in defining and confronting speciesism instead of ogling the legal paralysis on the issue.

Notes

1   Walt Kelly (1970).
2   I refer to animals as 'animals' and humans as 'humans' throughout, aware of the inherent ontological problem under discussion.
3   Nietzsche wrote, 'We do not regard the animals as moral beings. But do you suppose the animals regard us as moral beings? – An animal which could speak said: "Humanity is a prejudice of which we animals at least are free"' (Nietzsche 1982: 329). Echoing John Gray, 'moral status' has alternatively been described 'an obfuscating piece of philosophical nonsense' (email from Prof. Hursthouse, dated 3 January 2011).
4   James Rachels and Joan Dunayer have posited this reduction.
5   Haraway cites Anna Tsing's observation that 'human nature is an interspecies relationship'.
6   Professor Steven Wise heads the Nonhuman Rights Project. I am grateful to have served as a member of the NHRP from 2010–2012.
7   Haraway is referring to both Heidegger's and Derrida's discussion of the difference between humans and animals in terms of a theorized capability to *respond* rather than merely *react*.
8   Prof. Bryant managed to change the status concerning the conditions under which some shelter animals were sacrificial in California through legislation by drafting 'Hayden's Law', which requires that shelter animals be released to available rescue organizations in lieu of euthanasia.

9   Reminiscent of Orwell's observation in *Animal Farm* that 'some animals are more equal than others'.
10   See, for example, 510 Ill. Comp. Stat. Ann. 70/16.3; *Plotnick v. Meihaus*, 208 Cal. App.4th 1590; 146 Cal. Rptr. 3d 585; but see *Strickland v. Medlin*, 12–0047 Sup. Ct. Texas (5 April 2013).
11   Email from David Favre, 14 April 2013.
12   *False Claims Act*, 31 U.S.C. §3729. See also *United States ex rel. Patricia Haight, et al., v. Catholic Healthcare West, et al.*, 2010 U.S. App. LEXIS 2381.
13   N.C. Gen. Stat. §19A-1 et seq., see also *ALDF v. Woodley*, 640 S.E.2d 777; 2007 WL 475329.
14   *Grundgesetz für die Bundesrepublik Deutschland*
15   https://www.btg-bestellservice.de/pdf/80201000.pdf (accessed 21 August 2013).
16   *Bürgerlichen Gesetzbuche* http://www.gesetze-im-internet.de/englisch_bgb/englisch_bgb.html (accessed 21 August 2013).
17   Kelch cites the *Constitution Federal de la Confederation Suisse*, April 18, 1999, Arts. 74, 80 and 104.
18   http://paçtiss.org/2008/05/28/should-the-great-apes-have-rights (accessed 24 August 2013).
19   William Shakespeare, *Macbeth*, Scene V.
20   http://www.elmundo.es/elmundo/2006/04/24/sociedad/1145890969.html (accessed 24 August 2013).
21   http://www.nonhumanrightsproject.org/2012/03/05/ask-the-animal-rights-lawyer-%E2%80%9Cdo-great-apes-have-legal-rights-in-spain%E2%80%9D/ (accessed 24 August 2013).
22   http://www.nonhumanrightsproject.org/2012/03/05/ask-the-animal-rights-lawyer-%E2%80%9Cdo-great-apes-have-legal-rights-in-spain%E2%80%9D/ (accessed 24 August 2013).
23   http://www.brusselsjournal.com/node/1031 (accessed 24 August 2013).
24   http://cza.nic.in (accessed 24 August 2013).
25   http://www.abolitionistapproach.com/the-great-ape-project-not-so-great/#.UfsuFG1i11z blog post 20 December 2006 (accessed 21 August 2012).
26   *Somerset v Stewart* 98 ER 499 (1772).
27   http://cza.nic.in (accessed 24 August 2013).
28   See e.g.: Mt. *Graham Red Squirrel v. Yeutter*, 930 F. 2d 703; *Palila v. Hawaii Dept. of Land and Natural Resources*, 852 F. 2d 703; *Northern Spotted Owl v. Lujan*, 758 F. Supp.
29   http://www.nz01.2day.terabyte.co.nz/ots/DocumentLibrary%5CWhanganuiRiverAgreement.pdf (accessed 30 July 2013).
30   Steven Wise, 'Are You a Legal Person or a Legal Thing?' http://www.nonhumanrightsproject.org (accessed 27 April 2013).
31   http://www.nonhumanrightsproject.org (accessed 20 April 2013).
32   http://www.nonhumanrightsproject.org/2013/12/02/lawsuit-filed-today-on-behalf-of-chimpanzee-seeking-legal-personhood/ (accessed December 2, 2013).
33   http://www.unesco.org/mab/doc/grasp/E_KinshasaDeclaration.pdf (accessed 5 April 2013).
34   http://fcmconference.org/img/CambridgeDeclarationOnConsciousness.pdf (accessed 27 April 2013)
35   *Dred Scott v. Sandford*, 60 U.S. 393 (1857).

36 16 U.S.C. Sec. 1361 *et seq.*

37 *CEASE v. New England Aquarium*, 836 F. Supp. 45 (1993).

38 *Id*, at 49.

39 TILIKUM, the first named plaintiff, is an Orca. His confinement is the subject of much of the film *Blackfish*.

40 *TILIKUM v. Sea World Parks & Entertainment, Inc.*, 842 F. Supp. 2d. 1259.

41 U.S. Const. Amendment XIII states in part 'Neither slavery nor involuntary servitude, except as a punishment for crime whereof the party shall have been duly convicted, shall exist within the United States'.

42 U.S. Const. Art. III

43 *Slaughter-House Cases*, 83 U.S. 36 (1872).

44 *TILIKUM v. Sea World, supra. at 6.*

45 PETA had put the cart before the horse.

46 Guardians specifically for animals may be appointed in the U.S.

47 http://hudoc.echr.coe.int/sites/eng/Pages/search.aspx#{%22fulltext%22:[%22 Matthewl%22],%22documentcollectionid2%22:[%22GRANDCHAMBER% 22,%22CHAMBER%22 (accessed 5 April 2013).

48 *In Favor of Suiça*, 9th Salvador Criminal Court, 9th Criminal Jurisdiction, Salvador, Bahia, Brazil (26 September 2005), petition case number n 833085– 3/2005.

49 'One can not ask for a writ of *habeas corpus* on behalf of animals because the law only allows the granting of *habeas corpus* in favor of humans' (email dated 10 April 2013 from Prof. Gordilho).

50 Jimmy, N.° 0002637–70.2010.8.19.0000, 5 November 2010.

51 See, *Ministério Público Do Estado Da Bahia, Associação Brasileira Terra Verde Viva E Associação Célula Mãe v. Portugal Produções Artísticas Ltda 'Circo Portugal'*, 12th July 2010. I am grateful to Prof. Gordilho for his insight.

52 See, *Constitution of Brazil*, Constitutional Amendment n. 45/2004, Art. 103-A.

53 Emails from Prof. Gordilho, dated 14 April 2013 and 16 April 2013.

54 *United States v. Libellants and Claimants of the Schooner Amistad*, 40 U.S. 518 (1841).

55 "Video on the website of Dr. Steve Best" http://drstevebest.wordpress. com/2011/10/29/dr-steven-best-fuck-the-law-riot-now/ (accessed 28 November 2013). Steve Best, *Fuck the Law-Riot Now* http://www.youtube.com/ watch?feature=player_embedded&v=oPbOLlad1nk (accessed 30 April 2013).

56 Steve Best, *Gaps in Logic, Lapses in Politics: Rights and Abolitionism in Joan Dunayer's Speciesism* http://www.drstevebest.org/essays.htm (2012) (accessed 17 April 2013).

57 Animals were liberated from the Greenhill breeding facility on 28 April 2012 in Montichiari, Italy.

58 Steve Best, *Gaps in Logic, Lapses in Politics.*

59 *Brandenburg v. Ohio*, 395 U.S. 444 (1965).

60 See, for example, *US v. SHAC*, (Civ. No. 04-cr-00373 USDC D NJ).

61 Etymologically, the idea of 'animal justice' presupposes a form of justice for animals separate and apart from social justice for humans and the environment, which is problematic.

CHAPTER THREE

'Beyond' the Singular?
Ecology, Subjectivity, Politics

Danielle Sands

*The political question for the twenty-first century will center
around the extent to which a transcendent, universal form of
subjectivity can be removed from the political lexicon.*

ANDREW M. KOCH (2007: 129)

Rights, justice and the singular subject

In her essay 'Injustice and Animals', Cora Diamond uses Simone Weil's
late reflections in 'Human Personality' to tease open the relationship
between 'justice' and 'rights'. For Weil, the term 'rights' represents the
commodification of a much deeper network of human relationships and she
traces its origin to Roman property law, reminding us that in this context,
property often referred to enslaved humans. She is characteristically frank:
'It is singularly monstrous that ancient Rome should be praised for having
bequeathed to us the notion of rights' (Weil 2005: 82). Central to the liberal
tradition, the discourse of rights has become enshrined in Anglo-European
law, reinforcing a structure whereby the 'subject' – rational, autonomous and,
without exception, human – is accorded a certain social standing. Despite
the problems with rights discourse and with the framework it represents –
not by any means confined to Weil's repulsion at its origins – it remains
pervasive, and, incongruous as it may seem, has provided the grounding for
significant attempts to refashion the relationship between human and non-
human animals.

The most famous of these was made by Peter Singer, whose purportedly
anti-speciesist argument in the ground-breaking *Animal Liberation* can be

summarized by the claim that beings who have the capacity to suffer have an interest in avoiding suffering and, therefore, have the right to have this interest acknowledged and protected. Singer's account is doubtless more nuanced with regard to the attribution of rights than his critics would suggest; however, his focus on rights seems itself misguided. Whilst protecting those who are included, the designation of a category of beings who are deserving of rights inevitably devalues those who escape this category, often resulting in their abuse. To expand the ethical community to incorporate some non-human animals is simply to displace the abuse and overlook the history.

Singer's adoption of the concept of interests provides scope for further questioning. As Deborah Slicer perceives, rights theories 'reduce individuals to that atomistic bundle of interests that the justice tradition recognizes as the basis for moral considerableness. In effect, animals are represented as beings with the *kind of capacity* that human beings most fully possess and deem valuable for living a full *human* life' (Wolfe 2003: 36). This focus on interests not only renders non-human animals subject to a singularly human value system, it also suggests a certain economization of value. Concerns about the implications of this form part of Weil's critique. She observes:

> The notion of rights is linked with the notion of sharing out, of exchange, of measured quantity. It has a commercial flavour, essentially evocative of legal claims and arguments. Rights are always asserted in a tone of contention; and when this tone is adopted, it must rely upon force in the background, or else it will be laughed at. (Weil 1986: 81)

Weil looks to challenge the conflation of rights and justice, suggesting that, as Diamond notes, 'when genuine issues of justice and injustice are framed in terms of rights, they are thereby distorted and trivialised' (Diamond 2001: 120). For Weil, rights and justice belong to 'different conceptual realm[s]' (Diamond 2001: 120). Weil's conception of justice is sheared from the language of economics and law, and thus feels shocking. She tells us that 'Justice consists in seeing that no harm is done to men' (Weil 2005: 93), a claim which, while notably speciesist, contrasts with the familiar liberal justice position, expressed for example by James P. Sterba as, 'Justice requires giving what is deserved' (Sterba 2006: 148). In comparison, the latter feels limited, inaccurate, even mean.

A gloss on this disparity within the notion of justice, or in the tension between rights and justice, can be found in terms of the relationship between law and justice in the opening section of Jacques Derrida's essay 'Force of Law: On the Mystical Foundation of Authority'. Derrida's perception of justice in this essay has much in common with that of Weil. Justice is that which is excessive and non-economic, evading calculation. It cannot be sedimented into law or generality; it is 'without economic circularity, without calculation and without rules …' (Derrida 2001: 254). It exceeds and haunts the law – which is economic, limited, generalizable – and renders it always incomplete.[1] Nevertheless, for Derrida, law and justice are inseparable, existing in a non-economic relationship which means that one can never be reduced to the other. The consequence for Derrida, who responds to Pascal's claim that 'la justice sans la force est impuissante', is that justice cannot be severed from the law and held in a state of passive, transcendent purity, rather, 'justice is not justice, it is not achieved if it does not have the force to be "enforced"; a powerless justice is not justice, in the sense of law' (Derrida 1995: 238). This strange yoking of the seeming opposites of law and justice is not altogether different from Weil's understanding of the disjunction between rights and justice as 'a difference in grammar' (Diamond 2001: 120). The two terms speak of different, even incompatible conceptual frameworks, but are drawn together; 'in their very heterogeneity', they are 'indissociable' (Derrida 1995: 257). The lesson here is perhaps that we should never settle for a self-satisfied version of law (or indeed of its expression as 'rights') which professes to be just or complete, rather we should always strive to attend to the complexity and singularity of each instance.

A second, equally illuminating expression of this problem can be found in Derrida's account of democracy. The heterogeneous indissociability of law and justice here emerges in the two orders or truths of democracy. Derrida depicts the first using images of circling or revolving; it is an economic movement which aspires to a return to same or self. This refers to the way in which democracy measures itself out, offering equal rights and equal access to opportunities. Derrida maintains, 'it seems difficult to think such a desire for or naming of democratic space without the rotary motion of some quasi-circular return or rotation toward the self, toward the origin itself' (2005: 10). However, this sense of equality and similarity does not fully capture the meaning of democracy. Rather, Derrida asserts that 'the relationship between the commensurable and the incommensurable is what is at stake in democracy' (2005: 111), with the latter element, incommensurability or incalculability, consisting of heterogeneity, licence and openness to the other. This sense of freedom and openness, of difference, can be seen in the need for democracy to remain open to anything, even to the rejection of democracy itself. These two movements are both constitutive of democracy yet cannot be thought together; freedom and equality 'are reconcilable, so to speak, only in a turning or alternating fashion' (Derrida 2005: 24). Derrida takes up Plato's claim that democracy can never name a regime or constitution, and suggests that it cannot be a concept either, as this schism between its two modes denies it a 'proper' or self-same identity. This is not to be confused with a gap between the theory and practice of democracy; for Derrida, the 'opening of indetermination and indecidability' is *in the very concept* of democracy' (2005: 25).

Derrida's account of democracy gives us a broader sense of the framework from which rights issue and a clearer idea of the problems which may arise in the development of an ethics of non-human life. These problems arise not only from the idea of rights themselves, but from the democratic frameworks – not only familiar but assumed irreproachable – in which they are situated. Derrida's first sense of democracy, with its stress on equality and calculability, is central here. In order to 'count' or be recognized within this system, being must appear in the form of a singular subject with certain capacities. Democracy does acknowledge difference and non-identity (Derrida's second truth), yet it is only in the first sense, where everyone is equal to every other one, that ethical status becomes formalized in law. As we have seen with rights, that which is not included – and the system is only structurally coherent if there is an excluded term – is immediately disregarded. Although democratic systems have clearly made considerable progress with regard to respect for non-human animal life, this appears to be limited, not least by their role in perpetuating a model of individualist subjectivity which separates and elevates the human community, according its subjects only with full ethical value. It is notable that in Derrida's later work democracy becomes a synonym for politics; in Western democratic societies – for good or ill – it has become impossible to envisage a political system outside of this framework.

In what follows, I shall consider three approaches to non-human life which navigate these issues of subjectivity and political representation. The first, Derrida's own account, presents a challenge both to philosophical histories of 'the animal' and to rights-driven positions. However, it is, I shall argue, inhibited by its dependence on the concept of 'unsubstitutable singularity' which reinforces a model of individualist subjectivity, consequently short-circuiting any properly radical approach to the question of non-human life. Turning to ecological accounts for a more potentially radical approach, I shall focus first on Val Plumwood's quest for alternative and plural rationalities, discussing how her shift of emphasis from consciousness to intentionality offers us an alternative subjective framework. I shall argue, however, that she struggles to translate this into an effective political position as she remains within current political discourses which alienate non-human others and fails to envisage real change to current democratic structures. Plumwood's account, however, is the only one which attempts to sketch out the practicalities of political change. Turning finally to Timothy Morton's (2007: 67) critique both of conceptions of 'nature' and of the ways in which environmental writing sustains 'ideological fantasy' and reproduces the structures and relations which it looks to challenge, I shall both endorse his critique – which problematizes any reductive account of intersubjective relations – and reveal its limitations. Both Derrida and Morton tend to confine themselves to a realm of abstraction, to the 'political' which haunts or shadows the practicalities of 'politics', in the same way that justice stalks and exceeds law. This approach, I shall argue, is insufficient, as it fails to account for the duality of this movement, the ways in which the practical truths of current political structures condition the abstractions and grounds of political thought itself.

Derrida: The limitations of 'unsubstitutable singularity'

In *The Animal That Therefore I Am*, a corrective to philosophical misrepresentations of animal life, and concomitantly, to humanity's ill-formed autobiography, Derrida looks to challenge our understanding of the term 'animal':

> Animal is a word men have given themselves the right to give. These humans are found giving it to themselves, this word, but as if they had received it as an inheritance. They have given themselves the word in order to corral a large number of living beings within a single concept: 'The Animal', they say. (2008: 32)

Derrida's (2008: 88) work here is long overdue, as he tracks and critiques the 'post-Cartesian genealogy' of thinkers who follow Descartes' separation of man as rational, linguistic animal from all other animals, which are dismissed as mere 'animal-machines' (22). For Derrida, such thinkers include Kant, Heidegger, Lacan and Levinas, thinkers who all employ a discourse which ignores animal difference, disregards the subjection of animals as well as advances in 'ethological or primatological knowledge' (Derrida 2008: 89) and perceives the animal as that which is deprived of language, agency, subjectivity and the ability to meet and match the human gaze. Derrida demonstrates the ways in which this ill-conceived discourse informs both the human–animal relation and the human self relationship; it is inseparable from the development of human subjectivity and ethics. He terms it 'the discourse of domination itself' (Derrida 2008: 89).

Groundwork done, Derrida (2008: 41) replaces the 'general singular' term 'animal' with the multi-faceted 'animot' and looks to develop an alternative methodology and discourse which respond to the otherness and multiplicity of animal life. This emphasis on otherness is characteristic of Derrida's later work, and speaks of the influence – complex and contested – of Emmanuel Levinas. The face-to-face encounter which opens and underpins Levinasian ethics is transformed into the human–animal encounter; Derrida describes: 'The animal looks at us, and we are naked before it. Thinking perhaps begins there'. For Derrida (2008: 29), what becomes evident in this experience is the animal's 'unsubstitutable singularity', which means that we must acknowledge each animal as an individual with unique needs, desires and interests, and we must respond accordingly. This, he suggests, would begin to challenge the processes of objectification and instrumentalization which perpetuate animal abuse. Here, however, Derrida sounds a little like Singer, his emphasis on interests and individual subjectivity pushing him towards an ethical extensionist approach. Alterity and singularity figure as placeholders for ethics in Derrida's work; before he encounters the 'animal', his model of 'ethics' is already in place. Rather than acknowledging that the non-human might challenge the very concept of ethics, Derrida (2008: 107) stretches the Levinasian account to incorporate that which is 'more radically other' than the other human, the animal. Ironically, it is due to its similarity with human life – its potential to possess some kind of individualist subjectivity – that it enters 'the ethical circuit' (Derrida 2008: 106).[2] The trope of 'unsubstitutable singularity' may well prove useful in unsettling assumptions about non-human life; however, Derrida fails to acknowledge that it originates from a certain anthropocentrism which restricts the possibility of a radical rethinking of human and non-human life and disavows the stranger, more challenging elements of deconstructive thinking in this area.[3]

Plumwood: From consciousness to intentionality

The focus on the singular individual has proved one of the key differences between the movements of animal rights and environmental ethics. Whereas, according to Kate Rawles, 'the animal rights/liberation movement is primarily concerned with individuals rather than collectives, and with individuals of a certain kind' (2007: 92), environmental ethics tends to focus on broader movements, and on collectivities rather than individuals. As critics have noted (Baird Callicott 2001: 5–15), this has generated something of a schism between the two in spite of their many shared aims. Whereas the focus on the 'animal' tends to make it more difficult to reconceptualize subjectivity, environmental accounts incline towards a more exploratory approach to the subject. One such account is that of Val Plumwood, whose environmental writing, although not avowedly deconstructive, exhibits a certain deconstructive flavour in its interests and strategies.

Similarities between Derrida and Plumwood are clear: she highlights certain oppositions, such as those between nature/culture, reason/nature and prudence/ethics, which she regards as having limiting or damaging effects; she looks to replace monologue with dialogue; rejects totalizing environmental solutions and, like later Derrida, looks to exchange a 'cult of reason' (Plumwood 2002: 4) with what Derrida might term 'heterogeneous rationalities' (Derrida 2005: 121). This method enables Plumwood to escape some of the pitfalls of environmental criticism, for example, the reductive inversion of anthropocentrism to ecocentrism. In this section, I shall consider how her approach, which begins from the environment rather than from the individual animal, may present an opening to different conceptions of subjectivity.

Plumwood's aim in *Environmental Culture* is twofold, combining 'the tasks of (re)situating humans in ecological terms and non-humans in ethical terms' (Plumwood 2002: 8–9). This she will achieve by dismantling the supremacy of a restricted and restrictive form of reason, 'economic, egoist and atomistic' (Plumwood 2002: 33), which is now widely recognized as the only form of reason. Consisting of a privileging of abstract or conceptual thought, of a vilification of the body and of corporeal knowledge, of an unshakeable faith in the salvific power of science and technology and of a tendency to reinforce privilege through its adherence to the whims of the market, this brand of rationalism reinforces the damaging dualism between humanity and nature. This promotes the image of human life as intrinsically separate from other forms of life and rendered superior by its capacity to reason. Any sense of mutual dependency is jettisoned here, 'nature', its multitudinous elements, capacities and requirements, dismissed as 'Other'. In service of her argument, Plumwood notes that blame for the current ecological crisis has been apportioned to nature, in the form of '"natural" human selfishness or greed' whereas reason 'in the form of scientific or technical fix' (2002: 6) emerges as the hero. For Plumwood, our unerring faith in science is irrational 'because it does not take due account of the possibility of being wrong, as any fully rational position must' (2002: 6). Further, the reliance on a scientific solution does little to rethink the grounds of our relationship with nature, viewing this as unchangeable.

This unchecked rationalism represents an entire political and philosophical structure which conditions our relationships. Plumwood (2002: 48) argues that 'The modern rationalist-empiricist model is explicitly about power, instrumentalism, individualism, and human-centredness' and reason has become a 'vehicle for domination' (Plumwood 2002: 5) over a passified and instrumentalized 'other'. The alliance of reason with profit and with maximizing self-interest has led to the global capitalism that we currently experience, to a world where value is economized and prudence is valued over ethics, which is itself increasingly individualized. The non-human is regarded as deserving minimal ethical attention, nature an inactive backdrop which must be remade in 'a more rational form' (Plumwood 2002: 25). The individualist 'master subject' (Plumwood 2002: 29) exists in a bubble, fuelled by the 'illusion of self-containment' (Plumwood 2002: 27), denying the contributions of human and non-human others. It is clear both how an ethical extensionist model of animal ethics might fit into this fiercely individualist model, and how this would simply shift the boundaries which determine who or what may be abused. Such a framework perceives species difference in anthropocentric terms, overlooking or dismissing non-human abilities. Plumwood is frank: 'Extensionist ethical strategies do not fit with an ecological awareness of the kinship and continuity of planetary life' (2002: 144). Moving away from extensionist strategies entails rethinking the primacy of the individualist subject and developing a broader, more self-critical rationality. This ecological rationality would include 'that higher-order form of critical, prudential, self-critical reason which scrutinises the match or fit between an agent's choices, actions and effects and that agent's overall desires, interests and objectives as they require certain ecological conditions for their fulfilment' (Plumwood 2002: 68).

Plumwood proposes various ways of re-visioning subjectivity and intersubjectivity. She looks to the humanities, where the studied other is not regarded passive and mindless, for a 'subject/subject' (Plumwood 2002: 52) configuration to replace the subject/object hierarchy. This too is limited, however, as it confines itself to the human. She urges that we minimize ranking and the establishment of hierarchies, extending respect to non-human others – as we do to other humans – without grading their 'rationality'. Following a feminist trajectory which has adapted the Heideggerian notion of *Mitsein*, and includes thinkers such as Luce Irigaray and Donna Haraway, she emphasizes the primacy of 'being with', arguing that the subject does not pre-exist its relationships with others, and putting renewed stress on relationality and embeddedness – without sacrificing difference – in her quest for a 'Counter-centric ethics' (Plumwood 2002: 124).[4] Here she accepts human *epistemological locatedness* (Plumwood 2002: 132) and rejects the Deep Ecological tendency towards a total rejection of human interests and needs, instead dispelling the myth that prudence demands egocentrism and rejecting the polarization of anthropocentrism and ecocentrism. She doesn't deem the category of the 'human' worthless and out of date, but rather stresses the human potential for dialogue and communication, insisting that 'in these contexts of interrelationship, not monological but different dialogical strategies aimed not at self-maximisation but at negotiation and mutual flourishing are rational' (Plumwood 2002: 33). We would have to devise new ways, which are not primarily linguistic, to communicate with non-human others and this would entail a more thoroughgoing experience of our embeddedness.

Perhaps most importantly, she argues that we should shift focus from the Cartesian position (or mechanist stance) where consciousness is seen as either/or to a broader understanding of intentionality, or the 'intentional recognition stance' which would be more receptive to non-human others. She explains:

A simple spectrum or scalar concept like consciousness has the disadvantage, additional to unclarity and obscurity, of having little capacity to recognise incommensurability or difference, and none at all if interpreted in terms of hegemonic otherness. Intentionality can allow us to take better account of incommensurability because there is enough breadth, play and multiplicity in intentionality to allow us to use diverse, multiple and decentred concepts that need not be ranked relative to each other for understanding both humans and more-than-humans as intentional beings. For example pheromone-based, sonar-based and pollen-based sensitivities and chemical communication systems such as those used by cells might appear as heterogeneous intentional capacities that cannot be treated as extensions of the paradigmatic human case, as narrow concepts like consciousness tend to be. (Plumwood 2002: 179–180)

Here she challenges us to reconceptualize the world as a web of intentionality, suggesting that 'a world perceived in communicative and narrative terms is certainly far richer and more exciting than the self-enclosed world of meaningless and silent objects, exclusionary, monological and commodity thinking creates, reflecting back to us only the echo of our own desires' (Plumwood 2002: 230). This approach, characterized as 'a weak panpsychism' (Plumwood 2002: 178), and first posited in *Feminism and the Mastery of Nature*, not only observes 'mind-like qualities' (Plumwood, 200: 178) throughout nature,[5] but argues that these are deserving of ethical and political consideration. She insists that 'whenever we can discern an autonomous intentional system or teleology the concepts of respect and moral consideration have a potential for application' (Plumwood 1993: 210). Here she calls for a re-ethicizing and re-politicizing of our relationships with non-human others, defining ethics as 'the domain of response to the other's needs, ends, directions, or meaning' (Plumwood 1993: 138), a phrase inflected with Derridean alterity but creating a much broader sense of 'other' than that which we find in Derrida's *Animal*. Plumwood issues one caveat: intentionality shouldn't just become another way of ranking, a test of individual value, but should change our aspect, increasing our openness to non-human intentionality and the capacity for communication and exchange. Plumwood advocates a change on two interconnected levels: both at the quotidian level of thought and language, and legally, creating a new system whereby non-human others are not routinely ignored or discredited.

Plumwood considers the latter at some length, assessing the viability and effectiveness of different forms of democracy in responding to the needs of non-human others. She critiques the concept of interest group liberalism, arguing that it propagates the idea of political subjects as private consumers and discourages a sense of collective responsibility. She insists that the current political system requires more than minimal changes to render it ecologically aware and responsible, and explores different forms of deliberative, communicative and discursive democracy. She argues:

> The kind of society whose democratic forms open communication and spread decision-making processes as equally as possible should, other things being equal, offer the best chance of effective action on these significant kinds of ecoharms. Thus systems which are able to articulate and respond to the needs of the least privileged should be better than less democratic systems which reserve effective participation in decision-making for privileged groups. (Plumwood 2002: 91)

She is acutely aware of the ways in which certain democratic models and processes privilege particular groups, and she reveals 'The hidden rationalist assumption here that social or redistributive inequality is irrelevant to political inequality' (Plumwood 2002: 94). However, this entire chapter

feels rather incongruous within the volume as a whole. It is doubtless one
of the most important, wrangling with the specific ways in which non-
human life may gain political recognition, yet it contains very little about
non-human life. Rather, it feels like a foray into political philosophy in
which political philosophy remains completely intact. Plumwood veers into
extensionist territory, regarding non-human life as another 'unprivileged'
group seeking adequate legal representation, another example of the 'voices
from below' (Plumwood 2002: 95). Aside from the extensionist issue, an
additional problem here is that Plumwood seems to ignore the logistical
difficulties of giving non-human life a voice; as Ted Benton (2003: 341)
articulates:

> If the emphasis on communication has to do with allowing the voice of
> non-human beings to be heard in our democratic decision-making, then
> this voice cannot be heard directly, but only by way of receptive human
> mediators. This is a very important difference between a liberation ethic
> for nature and the other liberation movements. (Benton 2003: 41)

Plumwood seems to deny that this is a 'very important difference', implying
instead that all forms of life, and all human groups, have different voices
and communicative styles which we must recognize and to which we must
adapt. However, she does not effectively defend this, and her rather vague
observations about listening to non-human voices, and her preference for
embeddedness over remoteness, are lost in the complexities of her account
of different democratic forms. As she herself states: 'A political structure
that aimed to hear the bad news from below couldn't just rely on hoping to
represent "below" in apparently fair communicative processes' (Plumwood
2002: 96). Plumwood is right here, yet in absenting the 'voice from below'
from this entire chapter she both fails her own test and demonstrates the
difficulty of incorporating non-human voices into a democratic structure
which fetishizes the individualist subject.

We might turn back to Derrida's account of democracy here, not only
to remind ourselves of its inescapable tensions – the two orders of equality
and difference which can only be realized intermittently – but also to
address the concept of equality itself. Plumwood gestures towards the claim
that equality in the form of voting rights is not in itself 'equal', as it tends
to favour certain groups over others. We have already seen how current
democratic forms exclude non-human life and recognize only individualist
subjectivity. One partial response to the problem, following both Derrida
and Plumwood, would be the development of a stronger, more influential
extra-legal, 'political', or 'ultrapolitical' zone where other, more varied
conceptions of equality and justice come to put pressure upon those currently
enshrined in law.[6] Like Weil and Derrida, Plumwood looks to a broader,
non-economic account of justice, arguing that 'One source of the neglect of
redistributive equality in liberal concepts of political equality are concepts

of justice and equality defined in terms of reason and the state' (2002: 94). An understanding of justice and equality which is constantly in process and which resists their economic re-appropriation is a useful starting point here, alongside Plumwood's call both for a broader understanding of agency and for a more communicative, engaged relationship with non-human life. Plumwood's work exposes the insufficiency of Singer's claim: 'We have to speak up on behalf of those who cannot speak for themselves' (1977: xii), yet it remains unclear how non-human voices may be heard rather than represented.

Morton: Ecology without nature

The questions surrounding representing and responding to non-human others form the basis of Timothy Morton's work. For Morton, 'Ecological criticism keeps beating itself against the glass of the other like a fly' (2007: 100). He argues that a recognition of the limitations of ecological writing might actually render us better placed to respond to non-human life. In *Ecology Without Nature*, he problematizes the concept of 'nature' and more recent, increasingly sophisticated variants on this concept which bypass the term but not the framework,[7] thus separating and idealizing the natural world.[8] The deconstructive inflection of Morton's work is reflected in his claim that he speaks in the name of an 'ecology to come' (2007: 6). This suggests not a distinct futuristic moment, but an aporetic structure, like that of Derrida's 'democracy to come', which speaks of tensions inherent in the concept of 'democracy'. Looking to politicize the aesthetic, Morton also trades on the political implications of the 'to come', which does not consign us to passive anticipation, but rather demands active engagement, that one 'should force oneself to achieve it'. (Derrida 2005: 74).

For Morton, *Ecology Without Nature* 'wavers both inside and outside ecocriticism' (2007: 9). He is nonetheless unequivocal about the implications of a fetishized concept of nature, asserting that 'putting something called Nature on a pedestal and admiring it from afar does for the environment what patriarchy does for the figure of Woman. It is a paradoxical act of sadistic admiration' (Morton 2007: 5). Turning back to Plumwood with Morton's eyes, we might see how her acceptance of an ontologically unquestioned concept of 'environment' underscores the problematic elements of her account, notably the model of political engagement and her failure to examine the complexities of the relationship between 'environment' and capitalist consumerism. Morton (2007: 67) maintains that environmental writing pursues a path of 'ideological fantasy' which further separates and misrepresents its subject. Taking Romantic accounts of self and nature as his starting point, Morton (2007: 135) unravels the complex techniques, the *ecomimesis*, by which art looks to render nature present and to dissolve the distinction between artist and subject, but succeeds only in creating carefully and complexly rendered artificial worlds and reproducing 'with a vengeance the Cartesian opposition between *res cogitans* and *res extensa*'. Rather than inviting new conceptions of subjectivity, environmental writing tends to reinforce the old.

In this way, 'nature' becomes a conduit for understanding the self and the intricacies of the internal landscape, and nature writing a discourse of idealism rather than materialism. This is perhaps to render vulgar the intricacies and historical sensibilities of Morton's position, which effectively demonstrates the need for critical vigilance and a scepticism towards the aesthetic, particularly the latter's tendencies to idolize, idealize and transcendentalize.[9] Morton also observes the ways in which 'nature' becomes a secular trope for God, asking: 'If it is just another word for supreme authority, then why not just call it God? But if this God is nothing outside the material world, then why not just call it matter?' (2007: 15) Reframing this more productively he describes: 'Nature wants to be both substance and essence at the same time. Nature opens up the differences between terms and erases these very differences all at once. It is the trees and the wood – and the very idea of trees (Greek *hyle*, matter wood)' (Morton 2007: 18). For Morton, a central problem is how to retain the urgency of the ecological crisis if 'nature' is transcendentalized.

As his image of the hapless fly suggests, much of nature writing, ostensibly written in glorification of the other, reinforces and celebrates a certain inherently separatist model of subjectivity. As he frames it, environmental writing appears as yet another expression of the solipsistic desire to outline and understand the human subject by plotting it against fictive notions of God, death and the 'other'. At first, Morton seems to find himself repeating familiar investigations into the human's abyssal relationship with itself. He states that '*Ecology without Nature* takes nature out of the equation by exploring the ways in which literary writing tries to conjure it up. We discover how nature always slips out of reach in the very act of grasping it' (Morton 2007: 19). Given this, it is hard to imagine how his work could provide anything other than the latest chapter in the human separatist autobiography. However, his insistence that we retain a certain focus on the human is crucial. He warns against the dangers of taking flight into an alternative vocabulary, be it Donna Haraway's 'natureculture' or the 'posthumanism' of Cary Wolfe and others; such a move would be too easy, implying yet not fulfilling a shift in framework. Accordingly, Morton goes to great pains to deny any association with posthumanism, asserting that:

> The ecological thought reserves a special place for the 'subject' – the mind, the person, even the soul. Posthumanism seems suspiciously keen to delete the paradigm of humanness like a bad draft...What if being human is the encounter with the strange stranger or in other words, at a certain limit, an encounter with the inhuman? (2012: 3)

There is clearly a little wilful misunderstanding here. As Kate Soper (2011: 56) recognizes, there are strong similarities between Morton's work and posthumanism. In part a consequence of the Derridean inheritance of both, the strongest connection emerges in the notion of the non-self-identity of the human; as Cary Wolfe, perhaps the most significant proponent of posthumanism, describes, '"we" are not "we"; we are not that "auto-" of the "autobiography" that "humanism gives to itself." Rather, "we" are always radically other, already in- or a-human in our very being...' (2009: 57). The difference here seems merely terminological – whether or not to retain the 'human' label – yet for Morton there is certainly more at stake. His work speaks directly against the idea that simply by adopting a different vocabulary we can leave the tensions and issues behind. Retaining the messy, misunderstood term 'human' serves as a reminder that there is no pre-lapsarian form of 'nature' to which we can escape. As Norman Wirzba discerns, 'Morton proposes that our best strategy is not to seek some elemental wholeness, unity or monism, since these invariably fail. Rather we should acknowledge the gap by exploring rigorously and patiently the otherness that is within our engagement with the world' (2008: 529).

In undertaking this process of exploration, Morton adopts an ironic stance, in which irony is synonymous with non-identity. In this, he again echoes Derrida, who, on acknowledging the desire to escape metaphysics as a metaphysical desire, instead looks to repeat the procedures of metaphysics *otherwise*, creating a certain doubling, or non-identity within metaphysics itself. This position, at once both less and more ambitious than ecological attempts to escape the nature/human, inside/outside or subject/object dualisms, might relieve the fly of its glass banging. It does mean, however, that Morton's (2007: 188) account feels less obviously transformative, as it consists of 'finding ways to stick around with the sticky mess that we're in'. This is nowhere more true than with regard to subjectivity, with Morton rejecting attempts to reframe the subject/object divide as 'intersubjectivity', arguing that these do nothing other than re-inscribe the same divide and fixate on the same, irresolvable problematic. He expands upon this further:

Wherever I look for my self I only encounter a potentially infinite series of alterities: my body, my arm, my ideas, place of birth, parents, history, society... The same goes for nature. Wherever we look for it, we encounter just a long metonymic string of bunnies, trees, stars, space toothbrushes, skyscrapers... Attempts to found a politics and philosophy on a view of self, however sublimated and radically alternative to a Cartesian view, involve us in an aporia. These 'new and improved' versions of identity never entirely get rid of the paradoxes of the idea of self from which they deviate. And yet the ultimate paradox is that wherever we look for the self, we won't find it. (Morton 2007: 176)

Not only are these 'new and improved' subjectivities neither new nor improved, they perpetuate the idea that there is a subject out there which we can grasp and conceptualize, that it's just a matter of finding the right nomenclature. Rather, a constant vigilance to the structural insufficiency of our models entails an awareness of the structural insufficiency of *all* models. Here, Morton's own model often strains his insistence upon irony; the more convincing his account, the more likely it is to be transcendentalized, framed as a view from the 'outside'. Hence the infinite need for doubling, deconstruction and critical vigilance.

Morton's account is ultimately frustrating. Grandiose, uncritiqued claims, such as 'This is the ultimate rationality: holding our mind open for the absolutely unknown that is to come' (Morton 2007: 205), often arrive without ironic counterpart. Whilst his critique of the ways in which the fixation on ideas of 'nature' and 'subjectivity' actually reifies relations is vital and slows overhasty attempts to easily free us from the tangle of subjectivity, his development from critique is disappointingly familiar, depicting ecological thought as 'the thinking of interconnectedness' (Morton 2007: 184) and subjectivity as collective rather than individualist (Morton 2007: 17). What he offers is a vague outline of certain responsibilities: to acknowledge the otherness and embeddedness of oneself; to illuminate the political nature of discourses on the environment; to challenge the retreat of art into depoliticized non-conceptuality; and to resist the desire to remake others in one's own image. The latter Morton frames as 'a melancholic ethics. Unable to introject or digest the idea of the other, we are caught in its headlights' (2007: 186). This transformation of the Freudian melancholic into something towards which we should aspire captures the sense of the ever-incomplete task of ethics and responsibility but it fails to pursue the material conditions of its realization.

The critique of politics/The politics of critique

Morton, Plumwood and Derrida are connected by their emphasis on critique. For all three, critique is ongoing and unfinished, a form of praxis which has ethical and political resonances. It is tied to non-identity, difference and otherness, to excessive, non-economic accounts of responsibility, justice and equality. This provides the context for human interaction with human and non-human others; for all three thinkers, we are called to respond in particular ways. Each goes some way to critiquing traditional conceptions of subjectivity and to revealing the complex ties which bind us to these models and which cannot be easily severed. Each critique at some point wavers, demonstrating again that critique is ongoing and unfinished, a collective project.

What is at stake with these thinkers is the status of critique and the relationships between politics and the political, law and justice. Plumwood's attempt to envision a democratic form which would incorporate her 'weak panpsychism' – such a challenge to the individualist subject – flounders, highlighting the radical discrepancy between the abstractions of political thought regarding non-human life and the political realities. Morton tells us that thought has left art behind, and given this discrepancy, it seems that thought has left politics behind too, a shell in which old beliefs have been reified. Much has been made of the wrongheadedness of asking deconstructive thought to provide a prescriptive politics,[10] or of assessing its functional value. It is clear, however, from the critiques developed by both Derrida and Morton, that deconstructive thought does have a political element. What is less clear, however, is how that political thought translates into political praxis. The problem arises, and this becomes clear in the case of human rights, when we try to think this relationship between politics and the political. In a remarkably clear discussion of this issue, Derrida posits:

> We must (*il faut*) more than ever stand on the side of human rights. We *need* (*il faut*) *human rights*. We are in need of them and they are in need, for there is always a lack, a shortfall, a falling short, an insufficiency; human rights are never sufficient. Which alone suffices to remind us that they are not natural. They have a history, one that is recent, complex, and unfinished ... To take this historicity and this perfectibility into account in an affirmative way we must never prohibit the most radical questioning possible of all the concepts at work here: the humanity of man (the 'proper of man' or of the human, which raises the whole question of nonhuman living beings, as well as the question of the history of recent juridical concepts or performatives such as a 'crime against humanity'), and then the very concept of rights or of law (*droit*) and even the concept of history. (2003: 132–133)

It is not enough to say that 'human rights are never sufficient' and that they must be supplemented from outside the law. Both Morton's and Derrida's accounts hover outside the law, outside politics, reluctant to sully their hands with practicalities, exploring instead the grounds of the political and the meaning of justice. Thus, it is no accident that when Derrida, in the quote above, does turn to the law – here, human rights as a pseudo-universal rather than state law – that radicality, and non-human life, remains in parentheses. Derrida's tendency to consider the constitution of justice rather than law (which remains an abstraction), the conditions of politics rather than politics itself, ironically means that when he does address the practicalities of law and politics he is less, rather than more, radical. Both he and Morton fail to acknowledge the mutuality of the relationship between the terms, emphasizing the way that thought (the 'political', justice) influences the materiality of law and politics but failing to acknowledge the influence in the other direction, from material conditions. This can be clearly seen in the quote above in which Derrida's radicality, and the challenge to the individualist subject, is consigned to the realm of the extra-legal, to a critique which is bracketed and secondary.

If we are to have an ethics which is not, or not only, underpinned by a singular relationship to a singular other, then this cannot exist entirely independently from the structure of the law. As we have seen from Plumwood's work, the vision of an 'other' law remains distant and difficult to formulate. This should not discourage us. In addition to acknowledging the tension between justice and law, which allows law to remain inflexible and always behind, we might also ask how a law in tension with itself might look, a law 'to come', which would acknowledge and incorporate the irresolvable tension between individual and collective subjectivities.

Notes

1   There are clear Kantian resonances here. See Neal Curtis's claim that 'Justice, therefore, is not something that we might know in the sense that it might be cognitively grasped and executed; it is rather an opening in thought' (Curtis 2006: 454).

2   Derrida's interest in the construction of the subject persists throughout his writing and is often a source of tension. Of particular interest here is *The Gift of Death*, in which Derrida traces the construction of an interiorized, individualized self to a real or fictitious encounter with 'God' (Derrida 2005).

3   Instances of this include moments where Derrida (2008: 104) gestures towards *Of Grammatology*, for example, his assertion that key deconstructive terms such as 'Mark, gramma, trace and *différance*' not only apply beyond the human and linguistic but 'refer differentially to all living things, all the relations between living and nonliving'. Matthew Calarco (2008: 106) pursues this line of deconstructive thinking, particularly the way in which the idea of the 'trace' challenges clear distinctions between human and animal. See also Cary Wolfe's deconstructive appropriation of the work of Maturana and Varela (Wolfe 2003).

4   For a discussion of the significance of an active relationality sustained by difference, see Plumwood (1993: 154–160). There are clear echoes of process thought here.

5   There is much to support this position. See, for example, Charles Birch's assertion:

> I would claim that to exhibit self-determination is to exhibit mind. It is to have some degree of freedom, no doubt at the molecular level. I am not saying that, having investigated the life of the cell, biologists have found mind. I am saying that what they have found is *more consistent with* the proposition that the cells and their DNA molecules are mind-like in the sense of having internal relations than with the proposition that they are machine-like. (Birch 2011: 328)

6   Plumwood gestures towards a plural understanding of equality, to 'a deep form of democracy that involves a justice dimension as redistributive equality, equality and plurality of communicative process, and complex equality' (2002: 91).

7   Morton's work is radical but not entirely unprecedented. See, for example, Kidner and Luke.

8   My analysis of Morton will focus primarily on *Ecology Without Nature*. I will not address Morton's recent work, influenced by OOO and Graham Harman.

9   There is a thoroughness here which is lacking in *The Ecological Thought*. See Kate Soper's claim that Morton 'targets a straw version of environmental thinking that is belied by the actual sophistication, complexity and diversity of contemporary eco-discourse' (2011: 56).

10   See, for example, Thomson (2005).

Animal Mediators: Philosophy, Film, Literature

PART TWO

Animal Mediators: Philosophy, Film, Literature

CHAPTER FOUR

Etre aux aguets: Deleuze, Creation and Territorialization

Charles J. Stivale

In *L'Abécédaire de Gilles Deleuze*, a significant video interview produced in 1988–1989 but not transmitted until 1994–1995, Gilles Deleuze discusses with Claire Parnet the crucial link between creativity, the very possibility of thinking, and animality, through the practice of *être aux aguets* (being on the lookout) for *rencontres* (encounters). In this chapter, I propose, first, to explore briefly the links that Deleuze makes implicitly between thought and creativity and the cluster of concepts to which Deleuze associates his practice of *être aux aguets*. Second, given Deleuze's explicit comparison of creativity to how animals live, that is, constantly 'on the lookout', I challenge the views enunciated by Donna Haraway (in the introduction to *When Species Meet*) against Deleuze's (and Guattari's) position on animals, a reactionary critique that eschews the very possibilities of innovation and thought expressed by Deleuze and Guattari. In the section 'C as in Culture' of *L'Abécédaire*, Deleuze maintains that whenever he is out in the world, at an art exhibit, or at a movie, he is ever searching for *rencontres*, for intensities that might touch him or affect him, to 'risk having an encounter with an idea'. Just as animals live constantly *aux aguets* and thereby must define their territory and existence in specifically delimited ways at every second, so too do artists and philosophers open themselves to possibilities of innovation and thought. In contrast to Haraway's myopic reaction, Deleuze (and Guattari) undertake to consider the mutations of space and time, like Artaud's search in cinema for the 'shock or vibration, which must give rise to thought in thought' (1989: 166, 169–171), Deleuze implicitly proposes a pragmatics for restoring a 'belief in the world' (1989: 172), that is, 'giving discourse to the body' (1989: 172). As different scholars have pointed out (notably, Brian Massumi and François Zourabichvili), this *philosophie de l'événement* helps us reconceptualize existence not only within the creative parameters of new worlds and new space, but also within renewed perspectives of ethics and resistance.

Clearly, given the key concepts I have just evoked – creativity, thinking, animality, *rencontres*, art, territory, event – this theme of *être aux aguets* constitutes a nexus for Deleuze's conceptual lexicon. I, therefore, need to be both selective and brief, and to do so, I start with reference to the opening section of *L'Abécédaire*. In 'A comme Animal', Deleuze explains his fascination with spiders, ticks and fleas because of how they reveal the power of their worlds, that is, their 'extraordinary, limited worlds', through reactions to very few stimuli. Through these reactions, they constitute a territory just as an artist does – not just through markings of territory (urinary, defecatory), but also through postures, colours (that animals take on) and sounds (the cry, the chant). So these determinants – colours, lines and songs – constitute art in its pure state. Moreover, Deleuze emphasizes the importance of different vectors of such territorialization, at once to leave the territory (deterritorialization), and also a return to it (reterritorialization), all expressed through an endless emission of signs (e.g. songs and colours), reactions to signs (e.g. the spider and the web) and production of signs (e.g. wolf tracks).

Then, to Parnet's query as to whether there is a connection between this emission of signs, territory and writing, Deleuze again evokes the key formula *être aux aguets*, always being on the lookout, like an animal, like a writer, a philosopher, never tranquil, always looking back over one's shoulder. He then implicitly refers to something he had already expressed to Parnet a decade earlier, in their *Dialogues* (*Dialogues II* [2002]: 75), when he says that 'One writes for readers, "for" meaning "à l'attention de," toward them, to their attention', but that one also writes for non-readers, that is, 'for' meaning 'in the place of', as did Artaud in saying he wrote for the illiterate, for idiots, in their place, and for animals, as did Hofmannsthal, 'who used to say he felt a rat in his throat' (1997: 75). Thus, says Deleuze, the writer pushes language to the limit of the cry, of the chant, and a writer is responsible for writing 'for', in the place of, animals who die, even by doing philosophy. Here, he says, one is on the border that separates thought from the non-thought.

So just as I did in the opening paragraph, Deleuze also weaves a web of his own, as it were, in 'A comme Animal' starting with the thematics of animality, and drawing together key concepts that include the major terms of territorialization, then the importance of semiotics and style for artistic creation understood in the broadest terms possible. In this light, I propose to point out some links that may be useful for further research on these thematics. Before *L'Abécédaire*, the first major reference for Deleuze on animal territoriality is Jacob von Uexküll, notably his monograph 'A Stroll through the Worlds of Animals and Men', to which we can add the very important study of von Uexküll by Paul Bains in his book *The Primacy of*

Semiosis. Deleuze and Guattari are drawn, in plateau 3 '10,000 BC: The Geology of Morals', to von Uexküll's study of associated milieus in the animal world, 'with all their active, perceptive and energetic characteristics' (1980: 51). Deleuze's favourite example, the tick, makes an appearance for its triadic set of factors – 'gravitational energy of falling, its olfactory characteristic of perceiving sweat, and its active characteristic of latching on' (1980: 51). But this function of milieus, at least in plateau 3, is but one aspect of the 'machine interlock' across strata of coding and decoding, of territorializing and deterritorializing.

Given my focus on animal affectivity, let me introduce an obvious reference, Deleuze's work on Spinoza in *Expressionism in Philosophy: Spinoza*, most notably the development of affective passions towards joy and beatitude (cf. Seigworth, 'From Affection to Soul' 164–168). In his *Dialogues* with Parnet, Deleuze speaks in moving terms: 'It is not easy to be a free man: to flee the plague, to organize encounters, to increase the power to act, to be moved by joy, to multiply the affects which express or encompass a maximum of affirmation' (1977: 62). Deleuze speaks of a 'Spinoza-assemblage: soul and body, relationships and encounters, power to be affected, affects which realize this power, sadness and joy which qualify these affects' (1977: 62). This Spinoza is, not surprisingly, 'the man of encounters and becoming, the philosopher with the tick' (1977: 62), and through this *rencontre*, this becoming, the soul and body are joined: 'on the road, exposed to all contacts, encounters, in the company of those who follow the same path,... teaching the soul to live its life, not to save it' (1977: 62).

To pursue this path within the milieus of creativity, animality and territorialization, we would do well to shift to *A Thousand Plateaus*. For not only do Deleuze and Guattari devote particular attention to animal activities within and across milieus (notably in plateau 11, '1837: On the Refrain'), but they also precede this study with the longest plateau, '1730: Becoming-intense, Becoming animal...' And not surprisingly, it is within this plateau that they offer their 'Memories of a Spinozist', first returning to the earlier reflection on strata and on nineteenth-century science (from 'The Geology of Morals'). They thereby juxtapose Darwinian scientific perspectives on degrees of speed and slowness to questions of composition, of elements and particles, 'a becoming or jump on the same plane of pure immanence' (1980: 255). This scientific perspective lies at the heart of Spinozism: on one hand, the longitude of a body, that is, 'the particle aggregates belonging to that body in a given relation' (1980: 256), and on the other hand, the latitude of a body, that is, 'the affects of which it is capable at a given degree of power, or rather within the limits of that degree' (1980: 256). Here, at the juncture of Spinozan ethics and post-Darwinian science, Deleuze and Guattari recall Jacob von Uexküll's search 'for the active and passive affects of which the animal is capable in the individuated assemblage of which it is a part' (1980: 257). Again, the tick serves as exemplar, but juxtaposed now to Ethics, to longitude and its relations, to latitude and its degrees: 'We know nothing about a body until we know what it can do, in other words, what its affects are, how they can or cannot enter into composition with other affects, with the affects of another body ... ' (1980: 257).

We reach a point to shift this development towards the critique section of this chapter, specifically the distinction between Deleuze's (and Guattari's) conception of animality as *être aux aguets* and Donna Haraway's harsh judgement of their views, which she states succinctly à propos of the becoming-animal section of *A Thousand Plateaus*, 'an insult because they don't give a flying damn about animals – critters are an excuse for their anti-Oedipal project' (Gane & Haraway 2006: 143). Here I must address matters of approach. Since one of my main objections is Haraway's manner of truncating Deleuze and Guattari's views through selective citations out of context (which I just did in my quote from Haraway's interview), I am faced with the choice: to emulate that method for the sake of brevity and efficiency, or to quote Haraway's critique as much as possible and thereby lengthen this aspect of my analysis. I choose the latter approach, but I will take my lead from Deleuze's own approach to creativity (which I discuss later), that is, *être aux aguets*, to be warily on the lookout regarding Haraway's strategies. Haraway does begin her reflections with a paragraph succinctly summarizing Deleuze and Guattari's project in *A Thousand Plateaus*, but she then states her disappointment at not finding in *A Thousand Plateaus* 'an ally for the tasks of companion species' and instead considers introducing this work with 'Ladies and Gentlemen, behold the enemy!' (2008: 27). Indeed, one purpose of this section of her introduction is to understand 'why Deleuze and Guattari leave [her] so angry when what we want seems so similar' (2008: 27).

Although I cannot succinctly explain this conundrum, the shortest version of my response would simply accede Haraway's key point, to wit: what Deleuze and Guattari propose in the plateau on 'Becoming-Intense, Becoming-Animal, ... ' may well valourize a divide 'between humans and other critters' (Haraway's term) that reveals their 'scorn for all that is mundane and ordinary and the profound absence of curiosity about or respect for and with actual animals, even as innumerable references to diverse animals are invoked to figure the authors' anti-Oedipal and anticapitalist project' (2008: 27). Fair enough as far as this opinion goes – and it provides little surprise for viewers of Deleuze and Parnet's *L'Abécédaire*, particularly the aforementioned section on animality. However, let us understand Haraway's angle of approach: her project, elaborated from the late 1990s onwards, studiously focuses solely on two small segments of *A Thousand Plateaus* (elaborated with Guattari during the late 1970s), hence deliberately ignoring the extensive developments between animality, creativity and thought elsewhere in this plateau and, more generally, in *A Thousand Plateaus*. She also chooses just as *studiously* to ignore any of Deleuze's subsequent statements on human relations with animals, and I emphasize the term 'studiously' since I believe that despite her repeated displays of discursive emotion and outrage, Haraway carefully and cynically employs this segment of *A Thousand Plateaus* to mask her real agenda.

Here, a detailed examination of Haraway's step-by-step dismissal of the Deleuze–Guattari conception of animality is necessary. According to Haraway, the opposition between wolf and dog provides 'the key to how D&G's associational web of anomalous becoming-animal feeds off a series of primary dichotomies figured by the opposition between the wild and the domestic' (2008: 28). After she cites Plateau 2, specifically a passage where Deleuze and Guattari stage the meeting between the Wolf-Man and Freud, '[The Wolf-Man] knew that Freud knew nothing about wolves, or anuses for that matter. The only thing Freud understood was what a dog is, and a dog's tail' (1987: 26, cited by Haraway 2008: 28–29), about which she then comments:

> This gibe [by D&G] is the first of a crowd of oppositions of dog and wolf in *A Thousand Plateaus*, which taken together are a symptomatic morass for how not to take earthly animals – wild or domestic – seriously. (Haraway 2008: 29)

For some reason, entirely unclear to me, Haraway must steel herself here, at least rhetorically, to continue, with the following appeal to the domestic:

> In honor of Freud's famously irascible chows, no doubt sleeping on the floor during the Wolf-Man's sessions, I brace myself to go on by studying the artist David Goines's Chinese Dog of the Year poster for 2006: one of the most gorgeous chow chows I have ever seen. (Haraway 2008: 29)

Then, having thus gained visual solace and/or inspiration, Haraway returns to Deleuze and Guattari:

> Indifferent to the charms of a blue-purple tongue, D&G knew how to kick the psychoanalyst where it would hurt, but they had no eye for the elegant curve of a good chow's tail, much less the courage to look such a dog in the eye. (Haraway 2008: 29)

Completing the paragraph, she then continues quite critically:

> But [she continues] the wolf/dog opposition is not funny. D&G express horror at the 'individuated animals, family pets, sentimental Oedipal animals each with its own petty history' (Deleuze and Guattari 1987: 240) who invite only regression. (2008: 29)

Notice throughout this citation the shift of registers and foci: Deleuze and Guattari seem to have offended Haraway for citing and ridiculing not just

Freud's knowledge, but especially his knowledge of dogs, and also for failing
to take seriously the deep relationship between man/woman and domestic
animal/pet/companion. Yet, Haraway chooses to cite only two sentences
from the plateau's opening paragraph, and neither situates Deleuze and
Guattari's reflections nor seeks to comprehend, much less explain, what the
purpose is of this second plateau in *A Thousand Plateaus*. That is, had she
sought to grasp why Deleuze and Guattari (after lengthy consideration in
Anti-Oedipus) again take up Freud nearly at the start of this massive tome,
she would see them developing a transition from the earlier volume into
some of the terminology already introduced in the opening 'Introduction:
Rhizome' chapter. However, by adopting a strategy to wilfully ignore this
context and purpose while displaying rhetorical outrage, Haraway can
better advance her own pre-ordained perspective.

Furthermore, I have paused after this paragraph's first sentence because
Haraway here inserts footnote 37 where, commenting on Steven Baker's *The
Postmodern Animal*, she claims that 'Baker misses the systematic nausea that
D&G let loose in their chapter in response to all that is ordinary, especially
evident in the figural wolf/dog contrasts but not reduced to them' (2008:
314). Then Haraway delivers a veritable finger-wagging homily, apparently
about her 'core worry in reference to D&G's becoming-animal':

> Multiplicities, metamorphoses, and line of flight not trapped in Oedipal
> and capitalist fixities must not be allowed to work that way. Sometimes
> the herculean [*sic*] efforts needed to dodge various versions of humanism
> catapult one into empyrean lines of flight proper only to the anomalous
> gods at their buffed worst. I'd rather own up to the fraught tangle of
> relatings called 'individuals' in idiomatic English, whose sticky threads
> are knotted in prolific spaces and times with other assemblages, some
> recognizable as (human and nonhuman) individuals or persons and
> some very much not. Individuals actually matter, and they are not the
> only kind of assemblage in play, even in themselves. If one is 'accused'
> of 'uncritical humanism' or its animal equivalent every time he or she
> worries about the suffering or capabilities of actual living beings, then I
> feel myself in the coercive presence of the One True Faith, postmodern
> or not, and run for all I am worth. Of course, I am indebted to Deleuze
> and Guattari, among others, for the ability to think in 'assemblages'.
> (2008: 314)

This morsel gives me pause since I am sincerely trying to understand what
Haraway's 'core worry' really is as regards 'becoming-animal'. Specifically,
in what way 'must' the untrapped multiplicities (etc.) 'not be allowed to
work'? Who says individuals don't matter? Who is accusing whom of
'uncritical humanism'? What is that anyway? The inference I make from this
footnote is that D&G (not to be confused with the admirable Deleuze and
Guattari) and their take on 'becoming-animal' at once discard the individual

for the collective and thereby render suspect any appeal to 'sufferings or capabilities of actual living beings' while also instituting some coercive, possibly postmodern (and no doubt oppressive) 'One True Faith'. I believe that Haraway is quite sincere here in seeking a feeling, kinder and gentler critical approach as well as human/animal exchanges, but her critique (and apparent ire) renders D&G's thought in a cartoonish fashion.

Moreover, in her 2006 interview and in this book, she still seems to think that Deleuze and Guattari's main preoccupations in 1980 are the concerns of the 1972 *Anti-Oedipus*. We can see this misconception in the text as the paragraph continues, where Haraway ignores the broader context of 'becomings' in order to use Deleuze and Guattari's slight to Freud and his chow as a means to assert the greater harm that 'D&G' do: 'All worthy animals [for D&G] are a pack; all the rest are either pets of the bourgeoisie or state animals symbolizing some kind of divine myth' (2008: 29), after which a new footnote, number 38, is referenced. Here, Haraway intervenes – 'unfairly, [she says] since D&G could not have known most of these things in the late 1970s in France or elsewhere' (2008: 314) – to suggest some examples of symbiotic and altogether laudable human–animal relations, for example, trained therapy dogs working with autistic children and teenagers with cerebral palsy; pet dogs visiting the elderly; as well as research on relations between humans and dogs. Then, back in the main text, Haraway continues to characterize D&G's approach to the animal:

> The pack, or pure-affect animals, are intensive, not extensive, molecular and exceptional, not petty and molar – sublime wolf packs, in short. I don't think it needs comment that we learn nothing about actual wolves in all this. I know that D&G set out to write not a biological treatise but rather a philosophical, psychoanalytic, and literary one requiring different reading habits for the always nonmimetic play of life and narrative. But no reading strategies can mute the scorn for the homely and the ordinary *in this book*.

She then singles out, and out of context, the phrase: '*Anyone who likes cats or dogs is a fool*' (Deleuze & Guattari 1987: 240, original emphasis, cited 2008: 29), as well as D&G's return to drub Freud, who 'knows only "the dog in the kennel, the analyst's bow wow"', to which Haraway responds: 'Never have I felt more loyal to Freud' (2008: 29). And she continues her enumeration of their 'disdain for the daily, the ordinary, the affectional rather than the sublime' (2008: 29):

> The Unique, the one in a pact with a demon, the sorcerer's anomaly, is both pack and Ahab's levitation in *Moby Dick*, the exceptional not in the sense of a competent and skillful animal webbed in the open with others, but in the sense of what is without characteristics and without tenderness. (Deleuze & Guattari 1987: 244 cited, without specific text)

And Haraway concludes this paragraph qua indictment with a generationally specific emotional rebuke:

> From the point of view of the animal world I inhabit, this is not about a good run but about a bad trip. Along with the Beatles, I need a little more help than that from my friends. (2008: 29–30)

While I confess to understand only quite vaguely what tripping and the Beatles have to do with this 'point of view', it is clear that Deleuze and Guattari – at least as caricatured as D&G through Haraway's selective citations – create a rhetorical locus that is altogether virtual, that is, at too far a theoretical remove from the actuality of Haraway's animal world of companion species. But as damning as this indictment has already been, the *coup de grâce* comes in the next paragraph, that I reproduce nearly in full, simply excising most of a lengthy quote from *A Thousand Plateaus*:

> Little house dogs and the people who love them are the ultimate figure of abjection for D&G, especially if those people are elderly women, the very type of the sentimental. 'Ahab's Moby Dick is not like a cat or dog owned by an elderly woman who honors and cherishes it....' [Deleuze & Guattari 1987: 244] 'My becoming' [referring to Lawrence's 'becoming-tortoise'] seems awfully important in a theory opposed to the strictures of individuation and subject. The old, female, small, dog- and cat-loving: these are who and what must be vomited out by those who will become-animal. Despite the keen competition, I am not sure I can find in philosophy a clearer display of misogyny, fear of aging, incuriosity about animals, and horror of the ordinariness of the flesh, here covered by the alibi of an anti-Oedipal and anticapitalist project. It took some nerve for D&G to write about becoming-woman just a few pages later! ([Deleuze & Guattari 1987]: 291–309). [footnote 39 inserted] It is almost enough to make me go out and get a toy poodle for my next agility dog. I know a remarkable one playing with her human for the World Cup these days. That *is* exceptional. (2008: 30)

Let me mention that the footnote 39 evokes (without specific references) critical commentary on inadequacies in 'the passages [*in A Thousand Plateaus*] on becoming-woman and becoming child' (2008: 315), and Haraway adds (again providing no references), 'however unintended, the primitivist and racialist tones of the book have not escaped notice either' (2008: 315). But then, having reached the far edge of her critique, she pulls back: 'In my calmer moments, I understand both what D&G accomplish and what this book cannot contribute to a non-Oedipal, antiracist feminism. Rosi Braidotti is my guide to fruitfully learning from Deleuze (who wrote much more than *A Thousand Plateaus*) and, in my view, offers much more toward an autre-mondialisation' (2008: 315). Providing references to

Braidotti and to 'a wonderful book [by Kathleen Stewart] partly shaped by Deleuze's sensibilities in *Difference and Repetition*' (2008: 315), Haraway seems to retreat from the absolute excoriation that preceded. However, her inaccurate attribution of authorship of *A Thousand Plateaus* solely to Deleuze and the repeated exclusion of any mention of Guattari (except as the letter G) suggest, I would argue, that she seems quite calm and nonchalant about casting blame, if only implicitly, for certain excesses in this collective work, on the less prominent member of the pair.

Having attempted to counter Haraway's strategy of selective citation by providing nearly all of her text, I argue that D&G (not to be confused with Deleuze and Guattari) function here as straw men, that is, serving as convenient rhetorical targets better to catapult forward Haraway's introductory development. Let us consider how she warms up to her critique of D&G with an earlier section on the 'good' philosopher, Jacques Derrida (2008: 19–23), who at least acknowledges his cat even if he falls short in Haraway's view. Derrida apparently

> failed a simple obligation of companion species; he did not become curious about what the cat might actually be doing, feeling, thinking, or perhaps making himself available to him in looking back at him in the morning.... What happened that morning was, to me, shocking *because* of what I know this philosopher can do. Incurious, he missed a possible invitation, a possible introduction to other-worlding. (2008: 20)

In Donna Haraway's animal world, then, the demands of attention, curiosity and courtesy to companion species are of utmost importance (which is an understatement), and the section on D&G provides her with a rhetorical bridge: on one side, the repugnant elitism of the virtual, the hypocrisy of the anti-Oedipal and anti-capitalist project that eschews adequate sensitivity towards fellow humans and animals; on the other side, examples of writers who provide Haraway with 'the flesh and figures that companion species need to understand their messmates' (2008: 30), writers, that is, who work more clearly with actual animals and create what Haraway values above all, 'the cobblings together that give meaning to the "becomings with" of companion species in naturecultures. *Cum panis*, messmates, to look and to look back, to have truck with: those are the names of my game' (2008: 32).

Now clearly, as Haraway has accurately suggested, Deleuze's views may well have little to do with actual ticks, fleas, or dogs and wolves. But then again, readers of Haraway's *When Species Meet* will never know really what she would have concluded in this regard since she never made the effort to study a text readily available to the curious and the scholarly alike, *L'Abécédaire*. The same obtains for the Deleuze–Guattari text that holds so much fascination and loathing for Haraway, *A Thousand Plateaus* itself. Not only does Haraway appear blind to the fundamental shift in *A Thousand Plateaus* beyond what she repeatedly calls 'the anti-Oedipal and anti-capitalist project' towards the more complexly multiple engagement with intersecting plateaus and assemblages. She also seems unaware that in other sections of the same plateau on 'becomings', notably in 'Memories of a Spinozist', 'Memories of a haecceity', Deleuze and Guattari develop the intersection of becoming-animal more broadly and philosophically with ethics, assemblages, creativity through *être aux aguets*. And in the next plateau, 'On the Refrain', they extend the previous lengthy development of 'becomings' towards the beautiful introductory evocations of the tune whistled by the child in the dark, alone, returning home; the housewife singing to herself as 'she marshals the antichaos forces of her work'; and the improvisation to meet 'the forces of the future' as 'one ventures from home on the thread of a tune' (1980: 311). In this way, they open the refrain as a reflection on the tensions between the forces of chaos and the fragile territory one might create on wings of song, all the while *être aux aguets*.

In contrast to this dismissive gesture by an otherwise respectable feminist philosopher, another text ignored by Haraway, *What Is Philosophy?*, offers an intensity on the milieu through Deleuze and Guattari's consideration of intersections of animality and art. Let us note in passing the temporal contiguity of *L'Abécédaire* (filmed in 1988–89) and *Qu'est-ce que la philosophie?* (published in 1991, but clearly under way at that time). Already in their final collaboration, under their reflections on 'percept, affect, and concept' in chapter 7, Deleuze and Guattari develop art and animality through links to territory, body, postures and colours, songs and cries – all blocks of sensations that are refrains, about which they argue:

> In this respect, art is continually haunted by the animal. Kafka's art is the most profound meditation on the territory and the house, the burrow, portrait-postures ... ; sound-music ... All that is needed to produce art is here, a house, some postures, colors, and songs – on condition that it all opens onto and launches itself on a mad vector as on a witch's broom, a line of the universe or of deterritorialization – *Perspective on a Room with Occupants* (Paul Klee)'. (1994: 184–185)

And not surprisingly, with the evocation of song and colour as percepts and affects criss-crossing territories, intersecting animal trajectories and creating junction points, Deleuze and Guattari refer again to von Uexküll's development of 'a melodic, polyphonic and contrapuntal conception of Nature' (1994: 185): relationships of counterpoint in bird songs, the spider's web and the fly, the dead mollusk's shell and the hermit crab, the tick and mammal linkage – all are simultaneously the 'two living elements' that combine to make art, 'House and Universe, *Heimlich* and *Unheimlich*, territory and deterritorialization, finite melodic compounds and the great infinite plane of composition, the small and large refrain' (1994: 185–186).

Let me return to Deleuze himself in this 1988–1989 interview in which he confirms Haraway's worst characterization (and takes full responsibility for it), that he cannot stand domestic pets, especially cats and dogs, which did not prevent him from having pets at home, brought there by his children. But, Deleuze relates his aversion to certain kinds of animals particularly to the way that humans interact with them, concluding in *L'Abécédaire*

> What I am going to say is completely idiotic because people who really like cats and dogs obviously do have a relationship with them that is not *human*. For example, you see that children do not have a human relationship with a cat, but rather an infantile relationship with animals. What is really important is for people to have an *animal* relationship with an animal. So what does it mean to have an animal relationship with an animal? It doesn't consist of talking to it... but in any case, I can't stand the *human* relationship with the animal.

Yet this is not at all Deleuze's final word on the animal–human relationship for, with Parnet's help, he explains the complex relationship between animals and art, writing, territory, semiotics and the all-important practice of 'being on the lookout' as a mode of creativity but also, for animals, as a means of survival. And had Donna Haraway cared to look into this explanation of animality, she might have found a moment, possibly no more acceptable than Derrida's, in which Deleuze can be seen to become-animal, to open himself to the becomings of an animal, as he contends that when humans die, they die like animals:

> Here we return to cats, and I have a lot of respect... Among the many cats that lived here, there was that little cat who died rather quickly, that is, I saw what a lot of people have seen as well, how an animal seeks a corner to die in... There is a territory for death as well, a search for a territory of death, where one can die. We saw the little cat slide itself right into a tight corner, an angle, as if it were the good spot for it to die in.

Again, we will never know how this reflection might or might not have corresponded to Donna Haraway's perspectives on animals, simply because she had no interest in making the effort to move beyond the 1980 collaborative text, *A Thousand Plateaus*, and then only in a highly selective and impressionistic manner. She, of course, has every right to employ and to analyse her sources as she sees fit, and I wish I could endorse Braidotti's suggestion that we might accept Haraway's views as 'a gentle but resolute betrayal' of the master's voice (2006: 203). However, I must argue for the perhaps outmoded perspective that she also has an ethical responsibility to undertake actual scholarship and to acknowledge, at the very least, the limitations of her chosen corpus. Instead, she employs *A Thousand Plateaus* as a foil, as a launching pad in order to leap forward in the direction she had already selected. Had she actually done this research, she might have paused, momentarily at least, over these words from Deleuze in *L'Abécédaire* about introducing the personal into one's writing (from 'A as in Animal'):

> When one writes, one is not pursuing some private little affair. [Such writers] really are stupid fools (*connards*); really, it's the abomination of literary mediocrity, in every era, but particularly quite recently, that makes people believe that to create a novel, for example, it suffices to have some little private affair, some little personal affair – one's grandmother who died of cancer, or someone's personal love affair – and there you go, you can write a novel based on this. It's shameful to think things like that. Writing is not anyone's private affair, but rather it means throwing oneself into a universal affair, be it a novel or philosophy.

In contrast, we can understand *être aux aguets*, not merely as a means of creating as well as critiquing, but also, and perhaps primarily, as *Lebenspraktiken*, that is, practices of life. For the becomings-animal that we have traced from the expression *être aux aguet* in 'A comme Animal' extends much more broadly, throughout *L'Abécédaire* certainly, but also back to *Logique du sens*, as a key practice of counter-actualization and the 'ethics of the mime', to which Deleuze associates his firm statement that we must 'be worthy of what happens to us', that is, to our events. This statement points to an ever-renewed, ongoing process, one circumstance at a time, reworking the actualization of personal lives, of 'everyday banality' (1969: 152), as a means to extend one's effectivity, so that the germs of innovative ideas might be picked up by other generations.

CHAPTER FIVE

Out of the Labyrinth, into the Métro: Becoming-animal, the Waking Dream and Movements of World in Raymond Queneau and Louis Malle's *Zazie dans le métro*

Colin Gardner

Raymond Queneau once described his fellow *Oulipans* (*Ouvroir de Littérature Potentielle*) as 'rats who build the labyrinth from which they plan to escape'. This labyrinth is often a rigid literary structure built on inherent formal constraints – for example, Georges Perec's eschewal of the letter 'e' in his 1969 lipogram, *La disparition (A Void)* or Queneau's own *Exercises in Style* (1981), which consists of 99 re-tellings of the same story, each in a different style. However, with all its constrictions and potential blind alleys, this labyrinth can also be seen as the foundation for a deterritorialized line of flight, in which every path is a potential avenue of escape, whereby conventional distinctions between here and there, inside and outside, male and female, above-ground and below-ground, animal and human start to collapse in favour of a more multiplicitous flux.

Through a close analysis of Queneau's seminal *Zazie dans le Métro*, published in 1958, and Louis Malle's 1960 film adaptation, this chapter will explore the liberating function of 'dis-unitary urbanism' through Gilles Deleuze and Félix Guattari's notion of becoming-animal. Here, the rhizomic metaphor of the Paris Métro (in effect an underground warren of tunnels which allows for a radically transverse, rat or rabbit-like trajectory across the otherwise uniformly schematic Haussmann-ized geography of the city) is forced to the surface (because of a transit workers' strike) through the anarchic daydreams of the 12-year-old Zazie.[1] In this respect, Zazie acts as a vengeful durational multiplicity in which her unleashed libido destroys the patriarchal and Oedipal structures of coherent individuation, transforming the urban plan(e) of organization into a deterritoralized plan(e) of immanence.[2] Through Zazie, each dream is a moving world, which is in turn marked by animal intensities and a series of inversions and perversions which serve to break the controlling Law of Oedipalization. For, as Deleuze and Guattari point out,

> it's not Oedipus that produces neurosis; it is neurosis – *that is, a desire that is already submissive and searching to communicate its own submission –* that produces Oedipus. Oedipus, the market value of neurosis. In contrast, to augment and expand Oedipus by adding to it and making a paranoid and perverse use of it is already to escape from submission, to lift one's head up, and see passing above the shoulders of the father what had really been the question all along: an entire micropolitics of desire, of impasses and escapes, of submissions and rectifications. Opening the impasse, unblocking it. Deterritorializing Oedipus into the world instead of reterritorializing everything in Oedipus and the family. But to do this, Oedipus had to be enlarged to the point of absurdity, comedy. (Deleuze & Guattari 1986: 10)

This expansion is Zazie's designated role and she accomplishes it with slapstick relish.

I

Zazie dans le métro's basic story is straightforward enough. The novel's eponymous, foul-mouthed heroine (played by the irresistibly gap-toothed Catherine Demongeot in the film) arrives in Paris to spend the weekend with her female impersonator uncle Gabriel (Philippe Noiret) and aunt Marceline (Carla Marlier) so that Jeanne, Zazie's mother (Odette Piquet), may spend some alone time with her latest boyfriend. Gabriel tries his hardest to entertain his insolent charge, introducing her to his ménage of eccentric friends and acquaintances. These include Gabriel's ornery restauranteur landlord, Turandot (Hubert Deschamps) and his beloved parrot, Laverdure; his taxi driver pal Charles (Antonie Roblot) and the latter's fiancée, Mado Ptits-pied (Annie Fratellini); as well as Gridoux, the local cobbler (Jacques Dufilho). To say that Zazie is strong willed is putting it mildly. In fact, she is marked by total self-interest, a bundle of rampant desires fuelled by a consumerist frenzy – Coca Cola, blue jeans, and most importantly, a life-long desire to ride the *Métro*. As Gilbert Adair points out, Zazie lacks any interiority or exteriority in the novel – she is desire incarnate. In fact, in a seminal 1959 essay, 'Zazie and Literature', Roland Barthes argued that she was a barely a child at all, seeing her fictional infancy as a strictly linguistic construct, 'a form of abstraction which enables her to judge all language without ever having to mask her own psyche' (Adair 2000: xiii).

It's not long before the inquisitive Zazie escapes her uncle's vigilant eye and goes walkabout in search of the nearest *Métro* station. Unfortunately she's clean out of luck – the *Métro* workers are on strike and all stations are closed. Incensed, Zazie conspires to take out her frustration on those she perceives to be responsible – that is, all the adults she meets during the course of the weekend. By day's end she is a vengeful flâneuse traversing the streets of Paris as if on a continuous disunifying *dérive*, a form of Situationism taken to the extreme, to the point where, in Ivan Chtcheglov's words, 'The changing of landscapes from one hour to the next will result in complete disorientation' (Chtcheglov 1989: 4).[3] Thus begins a zany series of episodes as Gabriel, aided and abetted by Charles, attempts to rein in his anarchic niece before she brings Paris to a standstill. To keep her distracted, they climb the Eiffel Tower and go joyriding with a busload of foreign tourists, which leads to Gabriel being 'kidnapped' by a group of attractive German 'Gretchens'. In addition, they have repeated encounters with a typical Queneau *type* (amusingly played by Vittorio Caprioli) who reappears in multiple guises, including the *sergent de ville* Trouscaillon, who is in turn pursued by the amorous widow, Mouaque (Yvonne Clech). The weekend culminates in a chaotic brawl at a local Pigalle brasserie before Gabriel and his cohorts are rescued by Marceline, just as the Métro strike comes to an end. Both book and film conclude with an exhausted Zazie's safe return to her mother at the Gare de L'Est:

'Did you see the Métro?'
'No.'
'What have you done then?'
'I've aged.'

Although *Zazie*'s use of formal constraints is far less apparent than in most Oulipo novels, there are inherent (albeit hidden) numerical structures that help shape its narrative organization. Thus, for example, there are 19 chapters in all, Laverdure the parrot repeats his phrase, 'Talk, talk, that's all you can do', 19 times, while Zazie pronounces 'mon cul' (my ass) 18 times and makes the 'gesture' once, making a total of 19. Similarly, Chapter 7 names seven different characters and the last to speak, Gridoux, has a name composed of seven letters. While such mathematical hermeneutics may make for a fun parlour game, perhaps a more fruitful approach to the book lies in a more immanent, ontological analysis, particularly through the lens of Deleuze and Guattari's concept of a minor literature, outlined in their joint project, *Kafka: Toward a Minor Literature*, and more specifically its characteristic trope of becoming-animal. What exactly is a minor literature? According to Deleuze and Guattari, 'A minor literature doesn't come from a minor language; it is rather that which a minority constructs within a major language' (1986: 16). It is defined by three major characteristics: (1) A high co-efficiency of de-territorialization: for example, Prague German in the case of Kafka; Irish English via French for Samuel Beckett; or the use of phonetic speech, slang and barely assimilated Americanisms in the case of Queneau. (2) Everything in Minor Literature is political: each individual intrigue connects immediately to politics, so that, for example, the family triangle (Zazie and her mother/uncle) connects to other triangles – commercial, economic, bureaucratic and juridical (each rhizomatically connected to the shifting and overlapping role of Caprioli's devious *type*). (3) Everything takes on a collective value and enunciation: in short literature is always the concern of the people, a pack or a multiplicity, whether literal or yet to come. Thus, as Deleuze and Guattari note in relation to Kafka's *The Trial*,

> The letter K [or Zazie, in our particular case] no longer designates a narrator or a character but an assemblage that becomes all the more machine-like, an agent that becomes all the more collective because an individual is locked into it in his or her solitude (it is only in connection to a subject that something individual would be separable from the collective and would lead its own life). (1986: 18)

Of course, there are many different strategies for creating a minor literature. Whereas, for example, Kafka and Beckett work through a process of willed poverty, a minimal sobriety of both style and substance that exhausts conventional signification to a point where both character and narrative will-to-power are undermined, leaving only non-signifying intensities and deterritoralized flux, Queneau's *Zazie* is much closer to the work of James Joyce. Both re-territorialize the dominant language through 'exhilaration and over-determination', piling on signification in order to unleash metamorphosis and movement for its own sake. As Deleuze and Guattari point out, 'Metamorphosis is the contrary of metaphor' (1986: 22).

However, none of this superfluity is necessarily apparent from a casual reading of Queneau's basic narrative. Barthes notes, for example, that at first glance *Zazie* is a well-constructed novel, a paragon of a major literature. It is essentially classical in its temporal frame (the duration of a *Métro* strike), its epic duration (an itinerary, a series of way stations), its objective narrative (it is told from Queneau's omniscient point of view), its full cast (hero, heroine, villain, secondary figures, walk-ons), its unified social setting (Paris), and the variety and balance of its fictional methods (narrative and dialogue). However, Queneau couples these positives with an insidious void:

As soon as each element of the traditional universe solidifies, Queneau dissolves it, undermines the novel's security: literature's solidity curdles; everything is given a double aspect, made unreal, whitened by that lunar light which is an essential theme of deceit and a theme characteristic of Queneau. The event is never denied, i.e. first posited then negated; it is always *divided*, like the moon's disc, mythically endowed with two antagonistic figures. (Barthes 1972: 118)

This division or bifurcation often takes on a rhyming form, through doublings and repetitions. As David Gobert notes, 'Rhyme for Queneau describes not only regular reappearance of characters, situations, places, but also pairings and contrasts between characters' (1986: 92). Thus, the playfully romantic engagement between Charles and Mado is paralleled by the more crudely debased attempts at seduction by both Trouscaillon and the widow Mouaque. Similarly, Gabriel is doubled by his female alter ego, the night club drag queen Gabriella, but his wife, the gentle Marceline, also turns out to be a transvestite, appearing heroically at novel's end as the biker-clad Marcel as he/she delivers Zazie safely back to her mother, whose own sexual getaway has been less than fruitful. For Gobert, 'Gabriel/Gabriella and Marceline/Marcel are a curious combination, transvestites who have apparently found happiness in union, in a comfortable and routinized status-quo constituting *les petits bonheurs*' (Gobert 1986: 92). In fact, the novel never makes clear whether Gabriel and Marceline constitute a heterosexual couple who happen to have cross-gender alter egos; whether they are two men, with Marcel playing the role of the wife; or two women, with Gabriella taking on the function of the husband.[4] This dividing also extends to the character of the essential *type* who, like Zazie, belongs to the demonical breed, an animalistic trope who invades the comfortable existence of Gabriel and Marceline and acts as an agent of deterritorialization. He is completely multifaceted, beginning the novel as Pedro-Surplus, a simple flea market peddler-cum-flic who also doubles as satyr-like paedophile on the prowl, seducing the innocent (yeah, right!) Zazie with the promise of army-surplus blue jeans before becoming besotted with Marceline. He then morphs into the *sergent de ville*, Trouscaillon, who helps to track down the 'kidnapped' Gabriel, reappears as Bertin-Poirée, a plain-clothes detective who tries to seduce Marceline in Gabriel's dressing room, and finally disperses the crowd during the final brasserie brawl in what he believes to be his true guise, the oriental prince, Aroun Arachide. Similarly, in the eyes of Gabriel and Charles, places and monuments have an equally uncertain identity: the Pantheon becomes, by turns and interchangeably, the Gare de Lyon, Sainte-Chappelle, Les Invalides and the Chamber of Commerce. Ironically, there would be no such doubt when riding the Métro as each landmark tends to have its corresponding stop clearly marked both on the station platform and the system map.

For Barthes, however, the key to the novel lies less in its metonymic skidding and more in its ability to attack all kinds of writing – epic, Homeric, Latin, medieval, psychological, anecdotal – not through semantic high-handedness but through frivolity. Zazie dislocates language *en passant*: 'Queneau's is a parody sapped from within, its very structure masking a scandalous incongruity; it is not imitation (however subtle) but malformation, a dangerous equilibrium between verisimilitude and aberration, a verbal theme of a culture whose forms are brought to a state of perpetual deceit' (Barthes 1972: 119). Figures of speech – that is, the very Frenchness of the major language – are undermined into stateless vocables. Queneau achieves this by distinguishing the language object – which dissolves into action itself and makes things act through the intercession of Zazie and through the oneiric world of dream – from metalanguage. Zazie never destroys the former, only the latter, *the* dominant arboreal language of the grown-ups: 'Zazie *wants* her Coke, her blue jeans, her Métro; she uses only the imperative or the optative, which is why her language is safe from all mockery' (Barthes 1972: 120). It's from this base that she destroys the language of Gabriel's cohorts, which doesn't speak things, but only *apropos* of things – that is, it's indicative, not active, it *represents* reality, it doesn't *change* it. However, as in all Oulipo texts, this contestation is always ambiguous. Queneau is not a judge of the novel but an active participant in its methods. For Barthes, he lacks good conscience – he lives with literature in a perpetual state of insecurity, all the better to commit a form of literary heresy against its longstanding shibboleths.

II

This textual insecurity is accomplished in two major ways. Firstly, one notes Queneau's use of foreign words as they might be pronounced phonetically by everyday Parisians – 'blue jeans' becomes *bloudjinzzes*; 'happy birthday to you' becomes *api beurzdé touillou*, etc. Indeed, the book opens with Zazie's Uncle Gabriel uttering the almost untranslatable sound *Doukipoudonktan* ('D'où qu'ils puent donc tant?'), that is, 'From where do they stink so much' (basically 'What a stench!'). Secondly, Queneau employs a strategy of becoming-animal, not in the sense of literal metamorphosis, but as a line of flight or means of escape, as a combination of de- and re-territorialization, usually as a form of waking dream or reverie. The result, for Deleuze and Guattari, is that 'There is no longer man or animal, since each deterritorializes the other, in a conjunction of flux, in a continuum of reversible intensities' (1986: 22). Moreover, with becoming-animal, there is no longer a subject of enunciation or a subject of the statement but instead a collective assemblage: 'Language stops being representative in order to now move toward its extremities or its limits' (1986: 23). In other words, language transforms into an assemblage of *intensities* akin to a painful warbling, an animal cry or resonant, low-pitched hum. In *Zazie*, as in Kafka, this is never entirely successful as a process, for as Deleuze and Guattari argue, 'We would say that for Kafka, the animal essence is the way out, the line of escape, even if it takes place in place, or in a cage. *A line of escape, and not freedom. A vital escape and not an attack*' (Deleuze & Guattari 1986: 35). This is particularly true in *Zazie*, where the superimposition of the underground world of the Métro, with its labyrinthine tunnels and transverse connectors between different lines of deterritorialization (a world much like that described in Kafka's *The Burrow*) disrupts (rather than transforms) the surface world in the form of impossible splittings and divisions. Thus in Malle's film adaptation, Zazie escapes Pedro-Surplus by literally becoming multiple bodies transcending coherent time and space (and on one occasion metamorphosing into an alley cat); while traffic patterns are subverted by literally piggy-backing vehicles on top of other cars. As Deleuze and Guattari remind us,

> the metamorphosis is a sort of conjunction of two deterritorializations, that which the human imposes on the animal by forcing it to flee or to serve the human, but also that which the animal proposes to the human by indicating ways-out or means of escape that the human would never have thought of by himself (schizo-escape); each of these two deterritorializations is immanent to the other and makes it cross a threshold. (1986: 35)

It shouldn't surprise us that this line of flight – particularly in the cinematic realm of Malle's film – often takes the form of a dream, or more accurately, the dream within the dream. In a significant passage in the novel, Gabriel muses philosophically after descending the Eiffel Tower:

> Being or nothingness, that is the question. Ascending, descending, coming, going, a man does so much that in the end he disappears. A taxi bears him off, a métro carries him away, the Tower doesn't care, nor the Pantheon. Paris is but a dream, Gabriel is but a reverie (a charming one), Zazie the dream of a reverie (or of a nightmare) and all this story the dream of a dream, the reverie of a reverie, scarcely more than the typewritten delirium of an idiotic novelist (oh! sorry). (Queneau 2000: 72)

For Deleuze, writing in *Cinema 2: The Time-Image*, this is an example of the implied as opposed to the explicit dream. It includes reverie, the waking dream, strangeness and enchantment, an audio visual language where the optical and sound image is cut off from its motor extension but is unable to compensate via relation with explicit recollection-images or dream-images. Instead, they extend into a 'movement of world'. In this case there is a return to movement but 'it is no longer the character who reacts to the optical-sound situation, it is a movement of world which supplements the faltering movement of the character' (Deleuze 1989: 59). This depersonalizes movement via what Deleuze calls 'worldizing' or 'societizing'. Now the world takes responsibility for the movement the subject can no longer make: 'The frightened child faced with danger cannot run away, but the world sets about running away for him and takes him with it, as if on a conveyor belt. Characters do not move, but, as in an animated film, the camera causes the movement of the path on which they change places, "motionless at a great pace"' (Deleuze 1989: 59).

This is a perfect description of the fast motion background contrasted with the normal motion of Gabriel and Zazie as they walk along the street early in the film, as well as the frantic rush – exacerbated by rapid parallel cutting – by the main characters as they race to the nightclub to finally witness Gabriel's drag act. This scene is actually dreamt by Zazie as she leans exhausted on the bonnet of a car, a reverie within the larger reverie of the film as a whole. However, Zazie is less the fearful, passive receptacle of this worldizing movement than its all-knowing, mischievous catalyst. Indeed, she is able to expand the totality of space and stretch the limits of time almost at will. Thus Malle initially presents the characters in simultaneous real-time through parallel editing: Gabriel rocking nervously back and forth in his dressing room chair as he waits anxiously for his wife to bring his new dress in time for his act; Marceline in turn racing through the city streets on her motor scooter; Trouscaillon as a traffic cop deftly attempting to avoid the widow Mouaque, who accosts every gendarme she sees; Mado and Gridoux in Charles's taxi; the 'Gretchens' on the tour bus. Then, through a series of jump cuts, Zazie is subjectively able to conjure them all in each other's designated role – subverting their already fluid identities within the narrative – so that the movement of world becomes the catalyst for Rimbaud's famous dictum: 'I is another'. Indeed, at one point, Zazie dreams the characters dancing hand-in-hand in front of a city fountain, evoking the silhouetted 'Dance of Death' along the horizon in Bergman's *The Seventh Seal*. Zazie has, in effect, turned the entire cast of characters into her own pliable multiplicity, her own wolf-pack, for 'A becoming-animal always involves a pack, a band, a population, a peopling, in short, a multiplicity' (Deleuze & Guattari 1987: 239). As Deleuze and Guattari argue in *A Thousand Plateaus*,

> The distinction to be made is not at all between exterior and interior, which are always relative, changing and reversible, but between different types of multiplicities that coexist, interpenetrate, and change places – machines, cogs, motors, and elements that are set in motion at a given moment, forming an assemblage productive of statements. (1987: 36)

Deleuze correctly notes that Malle – particularly in a film like *Black Moon* – commonly uses depersonalized movement of world, so that bodily states may link up with this movement as a form of dream-like becoming-animal, as a potential line of flight. 'Each is marked by animals', notes Deleuze,

> and is peopled by inversions (sound inversion of speech, aberrations of behaviour such as when [in *Black Moon*] the old woman talks to the rats and sucks the girl's breast). In Malle, it is always a movement of world which brings the character to incest, prostitution, or disgrace, and makes him capable of a crime like the one dreamed of by the old man who tells tall stories (*Atlantic City*). (1989: 60)

Zazie is no exception, for this is a true cinema of enchantment where depersonalized movements, whether slow-moving or, as in this instance, rushing frantically, pass directly through nature as an animal-human hybrid. Thus, for Deleuze,

> what matters is not at all the relative slowness of the becoming-animal; because no matter how slow it is, and even the more slow it is, it constitutes no less an *absolute deterritorialization* of the man in opposition to the merely relative deterritorializations that the man causes to himself by shifting, by traveling; the becoming-animal is an immobile voyage that stays in one place; it only lives and is comprehensible as an intensity (to transgress the thresholds of intensity). (1989: 35)

In other words, in the labyrinthine world of *Zazie*'s transverse logic, you can literally age without actually having to go anywhere, by *Métro* or otherwise, because becoming is always a multiplicity *en acte*.

Notes

1   The Situationists were particularly critical of Baron Georges-Eugène Haussmann's wholesale destruction of medieval Paris, correctly seeing his late nineteenth-century plans for urban renewal as a cynical attempt to transform the city into a controlled environment. Guy Debord, for example, noted that 'The concern to have open spaces allowing for the rapid circulation of troops and the use of artillery against insurrections was at the origin of the urban renewal plan adopted by the Second Empire. But from any standpoint other than that of police control, Haussmann's Paris is a city built by an idiot, full of sound and fury, signifying nothing' (Debord 1989a: 5). In that sense, *Zazie* – the apotheosis of vacuous sound and fury – is an anarchic spoof of both Debord's condemnation and Haussmann's original conception.

2   In effect, Zazie constructs a smooth space by re-striating the pre-existing striations of Haussmann's boulevards via the transverse trajectories and correspondences of the interconnecting Métro lines.

3   Debord defines the *dérive* as 'a technique of transient passage through varied
     ambiences. The *dérive* entails playful-constructive behavior and awareness
     of psycho-geographical effects; which completely distinguishes it from the
     classical notions of the journey and the stroll' (Debord 1989b: 50).
4   This multiple division is harder to pull off in Louis Malle's film adaptation,
     largely because Philippe Noiret's Gabriel is more clearly coded as male due
     to the actor's instant recognizability to contemporary audiences (although
     he has subsequently played homosexual characters in André Téchiné's 1991
     J'embrasse pas and Giuliano Montaldo's 1987 *The Gold-Rimmed Glasses*).
     Meanwhile, cover-girl Carla Marlier is too obviously feminine to be anything
     other than a female impersonating a male as Marcel (renamed Albert in the
     film).

CHAPTER SIX

The Animal That Therefore I Am Not: Inhuman Mediations on the Ultimate Degeneration of Bios and Zoe via the Inevitable Process of Phenomenophagism

Charlie Blake

Although the void devours the solid, the solid feasts on the void, i.e. its outsider. In compositions, the solid becomes hysterically gluttonous for the void. This is what intrigued the Cult of the Old Ones in their mission to perform their awakening ritual. If the Old Ones are to fly through holey space, bubbling up through the carrion black pit and turning their tentacles into interconnected burrows and lubricious warrens, then the only strategic technique to speed and facilitate their return is to mess with the ()hole complex, that is to say, the zone of emergence.
(Negarestani 2008: 45)

In order to produce werewolves in your own family it is not enough to resemble a wolf, or to live like a wolf: the pact with the Devil must be coupled with an alliance with another family, and it is the return of this alliance to the first family, the reaction of this alliance on the first family, that produces werewolves by feedback effect. (Deleuze & Guattari 1988: 246)

One can imagine the surface of the text given over to the gnawing, ruminant, and silent voracity of [such an] animal-machine and its implacable 'logic.' This would not only be simply 'without spirit,' but the face (figure) of evil. (Derrida 1989: 134)

I was a blasphemer, an atheist, a madman, a fury, a savage beast, a wolf. (Rousseau 2000: 577)

It has long been a characteristic of the novel or of its more shadowy cinematic sibling, and especially where certain Gothic shades and colours are to be explored or extrapolated, to evoke the idea of the found manuscript or object which, once obtained by the narrator or central character, has a transformative effect on his or her fortunes. In some cases, as in Honoré de Balzac's fable of poverty, despair and imagined wish fulfilment in *The Wild Ass's Skin*, the result may be to lead the reader to reflect on the moral and ethical dimensions of fortune and desire with potentially benign consequences for his or her subsequent behaviour. In other, rather less uplifting exercises, as in the second version of *Evil Dead* (Raimi 1987), in which a group of hapless youths chance upon and activate an ancient book of demonic inscriptions in an isolated forest cabin with decidedly visceral results, the consequences for the viewer may be said to have no real moral or ethical content whatsoever, aside from possibly leaving her or him with a mild and yet queasy sense of disquiet at the ultimate pointlessness of virtue. I make no claim one way or the other for the document that follows and confess to finding the motif of the found text or object, like that of the double or ancient relic or curse, or the story within a story within a story, to be something of a cliché, especially when it concerns or relates to matters of serious philosophical enquiry. Suffice it to say, however, that the document under consideration was passed on to me by a colleague whose work can at times be a little dense and obscure, but whose peregrinations on matters both critical and clinical I have always found to be worthy of sustained attention. On this occasion, however, he did seem somewhat perturbed, more so than usual, and, almost in imitation of the author for whom he had composed the rigorous introductory essay that you are about to read, and before leaving rather suddenly and without explanation, he asked – indeed pleaded, – to remain anonymous. He was also insistent that these notes and his introduction be published and distributed widely and he was confident that I would find the means to accomplish this without requiring an explanation for his unusual behaviour and urgent request. Accordingly, it has been left to me to explain that his introduction may be found in Part One and his appended notes and bibliography at the end of the document, and that the sections in between in Part Two (respectively entitled *The wolf and the void*, *The beast machine* and *Becoming ahuman becoming*) are the result of what he was able to retrieve and then reconstruct from a set of discovered notes by a further unnamed author. Perhaps the reasons for this desire for serial anonymity will become clear to the reader in due course. All I can offer here, however, and by way of proxy and a favour to my former colleague is, in Part One, and without any explanation of the means or events leading to the discovery of this document, a two-stage introduction via a number of recent thinkers such as Jacques Derrida, Giorgio Agamben, Gilles Deleuze and Félix Guattari and Reza Negarestani, to what I understand he believed to be a synthetic discovery of considerable and urgent significance to the philosophical contemplation of the human, the animal, and the decidedly ahuman cosmic other that will inevitably displace and consume it. Thus it is that he begins his *prolegomena to phenomenophagism* with a critical account of, and pre-emptive commentary upon, the philosophical sources and passages and indeed thresholds of the found manuscript under consideration and then continues in his *Schizo scherzo* to contextualize these figures and their diversions by way of a preamble and a necessarily muted warning to the curious. The rest, from the section on *The wolf and the void* onwards, belongs to the found manuscript itself, which I will therefore leave, a little abruptly perhaps (rather as the runic script in M. R. James' famous tale of textual transmission and contagion is despatched to its unsuspecting recipient), in the hands of the reader, and then depart.

McMurdo Sound. Ross Island. Antarctica.

***Part one

A prolegomena to phenomenophagism

In his final published seminars, *The Beast and the Sovereign*, and by way of reflection on Giorgio Agamben's study of life and the exception in *Homo Sacer*, Jacques Derrida meditates briefly and critically on the nature and valencies of thresholds. In characteristically Derridean fashion, he is by turns interrogative, evasive and digressional, but one paired image in this elliptical meditation is, and however covertly applied, strikingly tenacious for the anonymous writer of the following essay: that of zoological gardens and mental hospitals as primary spaces of threshold and distinction.[1] Derrida's general thinking at this stage is based on some fundamental questions he wishes to pose on, to and then explore about sovereignty and the concept of the beast, about Thomas Hobbes's political project in *Leviathan* and its connection with animality, stupidity and the construction of the political. It is also, taking its cue from Hobbes, very much about wolves and werewolves and metamorphosis, and in this sense is part of an extended consideration of what he at several points in his later works affirms as the foundational question of philosophy, or rather group of questions, as they hover around that particular threshold which supposedly differentiates the human from the non-human, and more specifically from the non-human animal. In addition, and perhaps inevitably, these seminars also continue a lingering conversation with several notable figures from the past of philosophy as well as its extended present, for whom the beast is a concern: Hobbes obviously, Jean-Jacques Rousseau, Michel de Montaigne, Niccolò Machiavelli and of course Aristotle on the themes of life and politics, not to mention Agamben (of whom he is cruelly critical) and two of Agamben's most important intellectual sources, Martin Heidegger and Carl Schmitt, as well as Derrida's contemporaries, Michel Foucault, Gilles Deleuze and Félix Guattari. His play around the motifs of the lupine, the lycanthropic and the threshold are inevitably intricate, but for the purposes of the ruminations that will follow, possibly the most important element to be considered at this stage is his interest in the ways in which zoos and mental hospitals might be said to emphasize the specific resonance of certain kinds or qualities of threshold, and by association, the ways in which lycanthropy in particular is associated, via melancholy, with another crucial place of threshold: the cemetery.

The significance of the cemetery and its association with melancholy (as a path to madness, and thereby a path to the fragmentation of reason that illuminates the nature of reason), lycanthropy (as a path to a non-human animality which also reveals the animality that is within and thus constitutive of the human) and of course those perennially morbid and yet often exquisite themes of death, decay, loss and mourning, is not lost on Derrida, although he does not consider that significance in this volume. It is a significance especially pertinent to Hobbes and his contemporaries such as the great taxonomist of melancholy Robert Burton, certainly, in connection with the wolf or werewolf, but this connection between the lupine and the various machineries of mortality, melancholy and madness has been discussed with eloquence and erudition by a number of scholars in several disciplines and I will not, therefore, be going into those studies or that significance here.[2] Suffice it to say that what here links Burton, say, with Agamben and thence Derrida and Deleuze and Guattari is a sense of the lone man-wolf or human-wolf or werewolf or *loup-garou* (rather, that is, than the perhaps more genuine wolf of mobile colonies, packs or nomadic multiplicities – the anthropocentric gathering of a concept of 'wolf' and 'wolf-ness' for decidedly 'human' ends, in other words) as a creature of excluded status. For Agamben, this is the outcast status of the exception as elaborated in the chapter just prior to the 'threshold' of part two from *Homo Sacer*, a chapter that Derrida draws the reader's attention to and whose title translates as 'The Ban and the Wolf'. Here, in a footnote to his analysis of exclusion and power, Agamben refers in passing to a lay of Marie de France, in which, he claims: 'both the werewolf's particular nature as the threshold of passage between nature and politics, animal world and human world, and the werewolf's close tie to sovereign power are presented with extraordinary vividness' (Agamben 1998: 64). Agamben's assertion in *Homo Sacer* of a symmetry between the outcast or werewolf and the sovereign, a symmetry which – along with that between *bios* and *zoe* – provides the dialectical machinery of his anthropological exegesis of power, is a problem for Derrida. It is a problem for him because he is not convinced that either the symmetries or the dialectic activated by those symmetries perform as they are claimed to perform, neither does he hold with Agamben's derivation and deployment of bios and zoe (political life, roughly, and bare life, approximately) from Aristotle as holding up to philosophical or philological inquisition. The images of the wolf or man-wolf or werewolf, however, do remain as an important point or line of invention or reclamation for and between both of these philosophers, as these figures do also for Deleuze and Guattari in two significant moments from *A Thousand Plateaus*. There, for instance, at one stage, they note rightly – albeit indirectly – that no true wolf can ever be singular (Deleuze & Guattari 1988: 29), but must always be a becoming wolf of multiplicities, of packs, or, as they put it with typical baroque inflection:

> The wolf, as the instantaneous apprehension of a multiplicity in a given region, is not a representative, a substitute, but an *I feel*. I feel myself becoming a wolf, one wolf among others, on the edge of the pack ... don't think for a minute that it has to do with believing oneself a wolf, representing oneself as a wolf. The wolf, wolves, are intensities, speeds, temperatures, nondecom-posable variable distances. (Deleuze & Guattari 1988: 32)

This characteristic rejection of representation/identity and affirmation of expression/multiplicity is from their infamous chapter or plateau, 'One or several Wolves?', which includes a series of observations on and digressions from Sigmund Freud's study of the Russian aristocrat Sergei Pankejeff, first published as *The 'Wolfman'* in 1918. As a case study, *The 'Wolfman'* has often been used to illustrate Freud's reductive tendencies and those of psychoanalysis in general, in that he explains his patient's dream of an uncountable group of white wolves sitting in a walnut tree outside a window as a screen for the trauma induced by the primal scene of his witnessing his parents engaged in sex *a tergo* – possibly read by the patient at the time as an act of anal penetration, but decidedly in *more ferarum* or 'the manner of the beast'. Subsequently, Freud speculates that he might have even witnessed an actual act of zoophilial sex, both of which possibilities the patient later dismissed as absurd. For subsequent critics such as Nicholas Abraham and Maria Torok (1986), and of course Deleuze and Guattari, the improbability and/or reductiveness of Freud's account provides a valuable point of dissension from such psychoanalytic orthodoxies. In the case of Deleuze and Guattari, the figure of the anus, the orifice in question in one reading, is intimately related to that of the wolf or wolves as an approaching-nothing and an approaching-zero degree of intensity. For as they observe:

> A swarming, a wolfing. Who could ever believe that the anal machine bears no relation to the wolf machine...? For in the end the anus also expresses an intensity, in this case the approach to zero of a distance that cannot be decomposed without its elements changing in nature. *A field of anuses just like a pack of wolves.* (Deleuze & Guattari 1988: 32)

From this rather startling image, they continue with a brief passage which contains many of their most significant ideas of this period in a reasonably compressed form:

> Lines of flight or of deterritorialization, becoming wolf, becoming inhuman, deterritorialized intensities: that is what multiplicity is. To become a wolf or to become a hole is to deterritorialize oneself following distinct but entangled lines. A hole is no more negative than a wolf. (Deleuze & Guattari 1988: 32)

First, it should be stressed that the connection between the wolf and the hole or anus or zero is not a necessary connection, but one based on the productive contingencies of connecting and disconnecting, and thus dependent upon circumstance and situation, but also, and more consistently, on notions of multiplicity and becoming and the unceasing ebb and flow of relentless desire. In the case of our anonymous author, it should also be pointed out that this connection links very powerfully to a notion of cosmic extinction or what he refers to (in what can be reconstructed from his notes) as 'a cephalophilial cosmicide', which is also a metamorphosis but a metamorphosis as absolute regressive multiplicity. Second, and crucially, this apparent identification (which his notes seem to indicate as more precisely a *non*-identification, or possibly a disjunctive synthesis of expressive multiplicities, than an identification as such) – therefore, this non-identification between a becoming-wolf and a becoming-hole or a becoming-void shifts quite dramatically in its flight between two plateaus from a portrait of a field of orifices or anuses as a pack of white wolves to a more chaotically rendered image of crowds and contagion as clouds of self-organizing antioedipal crystals and plains or planes of infinite velocity. It executes this shift, moreover, via the temporarily more stable image of the werewolf as this latter figure then appears to transmute via its chronic and chthonic connection with the dark fluids released by the rapidly ungrounding Earth,[3] alongside undead vampires, swarming bees and other desultory haecceities in a section of a plateau on becoming animal and intense and imperceptible, subtitled 'Memories of a Sorcerer, 1', in which the essence of their theory of the becomings of packs, clouds, living densities and general multiplicities is expressed with uncharacteristic brevity and an almost child-like directness:

It is quite simple; everybody knows it, but it is only discussed in secret. We oppose epidemic to filiation, contagion to heredity, peopling by contagion to sexual reproduction, sexual production. Bands, human or animal, proliferate by contagion, epidemics, battlefields, and catastrophes. (Deleuze & Guattari 1988: 241)

Like the vampire or the wolf (or even, arguably, the gigantic wolf of chaos and global destruction, Fenrir, of Norse mythology), the werewolf is, then, a creature of contagion and multiplicities, conflict and catastrophe, chaosmosis and entanglement, beginnings and endings, not distinct in kind from the human but rather, another strand of a becoming-human by virtue of a becoming-*inhuman* which can also diverge along a different and distinct yet entangled path of becoming-*ahuman*. It is a travelling hither and thither via contagion and phase shifts, in other words: a becoming nothing as we walk into nothing out of nothing; a walk in the woods along distinct and yet distinctly entangled woodland trails. Always a walking, though. Always a becoming. Always a nothing to be approached perhaps infinitely through entropy, decay or the swerve. A zero. A (w)hole. A ()hole. A swerve to nothing and then back again to something, anything, everything, but more likely anything, something, and then back to nothing. Such are these travellings, at least in the bare life of Agamben's *zoë*, and before the predatory and political hunger of bios overwhelms the walker, for as Samuel Beckett has observed of this transition:

Where would I go, if I could go, who would I be, if I could be, what would I say, if I had a voice, who says this, saying it's me? Answer simply, someone answer simply. It's the same old stranger as ever, for whom alone accusative I exist, in the pit of my inexistence, of his, of ours, there's a simple answer. (Beckett 2010: 17)

It should be stressed, however, and moving between an image of polarities, an image of paths and an image of holes, that the decision to take one path or road does not, in this understanding, cancel the other one out or consign it to my inexistence, or his, or hers, or ours. A hole is no more negative than a wolf in this sense. It is not a question of simple bifurcation, of a binary choice between one path or another as we might initially surmise when finding ourselves in a garden of forked paths, although it may sometimes appear to be that.[4] Neither is it a simple choice between matter and void, Earth and emptiness, as one might be said to consume the other in the resonant imagery of decay associated with Reza Negarestani or Nick Land.[5] It is rather a multiplicity of bifurcations and then a bifurcation, trifurcation (and so on and so on), of these multiplicities (and so on and so on to the paradox of infinite identity and so on). In this particular case, moreover, we have the guiding image of a comparatively simple model and mode in which the human, inhuman and the ahuman are linked together as in a diagram or map of three roads meeting at a crossing, distinct and yet entangled at an opening or clearing (Heidegger's *lichtung*, the murderer's glance, the glint of a knife in a velvet glove, a single pink rose, the missing heart of a travelling funfair). This crossing might be compared to the place of trivia sacred to the number three and the ancient Greek goddess of lunar transitions, Hecate, more, that is, than to the traditional crossroads associated with the stellar and multiplicitous Papa Legba, guardian of portals in the Voudon tradition of Haiti (Métraux 1972: 80–81, 90–91, 101–102), or that connected with the etiolated, phallic devil of Christianity who supposedly gave Robert Johnson his skill on the guitar in exchange for his soul at a secret meeting at a crossroads outside Clarkesdale. Perhaps closer, also, however unintended, to the twin paths indicated by Derrida through the figure of the werewolf, or beast more generally, which as Nicole Shukin has argued, may seem to lead to either animality or spectrality, but actually entails a conflation of the two with consequences for what she has called animal capital (Shukin 2009: 49). These consequences are that for Derrida and post-Derridean theorists of the animal such as Akira Mizuta Lippit we end up with an 'animal specter that looks at Man from a paranormal time and space in which it is neither dead nor alive' (Shukin 2009: 40). In Derrida's case, this leads to the danger of a de-historicizing of the animal in which its 'bottomless gaze' spectralizes it to such a degree that any political emancipation that might be claimed for the Derridean approach is drained out of it. For Lippit, *a fortiori*, the animal has 'vanished from historical modernity' though 'a spirit or trace of animality' as code is 'salvaged by technological media' (Lippit 2000: 196; Shukin 2009).[6]

Shukin undoubtedly has a point and she pursues a vigorous advocacy which undoubtedly illuminates deeper ontological problems as it traces out political strategies, for in its sublunary transitions and ontological oscillations between man, beast and monster, on the one hand, and ghost or spectre, on the other, the werewolf below undoubtedly exemplifies that quality of being both within time and out of joint with time, like the ancestral relic of Quinton Meillassoux (2008: 9–27), but projected into our ahuman future rather than our pre-mammalian past, or quite possibly both, shattering the link between anthropological and cosmological time scales and creating an opening in which, as Wagner once put it, time becomes space. What is most immediately at stake for our anonymous author, then, between the werewolf as a figure of the beast trapped in time and its mirrored other beyond time, the creature that we are becoming, the hyper-swarming super-organism of the pack and the hive, the leviathan of superlunary dissonance and temporal disjunction that draws us towards itself, is the very ordinary distinction between the figure of myth and metaphor, on the one hand, and the very entity itself, on the other. What is at issue here is the beast in the mirror itself, the material *thing* that gazes back at us from beyond and within the shattered glass of our many compossible futures, from the shards of a magic mirror or crystal ball scattered across space and time that, as in the fable of *Snow White*, might enable us to see beyond the minor contingencies of space and time, but cannot as a medium predict our response to those visions. This mirror or medium is, as it were, a fragment ripped from the ancient Earth, indeed, a relic torn from both the ancient and future Earth, which as Negarestani has suggested of the notion of the relic per se, contra Meillassoux, is thus 'an operative of exhumation which confounds the chronological time by connecting the Now with abyssal time scales' (Negarestani 2008: 242).

Thus it is indeed that the beast looks back at us (more to follow) as we gaze at its gaze at our gaze across the abyss of time, just as Derrida's cat in 'The Animal that Therefore I am (More to Follow)' gazes at him across the more intimate abyss of domestic space as he steps naked out of the shower and into a world of seemingly mutual animality (Derrida 2002: 372–375). But as Derrida subsequently asks, what follows from this? What follows if we are looking at (and being looked back at by) vampires (who have, of course, a complex relationship with time and reflection), werewolves (who apparently do also in certain cases), or the more cephalopodic or spectral monstrosities that our author essays or indicates at various points in his ruminations? For what is also at stake here then is another dimension or surface of this threshold, but one that might also – if it is topologically possible – be reconfigured as a bridge or a rope or stream or strand between two otherwise dissonant ontologies, between that is, the animal for whom animality is an issue and the animal for whom it most decidedly is not (Abbott 2011: 87–99). Finally, of course, we must not forget the seemingly terminal threshold of speeds and intensities that we find in the graveyard or cemetery or necropolis, a place of apparent stasis and yet teeming with entities moving at infinite speeds and seemingly zero speeds as well; a place in the Western Christian tradition anyway,[7] of stone gargoyles and marble angels, of crypts and crosses, of fresh cut flowers and decaying leaves, of dissipative ghosts and hungry ghouls, as much as a place for vampires, vagrants, werewolves and mourners; a threshold that is sometimes seen as a bridge, whether one way or two way, but more often not: this being, of course, the threshold between life and death.

Schizo scherzo

This, at least, is how it appeared one afternoon to the anonymous author of the text which follows, an academic supposedly on sabbatical leave in England from an American university under the aegis of a Kinbote Scholarship, here ostensibly to write on the notion of the cosmic event in contemporary film, fiction and video games. This focus on an event of sublime magnitude for the invidious inhabitants of our small and desultory planet, whether through invasion, contagion, singularity, annihilation or some other spatio-temporal anomaly, was oddly appropriate for the

experience that he was about to undergo, for having recently digested
Derrida's first volume of *The Beast and the Sovereign* and some slightly
more recent essays in and on speculative realism, then having continued
this philosophical *rijsttafel* with a film based on the ambience rather
than the narrative of some short stories by that doyen of metaphysical
horror, H. P. Lovecraft, following this with a dessert involving a few rather
more whimsical tales of wolves and werewolves, he had an epiphany that
flickered provocatively around the affective dimensions of transition,
extinction and what we shall call here the *ahuman*. We must assume
from the clues presented to us – and I am admittedly making a leap of
assertion here, a knight's move, albeit one I feel to be fully justified – that
he must have felt for a moment rather like Friedrich Nietzsche's infamous
ringmaster-visionary in *Thus Spake Zarathustra*: the notorious figure who,
on descending from a mountain and arriving amongst a group of spectators
in a village waiting for a tightrope act to begin, starts to declaim, and then
bizarrely announces himself to be the evangelist of – or at least to intimate
or preface or pre-empt – a bridge (or a tightrope) between the apes and the
angels, or more accurately between the post-simian and the superhuman
(Nietzsche 2006: 5–7). Taking this image and notion away from its
nineteenth century audience and into the data-hungry deliquescence of our
still decidedly post-simian early twenty-first century, what our writer is
seemingly concerned with as a consequence of his moment of twenty-first
century epiphany and bricollage, albeit in a direct lineage from Nietzsche,
is a bridge (or perhaps tightrope or data stream) between, on the one side,
the wolves werewolves and similar therianthropes who haunt our myths
and fairy tales, our Palaeolithic cave temples, our primal consciousness, our
sedimented philosophy, our many pasts, and on the other side, the ghosts of
negative entropy and dark information, of alien hieroglyphs scratched onto
the surface of stars and subatomic particles, of vague spectral flickerings in
the cosmic darkness silently inducing a general sense of pan-dimensional
mal-ease and malaise, of the various pixelated polymorphs, cephalopods,
leviathan, wisps and whisperers, imps and elves, old ones and elder gods
who seemingly haunt our seemingly interminable future.

As our writer is acutely aware, bridges and tightropes and even data-
streams or rivers and the elaborate cyber-flora which flourish on their
banks may at times coexist uncomfortably with the idea of thresholds
or gates. Certainly in fictional adventures in speculative narrative and
film and the more speculative adventures in cosmology, we have become
accustomed to doors, gates and portals, wormholes and – in their more
ostensibly experimental and debatable topological modes – M-theory
sphincters, quantum vacuum bubble passages and even cosmic vaginas,
between or connecting worlds and dimensions, between or connecting
time zones and spatial spectra, and in extreme cases, between or connecting
parallel universes. These gates or portals or holes or cosmic invaginations
in some cases have a certain purchase in discussion of thresholds, of

course, as they can be configured less as boundaries than as openings between or within spatio-temporal zones, between, say, containment (or nature, form) and expression (or nurture, content), or alternatively as mere orifices that exist or subsist as part of a more generalized surface in a way that is topologically distinct – at least at first glance – from bridges or tightropes per se. Holes and holey space are surely distinct, in this initial understanding, from the probe, the speculum or the proboscis, or *a fortiori* from the rhizome, tendril or the tentacle. We are accustomed – programmed even – to view the probe as designed for entry into the holespace, as an agent of reciprocal topology, perhaps, indeed as penetration in this sense, or invasion in another related sense, as mitochondria is the trace of archaic penetration into the cell, but also as a fitting together of parts, or perhaps more fluidly as connection and lubrication, as narrative flow and flux, just as oil drips through and at the same time lubricates the ()hole space of the un-earthing Earth in its rampant Tiamaterialism in Negarestani's dangerously prophetic *Cyclonopedia*. Indeed, the kinds of thresholds that Derrida is playing with in *The Beast and the Sovereign* are arguably better served by the relation of parts and boundaries suggested by the narrator(s)of this work in relation to a discussion of holes, voids, solids and surfaces through the topological sub-genre of mereotopology, where, for example:

> ... on a mereotopological level (relating, that is, to topological interfaces of whole or whole-part relationships), changes or distortions on surfaces or the solid part are directly conducted to the compositional void and cause new convolutions and alterations by means of changing the ways or mechanisms through which the void is presented through the solid ... to make friends with the void, first one must submit to the rigid reign of the solid. (Negarestani 2008: 62–63)

Perhaps one of the problems with Derrida's allusive discussion of thresholds in *The Beast and the Sovereign*, for our author at least and in relation to zoological gardens and mental hospitals and by association cemeteries, is that, in the end (which, it has to be said, never actually arrives), it pays too little attention to what the commentator here in *Cyclonopedia* calls the reign of the rigid and in doing so avoids the void, and by implication a relation between parts and (w)holes and holey space and boundaries,[8] a relation which, it could be argued, potentially infiltrates Derrida's temporal disjunction (time out of joint) from his earlier *Specters of Marx* (Derrida 1994), in such a way that the convergence of the animal and the spectral is not in any way a conflation so much as a divergence of infinite speeds and absolute deterritorializations. From there, it is not too hard to discern that the political and cosmological implications of this infiltration, this contagion, this virulent infection of unbounded time (in which the political and the cosmological converge infinitely but can never be conflated), more than unsettles the already unstable symmetry between *zoë* and *bios* in Agamben, indeed they swiftly make it degenerate, at least that must surely be the case in any long term, projective, post-simian, ahuman sense in which, as in Zeno's fable, we infinitely approach but never arrive at the omega-point of zero or the zero-point of absolute void because we never even fired the arrow.

Animalities and schizophrenias, bestiaries and the edges of reason, gates and portals, holes and arrows, bridges and tightropes and· strange new topologies, as the writer of the essay to follow is clearly aware (at least, from the evidence of his notes), all of these tropes and motifs enfold and unfold the question of human identity and its determinations in this age we have perhaps somewhat arrogantly come to call the anthropocene. It is all too easy to be distracted by the immense gulfs of time our cosmologies tell us of, and the seemingly uni-directional quality of the arrow of time and entropy, against which messages from our distant future(s) are not quite impossible but are, nonetheless, deemed almost immeasurably improbable. Ours is not a mere tale of time and its vicissitudes, however, of reckless mortality or solar decay as some contemporary theorists have it (Brassier 2007: 205–239),[9] or at least not primarily, but a tale more cosmically aligned, a tale of space and void, of thresholds, of doors and windows, of buried cities, or ruined cities, of lights in the sky, of arbitrary cosmic events that split time as one arrow well aimed might split another in the shaft of its contingency, of Werner Herzog's deranged penguin waddling alone across the white plain towards the South pole (Herzog 2007), of lines of indeterminacy forming thereby like an alien script on the Antarctic snow and ice. Thus, it is that our unnamed narrator in the spirit of Arthur Rimbaud or of Judge Schreber and the Wolfman from Freud's exemplary fables of thought unhinged is both within and without the twin domains of madness and sanity, of reason and its other. This is a necessary destabilization for the task in hand, it is suggested, in that it requires human thought to first become deranged, to become inhuman, to pass through the inhuman, that is, en route to the unnameable which we currently and pre-emptively mark as the *a-human*, a figure which subsists for us in a projected shadow universe of the void of non-being, a meontological abyss around which imagination curls like black smoke on some remote desert island. But it is not on that imaginary desert island that we begin. Rather, and in the tradition of doughty characters from English literature such as Gulliver, Robinson Crusoe, Annie Bonnie or Captain Mission, it begins at the place before or at least other than the voyage itself, the space of another set of thresholds marking not only the passage or limit or line between land, air and ocean, between time and space, between history and fortitude, but also between the city and the wilderness, the planet and the stars, the stars and the cosmos, the cosmos and the void. It begins at the end. It begins in between the end. It begins here.

Providence. Rhode Island. USA

* * *

Part two

The wolf and the void

A few days before I began drafting these, my final notes, I was returning to my desk from a stolen afternoon in a cinema in a pleasantly hedonistic city on the south coast of England and by way of further momentary distraction I picked up a slightly battered copy of Sabine Baring-Gould's 1854 study of werewolves and wolf-lore in a second hand bookshop not far from the absurd, regency pavilion which stands just above the east pier. Pausing, then, in a windswept seafront café to check and reply to some messages that had been agitating my phone as I watched the recently reissued film (I am now, I believe, chronically unable to switch off my phone in all but the most extreme, romantic, socially or medically pressing situations), I opened the book at Baring-Gould's introduction and read the following:

> I shall never forget the walk I took one night in Vienne, after having accomplished the examination of an unknown Druidical relic, the Pierre labie, at Rondelle, near Champagni. (Baring Gould 1995: 1)

There are moments in one's life when concept, affect, memory, imagination, sentiment and experience, both past and projective, come together in a lightning flash, a flash that may even cleave the world into two or more pieces, revealing a hole in Being itself, a singular and divine emptiness, an ecstatic void of infinite possibility that is both savage and seductive and infinitely desirable, and this was indeed one such epiphany. Then, just following that moment, as thought returned like a ragged and yet raging tide and the sun dipped for a second or two beneath a dense bank of cloud and then seemed to ascend from behind a second and more dissipated bank of cloud, sending streams of dark light sweeping into and across the streets below and around the café's perimeter, several things struck me quite forcibly. The first, as, in a daze, I attempted to sip my macchiato and poke with little enthusiasm a piece of carrot cake under this striated and tenebrous flaring, was that so much of our lives as intellectuals, as scholars, as artists or academics, or at least, those aspects of those lives that could be said genuinely to still matter, have been based on what happens to us when we take a walk, whether in reality or metaphorically (Ingold 2010: 15–23).[10] It might be a walk around the block or a walk in the head. It might be a drift or a dream or a descent into the ribbed inferno. It could be a zigzagging schizo-stroll through the agora, or, and in keeping with psychopathology of walking more generally, it might be a promenade along the glistening shore-line of hysteria or the shadowy tree-line of paranoia or the line of flight that sometimes runs unaccountably between the two. Sometimes, indeed, we might find that we have taken a wrong turn on this oddly striated, slanted (transversal) traversal, might find, that is, that we have accidentally left the city of palaces and piers, of zoos, cemeteries and mental hospitals and crossed that shady and mutable quasi-arborescent quasi-rhizomatic boundary with all its sorcerers, witches and werewolves, as Gilles Deleuze and Félix Guattari characterize this space (1988: 246), and then discovered ourselves hopelessly lost in the deep dark woods, like Dante Alighieri or Snow White or Red Riding Hood or – and this must, of course, be appended with qualifications – Martin Heidegger. This is where we leave and lose sight of the path for a moment or perhaps for more than a moment. This is where both philosophy and fairy tales begin. This is where the heart beats fast.

At other times we are, in a brave new hyper-connected disjunctive Cosmopolis, more the digitally détourning disintegrative heirs of Louis Aragon or Walter Benjamin or Guy Debord than the delirious pedestrian of schizo spaces: online angels laden with GPS signatures and geopolitical hacks that we twist and turn and distort in the search for new patterns and parallels in space and time, new horizons, new transversalities, new geometries. This is where revolutions dream into new beginnings. This is where the heart beats faster. And at yet other times, when we descend to our deepest genetic and ontological levels, whether in imagination or otherwise, in those verdant forests or sailing above sultry oceans, in those glistening rivers and silent desert-landscapes of ice, rock, sand and crystal, beneath our feet and above our heads, in hotel rooms, in cars, in airports, in bars, in bodies, on bodies, between bodies, in fur, in feathers, in scales and fins: there hearts may become nuclei and nuclei cytoplasm and cytoplasm multiplicity and multiplicity multiplicities and multiplicities cryptonomies and as yet unimagined phenomenophagisms. Here we may travel not only vertically, horizontally and diagonally across space but forwards and backwards and even sideways in time, from here back to the prokaryotes then forward or sideways to who knows where?

At this point in my ecstatic ramblings, I observed a common house fly, a creature often associated with dirt and pestilence and even metaphysical evil by its human hosts, land on my piece of carrot cake and begin to feed (a decidedly uncommon sight in England these days, it seems, or at least since my previous visit, which tells perhaps of processes of extinction barely visible beneath the froth of life), and as I observed this invasion of my food space and thought of the delicate balance between hosts, guests and parasites, it occurred to me as it has so often and to so many others that perhaps in outer space, from outer space, from the great outdoors, one day others will come to us, or perhaps they will never come because they have never been. Perhaps if they do come, if they return, we will wish they had never been. Perhaps if they do come they will merely want to consume us, whether as flesh or phenomena or information or affect. But however we now choose to walk in and through our meditations and cerebrations on notions of dwelling and invasion, filiation and contagion, the figure who surely pre-empts our footfalls and clawfalls, wingfalls and finfalls, soarings and slidings risings and slitherings and hoppings, our pan-dimensional metamorphoses to come as well as those we have buried in the ash of dead cities and forests, is the heir of another walker of horror and abjection with whom he often identified, as did the original Parisian flâneur Charles Baudelaire, the anti-flâneur of Rhode Island, Howard Philip Lovecraft. This is the Lovecraft less of the unspeakable and the eldritch per se, although that remains important, than of the colours of space or of the mysterious city discovered deep in Antarctica by a group of academics (Lovecraft 2008: 422–503), a ruin and a relic composed of an architecture of sickening angles and volumes of solid space and impossible geometries of void, time, and fluidity, a place of an unendurable hieroglyphic density of image and icon. It is a space impossible at least for the human gaze to assimilate, or for human affect to resonate with except on a spectrum running from unease to disgust to unutterable terror, a place of silent topologies and ancient whisperings, of alien hungers and invisible desires. It is an absolutely inhuman and indeed an ahuman place, but a place not so much of ruins, perhaps, at least as in the ancient cities of human archaeology or the devastated cities of modern warfare, than of delirious and diabolical ruination itself, and in that latter sense, of delirious ruination and the insatiable desire to consume phenomena which accompanies that desire, and in this sense, the inhuman, the ahuman and the human would appear to meet like three paths in a forest clearing.

Thought of Lovecraft's mysterious city and its resistance to the human gaze connected my musings to the second, virtually simultaneous thing that struck me in that café in my moment of epiphany, which relates to the first through a winding tangle of rhizome and referent as much as it does through a straight line or threshold, which was that we live in an age of ruins. In itself, this observation was hardly revelatory – my reflection in the window glanced back at me quizzically for a moment, I noticed a dark spot on the side of my nose – ruins have been a preoccupation of a certain sensibility since at least the romantic era, if not back to the writings of Scipio on the sack of Carthage some 2000 years ago (Hell 2010: 169–192). However, what struck me here via this necessary qualification was that the quality of ruination since the romantics and subsequent romantically inflected modernists, since Walter Benjamin related the ruin to allegory,[11] or indeed, Benjamin's contemporary, Albert Speer, planned an architecture for the third Reich based on the assumption of its eventual imperial ruination – and this is what connects the notion of the twenty-first century ruin to Lovecraft – is that the desire for delirial ruination has become cosmic as much as textual or architectural. To make this generalization from the romantic to the cosmic via the inhuman or indeed ahuman is not, of course, to deny the imperial dimension of ruination which infects the gaze and dreams of both Scipio and Speer, separated as they are by nearly two millennia, but rather, to indicate ways in which contemporary notions of Empire, gradually attenuated over the past decade in a million tracts and blogs, from the grand designs of Michael Hardt and Antonio Negri into an ostensibly dispersive hegemony of desire, control and capital, flicker now between the fractured light of a demented politico-material aspiration to universal power and luxury above and within the libidinal economy, on the one hand, and on the other, the darkness of cosmic, planetary or at very least biological extinction (Hardt and Negri 2000). Thus the third thing that struck me, simultaneously, as I gazed out of the window at the murmuring city around me – related to the first and the second by its own peripatetic logic – was the instability and insubstantiality of the species, human or otherwise, that dreams of such universal power and control, in the face of absolute nothingness.

The beast machine

I finished my coffee, but not the carrot cake, which had been somewhat ruined by alien invasion, and then, still decidedly light-headed from my recent epiphany, went to the counter of the Soft Machine café to pay the proprietess, an attractive and obviously educated woman of indeterminate age with whom I was on nodding terms. I noticed as I had on a previous visit that she had a tattoo of a dark and twisting wolf with piercing eyes consuming the sun on her left arm and wore several items of jewellery relating to the mythos of Lovecraft, including a heavy Cthulhu belt and an ornate nose piercing on which I could just about discern some miniature and presumably Norse or Lovecraftian runes. Commenting on these, I mentioned to her the film I had just seen[12] and she smiled and returned that so far as this particular director was concerned her favourite was the one he had set in Antarctica – a place she had always wanted to visit. I agreed that I too had always nurtured a yearning for that vast and desolate place, and if possible, intended to use my next sabbatical from Miskatonic to visit the empty continent and study its literary and cinematic fauna and heritage from an anthropological perspective. She nodded, smiled a little more flirtatiously this time, and said that should I need a research assistant she would be more than happy to shut up shop for a few months and accompany me, and that she had always been intrigued by stories of a nameless city beyond the mountains and beneath the snow and ice. I smiled back, a little cautiously I suppose now (bearing in mind all that has happened since), and responded that I would certainly keep her offer in mind.

A little later that day after a stroll along the shingle beach which lies to the south of the city, bordering an ocean whose expanse so improbably connects England with that great southern continent of icy hurricanes and endless night, I returned to my study and, after glancing briefly in the faux art deco mirror which my landlady had begrudgingly dragged up from her basement (and in which I noticed with some alarm a slight lengthening of my canine teeth and a small hole which had appeared unaccountably on the side of my nose, and even more unnervingly, just where the proprietess's elaborate piercing had been), began reading an essay by Alberto Gualandi in the speculative journal *Collapse*, wherein the writer made the point that one of the central motifs in what we have come to call 'continental philosophy' was to effect a Copernican revolution within philosophy beyond that initiated by Immanuel Kant, and rid the discipline forever of its subject-ridden, anthropocentric, epistemological human-ness. As Gualandi notes, in this aim at very least, it failed miserably (Gualandi 2009: 508). What resulted, however, was not necessarily all bad. For Gualandi, the new 'Philosophy of Nature' that he associates particularly in French thought of the 1960s with the work of Deleuze, Gilbert Simondon and Michel Serres has a number of redeeming or at least retrievable features which connect it with the more enlightened aspects of contemporary neurobiologists such as Steven Rose (in contrast to the reductions of Richard Dawkins), especially in terms of the multidimensionality of the relation between genotype and phenotype. He then cites 'the celebrated page where Deleuze proposes to us an ontological model of the egg; or better, the egg as a model of the world' (Gualandi 2009: 510), the world is an egg – a passage that had appealed to me in the past but now merely made me feel restless, hungry.

I decided to return to this rich and interesting discussion later and poured myself a large bourbon, and then returned to my earlier thoughts in the café, posing myself some unusually angled questions which I hoped would take me to the heart of the problem I was attempting to formalize. How much does a werewolf remember of his or her wolfery once returned to the more desultory animality of the human, for example? This is, of course, a question that only makes sense in a fictional context, as werewolves don't exist in any substantial ontological sense, but subsist merely as ephemeral flickerings of brain chemistry or cinematic time-painting. Werewolves, in this understanding, certainly have a kind of existence, but it is – to use the term of Henri Corbin – an imaginal existence, not quite real in the material sense, and yet somehow more than merely a product of fantasy or whimsical imagining: hyperstition, is a more recent term for this, although the latter tends to suggest a way in which fiction transforms itself into reality, emerges into being, substantiates from text to flesh, rather than the intermediary zone of the imaginal. It was at this point that my phone rang once again and the noises started outside. I gazed out of the window and caught my reflection briefly against the dusty surface, looking like something archaic and slowly vanishing. There were lights flashing across the sky. Strangely intense iridescent colours in weird geometries spasmodically shrinking and stretching, shaping and reshaping and contorting themselves systole and diastole at unbearable speeds. Suddenly, my sabbatical plans ceased to have any meaning. I knew now what it was I had to do, which was to find a point at which three thresholds came together as a distinct and yet entangled place of opening so as to generate a relic for my parallel self. The cosmic event. Absolute contingency. An arbitrary hole in the universe through which larval selves swarm and group into ever more complex configurations of intelligence and signifying power, violence and desire, cruelty and curiosity, code and catastrophe, and yes, an endless and unbearable and insatiable hunger for everything and nothing. Phenomenophagism. I knew now what I had to do.

Becoming ahuman becoming

As I passed the mirror in the hallway (oh, magic mirror on the wall), I noticed with an equally passing concern that the hole in my nose had become even larger (who is the fairest of them all?), I noticed the soft fur on my cheeks (is it you?), I noticed the talons on my hands and my hands becoming paws (is it me?), I noticed the strong, musky, feral scent of the chase and its myriad trails and memories flowing from and out into the impending night, and I gazed back at myself for a moment and saw something else looming in the darkness too, behind and beyond the mirror in some weird, Lovecraftian space, something too terrible to recount or to record. It hardly matters now, anyway, the time of writing will have soon passed, after all, as writing and animality are, after all, one and the same, and very soon I will have consumed the world and then the sun, and then I will consume the universe and everything in it, and I will no longer be in any sense a creature of signification or information, an I or a me or a you, an animal, human or otherwise, a creature of organs or judgement, a creature with hands, a face, a mouth, a vagina, anus, nostrils, ears, eyes and pores, a creatures of loops and holes and language. I will no longer be in that sense at all. Lights like a double nebula or the glaring twin eyes of some gigantic beast are now tearing and wrenching the sky apart in search of the sun. I must run now, doggy style, leave the city, which is in a sense the same as becoming the city, becoming its missing heart, its murderer's glance, its pink rose, embodying its wound, colonizing the human absolutely by flooding its spaces with an integral ahumanity, flooding its animality with ananimality, with wild matter as much as with dreams or calculation or wild spirit.

It was a very good thing that I finally managed to save that stained and ravaged manuscript from its hastily scratched burial place on the edge of the cemetery by the old forest path, the place of thresholds where sorcerers who had always known that writing and animality were one and the same had once raised their chants to the cephalopod gods they worshipped who then consumed them. Had it been there any longer it would certainly have been destroyed by the radioactive rain at the very least, or the black oil seeping between the gravestones, or some other form of granular decay. Parts of it were already well beyond reconstruction by then, the pages apparently ripped by savage teeth and talons and then licked and sucked and nipped with lips and tongues and sharp incisors rather than tendrils, quills, feathers, fins or tentacles, as though some furry multiplicity were attempting to drink knowledge itself before it vanished like raindrops in a sea of entropy. Soon, though, the wounded, bleeding and dying sun will fall to the earth again and the all too pellucid moon will rise again and illuminate beautifully the ruins of the ancient city, will illuminate again the exquisitely disintegrating code and the vast, flailing tentacles of its new inhabitants, and we will become imperceptible again and again and again and again in the deep, dark woods as we always have and always will until until.() ...

Notes

1   The reference is to an article by Henri F. Ellenberger on zoological gardens and mental hospitals, as discussed by Derrida (2009: 297).

2   See, for instance, Diego H. Rossello's lucid analysis (2012: 255–279).

3   On dark fluidity and unearthing, see Nick Land (1992: 107).

4   Their criticism here (Deleuze & Guattari 1988: 241) of the author of that masterpiece of metaphysical fiction (amongst many others in his oeuvre), 'The Garden of Forking Paths', Jorge Luis Borges, is, to my mind, considerably less persuasive than most of their literary observations in the two volumes of *Capitalism and Schizophrenia* and elsewhere. For further discussion of this issue in regard to Borges and Deleuze and Guattari, see my 'In the Museum of Lost Objects: Absence, Affect, Entropy', forthcoming.

5   A useful overview of the question of decay in relation to geophilosophy and to Negarestani and Land in particular may be found in Woodward (Woodward 2013: 12–18).

6   Two other invaluable studies that discuss this general theme are Broglio (2011) and Wolfe (2013).

7   For a more general look at funerary rituals and geophilosophy, see Woodward (2013: 64–70).

8   For further information on this branch of topology, see Negarestani (2008: 230. n. 16).

9   For a different though related take on human extinction to Ray Brassier's bracing discussion in *Nihil Unbound*, this time via demonology, medieval scholasticism and horror, see Eugene Thacker's elegant thesis, *In the Dust of This Planet* (Thacker 2011).

10   I am here following in the exemplary tradition of the pedestrian (or possibly bicycling) tradition of thought and creativity in, for example, the work of Jean-Jacques Rousseau, Edgar Allen Poe, Charles Baudelaire, Samuel Beckett, Bruce Chatwin and more recently, Kraftwerk, Will Self and W.G. Sebald. On writing, reading, thinking and walking, see Rebecca Solnit's engrossing meditation on these interconnected themes in her *Wanderlust: A History of Walking* (2007). See also the illuminating discussion of 'mind-walking' by Tim Ingold (2010: 15–23).

11   'Allegories are in the realm of thoughts, what ruins are in the realm of things' (Benjamin 1998: 178).

12   As the more attentive reader may well have surmised, the film referred to here was *In the Mouth of Madness*, directed by John Carpenter from 1994. The main feature that day was preceded, it would appear, in true b-movie style, by a short and rather garish production called *Werewolf V Leviathan 2 – New Becomings* (date and provenance unknown).

CHAPTER SEVEN

The Taste of Living

Chrysanthi Nigianni

Prelude: The riddle of writing

The riddle of writing, the riddle of reading, is similar to the riddle of the Sphinx. It consists of all kinds of entrances: material (doorways/words/sensations), mental (ideas/concepts), spiritual (higher planes of wisdom), esoteric. It entails anticipation and a certain level of risk-taking, anguish and doubt (either we get in, or we get devoured). We are standing at the entrance of the gate. We cannot make the Sphinx say anything, we have to let it speak. She appeals to the ear. We need to be able to listen and we need to approach words with nobility and cautiousness: slowly (Regier 2004). It is within the words and their function that some truth will reveal itself, if only for a moment, and we need to be ready for that moment. The Sphinx is a man-eater: half-animal, half-woman, she questions the notion of a transcendent hu-Man knowledge and truth; she appears the moment a certainty of victory is reached only to turn it into a defeat.

The riddle called Clarice Lispector is the Sphinx of Rio De Janeiro (Moser 2009): a woman whose sight was a shock,[1] and whose work has often been dismissed as incomprehensible, enigmatic, hermetic, in the past. In today's Brazil, Clarice Lispector has become an icon with her face adorning postage stamps and her books being sold in vending machines in subway stations, whereas simply her first name is sufficient to identify Brazilian intelligentsia (Moser 2009). Her work – similar to her life – is a fascinating mystery and to contextualize it within the logic of genre or in a literary period would do little to solve the riddle of her writing. Literary theorists situate her work into the modernist tradition and more precisely, the third generation of modernism in Brazil, the 'generation of 1945' (Armstrong 1999: 62); a generation, which clearly broke away from a 'certain instinct of nationality' (Moser 2009: 126) that characterized the predecessors of the Brazilian modernist movement. Her stylistic experimentation of language, the highly subjective individualism and introspective mood that characterize her work, situate her within modernism's framework of experiments of consciousness and she has been compared to 'Joyce, Virginia Woolf, Katherine Mansfield, Dostoyevsky, Proust, Gide, and Charles Morgan' (Moser 2009: 127).

Clarice's work, like the Sphinx, is a man-eater: the immediacy and force of her enigmatic writing, the exhaustive phenomenological and existential crisis of her female characters, dismantle conceptual and cultural categories of the self, gender, subjectivity. For, these categories are based on concealments and exclusions of substantial and essential elements of living: dynamic matter, forces and sense-impressions that resist conceptual reduction, and ontological modelling. She opens the gate to a different understanding and perceiving that emerge from an excess of experience, an a-subjective, impersonal experience. Her texts always entail interpersonal struggles with 'impersonal cosmic forces termed "reality" or "God" (although not in any conventional religious sense)' (Peixoto 1994: 82), usually triggered by a violent encounter. In one of her best known novels, *The Passion According to G.H.* (1964), such an encounter takes place between a woman and a cockroach, where the cockroach becomes the catalyst for the woman's transformation and liberation from humanistic imperatives, norms, and ideals – an event that leads her to a different ethics, a different relating to the self and the world.

Writing (in the form of literature and poetry) relates primarily to ethics, and not epistemology, because it requires an encounter: it happens 'thanks to the other, and under dictation' (Derrida in Phillips 2011: 234), it moves in the direction of the other and upon the effacement of the 'I' – the death of the metaphysics of presence. An a-human ethics then, since the other that haunts writing (for Derrida) or impels writing as lines of escape (for Deleuze), lies outside the organization of the human and its colonization by Logocentrism. Writing reveals the tensions between (human) experience and language and it is through writing that language is pushed to its limits, its exhaustion. It is not primarily a medium of communication but that of creation and invention. Invention in the form of style[2] for Deleuze (1997) makes links between signs, events, life and vitalism, and inscribes becomings and transmutations that transgress the Law of Language. Or, writing as a trace (Derrida 1992) relates to a 'genealogical anxiety' that is nothing other than the question(ing): Who I am? Who is this 'I' that speaks or writes? (Bergo 2005) and refers to a pre-linguistic presence/experience. For both philosophers, literature and writing put phenomenology and a metaphysical concept of the human in crisis.

Rather than looking for representations of the ahuman, or posthuman[3] in the literary genre of sci-fi novels (a humanizing imaginary that appropriates the 'event' into normative forms of writing and conventional narratives, and assimilates the future into present possibilities), I have sought to work with a novel (*The Passion According to G.H.*) that departs form a humanistic point of view, only for this view to be gradually eroded as the narrative unfolds; the journey of G.H.'s dehumanization is full of joy and pleasure but also fear and anguish. In engaging with the book I let myself be guided by the text (and not by prior philosophical concepts), to read and be read.[4] The text that follows (hopefully) resonates with Clarice Lispector's powerful work and has developed within the lines of Cixous' notion *of écriture feminine*: it avoids conceptual overdetermination and practises a poetic (rather than analytic) and embodied style of philosophical thinking, where prior philosophical ideas and arguments (that inform my text) emanate from a close and experiential reading of Lispector's book. My aim has been to reveal the affective and mental tensions, the emotional extremity and ambivalence the character goes through in her struggle – a struggle between holding on to the known (her human identity) and a letting go (towards the ahuman), her struggle with language as both constraint and liberation. It is within this struggle that thinking happens and novel concepts are born. The text that follows aims to keep a living relation with language and my intimate experience of the book. It, moreover, wishes to remain open to different interpretations. Like with any riddle, the riddle of Clarice Lispector should remain unresolved, keep its mystery and a taste for the secret.

She gave me death to start with[5]

Why write? There is a moment of anguish before writing, before delivering words, words you do not entirely trust, yet you are left only with them. 'Why write' is always linked to the question 'what to write', instantly accompanied by a 'how to write it'. It is the *it* that troubles so much, both a necessity and an impossibility: how to write what remains unsaid is the paradox that puts one in the turmoil of writing. Not a psychoanalytic *it* stemming from the unconscious, a remnant of repression, but an *it* that goes far deeper, far lower.[6] It is more of a bodily symptom than a mental enquiry, emerging from the question 'what can a body do?' rather than 'what have I forgotten, repressed through oblivion?' To be able to write you have to be able to read the signs of the body, 'not those of the unconscious, which is already speaking – the unconscious is language – but the body signs that are of the same order as those of the unconscious, though before language' (Cixous 1993: 136). Writing departs from a pre-verbal exigency of the body, that expresses through stuttering and breaks the excess of human experience, an incompetence of language, an internal state of foreignness.

Like Hélène Cixous, I always liked writers of the extremity, the ones that stretch the limits of the livable, the possible, the thinkable. The ones that teach us how to die: the death of the given life, its determined forms, norms, habitual thoughts and clichés – the writers that strip us of our certainties. Cixous (1993), paraphrasing Montaigne, says writing like philosophizing is learning to die.

'To be human we need to experience the end of the world' (Cixous 1993: 10), we need to desire its end, to embrace the final disaster, to witness the ultimate crime scene, so that we can start to finally sense and see that the world is more than what we think it is, there is more to Life than our humanized lives. Writing is inspired by the lived and the taste of the living, an extra-subjective aesthesis that is dark, wild and repulsive, 'a very difficult pleasure; but it *is* called pleasure' (Lispector 1988: v) that needs to be communicated and shared for it weighs too much on us: the construction of the self proves to be fragile and cannot contain such extreme pleasure. It thus demands for words ('what is the word?'), and when it cannot find it, the word must be invented, for that pleasure needs to create its own linguistic style, so that it does not perish, or become deadly. 'Style in a great writer is always a style of life too, not anything at all personal, but inventing a possibility of life, a way of existing' (Deleuze 1995: 100).

If Deleuze is right in pointing that writing is an attempt to 'free life from what imprisons it' (Deleuze 1995: 143), then writing is a line of escape, a line of flight from the prison of the self. 'To get away. To get away, out! ... To cross a horizon ...' (Deleuze & Guattari 2003: 186). My favourite writers practised 'a certain type of writing that does not hesitate to go beyond the self, beyond oneself' (Cixous 1993: 36). Hence lines of writing pass between: between life and death, confinement and escape, I and you, my love and your love, where there is always a murder. 'Who is killing me?' It is not you, it is not me, but our betweenness. Death is only a question of love, the death of a loved one that gives and takes away. The only one who can kill me is the beloved one. Writing starts with death and loss and works as the catalyst that transforms loss into gain. A writer is always guilty of that. 'Mixed loss and gain: that's our crime. This is what we are always guilty of, guilt we can't do anything about with these unexpected and terrible gains' (Cixous 1993: 11). Writing is thus a forbidden act and equally reading is a forbidden pleasure, eating the forbidden fruit, making forbidden love.

'Death is associated with tears' (Bataille 1989: 32). Writing words is inscribing with ink the tears of Eros we fail to bring to the surface, remaining concealed in the depths of existing. My soul is sobbing. Tears that would wash the eyes out, wear down the sight, rendering us blind little Oedipuses, writing blindly with words, what cannot be known in advance but only after it has been written. The tears have not been shed, yet a salty taste stays in my mouth as a pre-knowing and not knowing, as a secret that wants to remain unavowable in order to escape forgetfulness. We seek that moment that will release our tears, our humanized tears because we know deep down that 'humanity is steeped in humanization [...] that false humanization (that) impedes man and impedes his humanity' (Lispector 1988: 150). We thus look for that moment of tears in books, in

the kind of books that wound and stab us ... If the book we are reading doesn't wake us up with a blow on the head, what are we reading it for?

[...] But we need books to affect us like a disaster, that grieve us deeply, like the death of someone we loved more than ourselves, like being banished into forests far from everyone, like suicide. (Kafka 1978: 16)

Clarice Lispector's work certainly falls into this category of books: books that 'wound and stab us', 'affect us like a disaster'. I came across Clarice Lispector's work a few years ago – although I felt instantly intrigued and drawn into her writing, I resisted it: it was a sense of powerlessness from my part that made me postpone and defer my rapport with it. It was not the right time. Unlike dreams, we can choose when to enter a text. 'What is magnificent about books is that they can wait for us' (Cixous 1993: 58). They give us time. It was only this summer that I opened the book and read it and then another followed and another. 'When we read a text we are either read by the text or we are in the text' (Cixous 1990: 3). Who is writing? Who is reading? 'A real reader is already on the way of writing' (Cixous 1993: 21). Like in the act of love, it has to do with passivity and activity, their interchange and intertwinement. Reading like writing is a love affair, an encounter where one loses oneself, takes a step beyond the self. And 'if I'm brave, I'll let myself stay lost' (Lispector 1988: 4), continue the reading, from one line to the next and the next, deciphering the unknown world of the beloved. 'The beloved appears unknown to us, implying, enveloping, imprisoning a world that must be deciphered, that is, interpreted. [...] To love is to try to explicate, to develop these unknown worlds that remain enveloped within the beloved' (Deleuze 2000: 68).

In the beginning of the book *The Passion According to G.H.*, Clarice[7] addresses the possible readers with the following words:

This book is like any other book. But I would be pleased if it were read only by persons whose souls are already mature [...] These people and they alone will understand very slowly that this book takes nothing away from anyone. To me for example, the character G.H. gradually gave a difficult joy; but it *is* called joy.[8]

As Hélène Cixous notes, with her last lines 'this book takes nothing away from anyone. To me for example, the character G.H. gradually gave a difficult joy', Clarice sides with the reader, becomes herself a reader and stands like us before the book. This is not unusual for Clarice Lispector. In her last work *The Hour of the Star*, she begins her book with a long reflection and meditation on the act of writing itself and what it is to be the author of a text (questioning and negating the writer's authority and the corresponding notion of the text as a property of the author). This is achieved by creating a character, who is the writer of the story we are about to read. Clarice employs here the literary device known as a 'story within a story' (in French 'mise en abyme') producing a 'book within book' or a book of a book, where the author takes distance from herself-as-the-author (even to the point of effacing herself) and multiplies the authorial voices, raising questions of who is the author and who is the reader, as well as, who is the subject and who is the object (the notion of the fictional object/character produced by the writer's imagination). With this gesture, Clarice blurs the boundaries between writing and reading, subject and object, while she does not allow the readers any sense of realism: we are reminded constantly that what we are going to read is fiction that nonetheless is no less real. For Cixous, it is the feeling of secret, or the feeling of truth that we approach better in dreams and fiction.

'"What is truth?" "Does truth exist?" Let us imagine that it exists. The word exists therefore the feeling exists' (Cixous 1993: 36). Whereas, Clarice exclaims in her novel: 'But the truth has never made sense to me. Truth doesn't make sense!' (Lispector 1988: 11). In *The Hour of the Star* she writes: 'I write because I'm desperate and weary. I can no longer bear the routine of my existence [...] I have experienced almost everything, even passion and despair. Now I wish to possess what might have been but never was' (Lispector 1992: 21). Cixous allies truth with the verb to 'unlie', 'not to lie'. This is the direction of truth, the direction of writing, a dangerous path since it means a relinquishing of everything that has sustained our lives, 'all the lies that have helped us live' (Cixous 1993: 37). It is only in the last moment that we can speak, we can say what could not be said before, though we never know when is the last moment. Clarice moves to the direction of the last hour, leaves her world to enter into the world ('what might have been but never was') only to confront the enormous space she had discovered: 'the space of truth?' (Lispector 1988: 11). The nakedness of truth, the nakedness of human experience,[9] the neutrality of the world, which is no longer my familiar, humanized world. In the vastness of this world the self shrinks, gets lost, 'the ready-made person idea' cracks, dies, and it would have been easier if 'I pretended to write for someone ... If I imagined that someone is holding my hand ... Give me your hand' (Lispector 1988: 9) – the need of the author for her character, similar to my need for you and that of the self for the other. 'I m in love with a character I invented' (Lispector 2012: 125). I am inventing your presence because I am afraid to die alone, and 'something allies truth to death' (Cixous 1993: 36). It is hard to lose oneself. 'With you I shall start to die until I am able on my own not to exist and then I'll let you go' (Lispector 1988: 11).

Letting go signals death. Loss and gain. She gave me death to start with and then words were invented. They address to mature souls.

It makes us feel, taste, touch life[10]

Tasting the living is an act of passion, an act of love and that of a lover in sexual intercourse. *The Passion According to G.H.* is the passion/love according to a woman (is it G.H or C.L?). It is also the passion according to the cockroach, the barata (in Portuguese), which is feminine. As the translator notes in the Preface of the book, the word 'passion' in Portuguese is 'the colloquial term for "love" and "lover", in addition to its designation of "passion" as an abstraction and of Christ's Passion' (Sousa 1988: viii), so that the title could also be translated into 'Love According to G.H', though the Biblical implications would be lost in that case.

It makes us feel, taste, touch life. The third (im)personal, neutral pronoun 'it' is devoid of human value. Sliding in meaning, it could stand for a series of substitutions: Clarice's writing, the novel, the room, the cockroach, the barata, the human-insect encounter, love, death, the vagina, the process of de-humanization. However, *The Passion According to G.H.* strikes us with its literalness (and not its metaphors).[11] 'The text says what it says which makes reading very difficult' (Cixous 1989: xxiii). G.H. wants to speak and share with us everything that has happened, all there is, though she finds it hard to find the right words: 'As soon as I say it, I'll have to add: "That isn't it, that isn't it at all!"' (Lispector 1988: 12). Living isn't tellable hence it requires creation that is different from lying. 'Yes to creation, no to lying' (Lispector 1988: 13). For Clarice, creation does not approximate to imagination but to reality, the risk one takes to come face-to-face with reality; an encounter which requires the abandoning of the security of our categorical thinking, and the disposal of the humanistic lenses of our anthropomorphizing perception and understanding: a linguistic perceiving that passes through metaphor and metonymy and which protects us from the violence of seeing and sensing.

A mobile army of metaphors, metonymics, anthropomorphisms: in short, a sum of human relations which became poetically and rhetorically intensified, metamorphosed, adorned, and after long usage, seem to a nation fixed, canonic and binding; truths are illusions; worn-out metaphors which have become powerless to affect the sense. (Nietzsche in Derrida 1974: 15)

What G.H. has seen is a 'raw truth' that cannot be translated into language – 'translate the unknown into a language I don't know and not even understand' (Lispector 1988: 13) – so that all she is left to do is a 'phonetic transcription', a physical vocal mimesis (in the form of monologue) of all that has taken place, of what she experienced – a mimesis that will attempt to reach a primitive meaning, always sensible and material.

G.H. wants to confess what she saw. She needs to speak, so that for a moment she is saved. It is the immensity of reality she was confronted with that paralysed her human understanding[12]: 'A world wholly alive has a Hellish power' (Lispector 1988: 15). Before entering the maid's room, she was a woman, recognizable with the initials G.H. Such a recognition and identity collapse the moment she gets into the room, a space that feels unfamiliar and possesses her with a feeling of estrangement. 'The room was so different from the rest of the apartment that going into it was like leaving my own home and entering another' (Lispector 1988: 34). She left her world and entered into another: a naked room, a dry and empty space, clean and shiny 'like a room in an insane asylum' (Lispector 1988: 30); the brightness of the sunlight lays bare the room's nakedness, its nothingness – a space of vast sameness and undifferentiation. 'It was of a sameness that made it undelimited' (Lispector 1988: 37).

It is a disturbance in her perception – 'why is it that just looking is so greatly disorganizing?'(Lispector 1988: 5) – and the accompanying feeling of shock, a shaking, out of fear and repulsion that puts G.H. gradually into a process of self-effacement: a distancing from the finished and complete person she was before crossing the doorstep; a process that leads her gradually to the final loss of her human constitution. Two events take place in the room: first, she comes across a mural hiding behind the door: three life-size figures of a nude man, a nude woman and a nude dog, drawn with charcoal thick lines, 'three isolated figures, the appearance of three mummies' (Lispector 1988: 31), stand as traces of a figurative failure, a 'sarcophagus' for the coming death of her humanistic form. Her second encounter is that with the cockroach hiding inside the old wardrobe:

> Then before I could even understand it, my heart turned white like hair turns white [...] No it wasn't nothing. It was a cockroach slowly moving toward the crack. By its enormity and slowness, it must have been a very old cockroach [...] Take away what I saw: for what I saw with a compulsiveness so painful and so frightening and so innocent, what I saw was life looking back at me. (Lispector 1988: 39, 49)

The room, the brightness of the light, the mural on the wall, the female cockroach, all acquire a magnanimous size, the dimensions of the living: they take on their own living force, forming an assemblage of an organic and inorganic life that assumes a frightful power. It is the realization and the confrontation with this life, with the living in its bare indifference that threatens her morality and human understanding. 'Living is supernatural' (Lispector 1988: 10): it breaks down our containers and categories that serve to render the world comprehensible.

'I m not sure I even believe in what happened to me. Did something happen, and did I, because I didn't know how to experience it end up experiencing something else instead?' (Lispector 1988: 3), G.H. asks in the beginning of the book. The sentence triggers an anticipation of what has already happened, something incomprehensible to G.H. and unknown to us. The sentence emerges from a certain violence already occurred, and the story is a detour to a primary event that also takes the form of a descending into 'the inferior realms', 'where the treasure of writing lies, where it is formed' (Cixous 1993: 172).

G.H.'s story is a story that does not meet our expectations of a usual narrative. As the narrative unfolds G.H's identity becomes undone, the narrative becomes a philosophical reflection on the relationship between language and human subjectivity (in its female incarnation that already denotes an otherness, an ahuman, not a full subject), between language and human experience; a psychical and spiritual journey though not psychological – 'I think I left the psychological stage behind with adolescence' (Lispector 1988: 17). The journey of G.H. proceeds as a rupture, a break-through, 'which smashes the continuity of a personality and takes it on a kind of trip through "more reality" at once intense and terrifying, following lines of flight that engulf nature and history, organism and spirit' (Deleuze 2006: 27). Lacking a full proper name, reduced to her initials, G.H. enters the maid's room only to get into a process of ef-*face*-ment,[13] where she loses her human face and becomes an object among others. In Lacan's terms, we could say that the subject of the symbolic is replaced by the subject of jouissance and the whole story develops as a questioning of the limits of the organizational power of language that sustains the category of the human. Such a questioning is not achieved through a philosophical reflection from the outside, but inside writing, through the literary style of Clarice Lispector; a style that escapes a traditional usage of language, characterized as it is, by an idiosyncratic use of syntax and grammar. With the violations of traditional grammar and syntax, Clarice makes a foreign language within her own language that destabilizes meaning and the notion of the self. At times, human communication gives way to an ahuman expressivity, the expression of the living force of things (both organic and inorganic).

In terms of structure, Cixous notes, 'the text does not proceed by chapters but rather sentence by sentence, or by small packages of sentences [...] The reader falls into a vertigo. They are here one after the other, in a paratactical model, without coordination, without subordination [...] Here we proceed by leaps, without coordination' (Cixous 1990: 110). Such a progression creates a sense of discovery to the reader. Each new section (or packages of sentences) begins by repeating the last sentence of the previous section. Every end becomes a new beginning. A series of beginnings and ends bound together through repetition and variation, interruption and disjunctions. As Conley argues: 'Cixous is most attuned to Lispector's ways of inscribing textual interruptions, into meditations about the "self", that is of marking limits, of linking self and other at all levels' (Conley in Cixous 1990: xii).

There is a slow mobility and inner movement in the text, that is, however, discontinuous; every now and then a dash appears in the sentence and breaks its continuity, signalling a leap or a letting go.[14] Cixous writes, 'Clarice is the champion of the sublime metaphor' (Cixous 1989: xxvi): she accompanies herself and follows herself through her writing, sentence-by-sentence, word-by-word. The text becomes a metaphor itself, 'a metaphor which is not a metaphor', a metaphor in the sense of metaphorisation (transferring or being transferred), a transference of sensation and affect, movement and energy.[15]

> The writer uses words, but by creating a syntax that makes them pass into sensation that makes the standard language stammer, tremble, cry, or even sing: this is the style, the 'tone', the language of sensation ... The writer twists language, makes it vibrate, seizes hold of it, and rends it in order to wrest the percepts from perceptions, the affect from affections, the sensations from opinion. (Deleuze & Guattari 1994: 176)

The rule of the text in *The Passion According to G.H.* consists of a release, a setting in motion of sensations and affects that escape and overcome human organization. Hence, G.H. gets gradually released from the human constitution and her humanized way of relating to the world – 'humanised life. I had humanised life too much' (Lispector 1988: 6). She comes to critically revise her previous self – a finished person – by dealing with her phobia of what is abominable, *immund*, which means impure, unclean, but also 'out of this world' (mundus: the world) (Cixous 1993: 117).

Clarice makes direct references to the Bible regarding the notion of the 'impure' – the law of a He-Bible as Ross (2004) comments – that comes to provide a moral definition of humanity by establishing a series of binary oppositions (pure-impure, clean-unclean, good-evil, proper-improper, right-wrong) with the first term being valorized at the exclusion of the other.

> I felt impure, as the Bible speaks of the impure. Why did the Bible spend so much time on the impure, even to making a list of impure and forbidden animals? Why, if, like all the rest, they too had been created? And why was the impure forbidden? I had committed the forbidden act of touching something impure. (Lispector 1988: 63)

Mary Douglas in her essay *Deciphering a Meal* (1972) claims an association between food, social relations and sexuality. Food is a code that depicts specific patterns of social relating, and more specifically, the social hierarchies, inclusions and exclusions and the boundaries that characterize a culture. She makes an association between eating and sex, since analogous restrictions are applied to each. In studying the Jewish religion, she deciphers a very rigid classification and a very clear definition of abomination. What is particularly interesting to the Mosaic code, according to Douglas, is that any living being, which falls outside the classification or comes to question its clear distinctions (either by falling into more than one category or by lacking defining features) is not to be touched or eaten. These creatures are perceived as 'anomalous' and abominable because they challenge the purity of the categories and the established cognitive boundaries and levels of holiness, humanness and bestiality. 'Creeping, swarming, teeming creatures abominably destroy the taxonomic boundaries' (Douglas 1972: 50). At the level of the individual living being impurity is 'the imperfect, broken, bleeding specimen' (Douglas 1972: 50).

The initial impure touching G.H. performs is in the act of looking/ seeing. She is 'standing in the presence of fear' (Lispector 1988: 59), that is, in the *presence* of the cockroach. Indignation, repulsion and fear take her over. 'What I have seen is unorganisabe' (Lispector 1988: 60). The cockroach, as this unorganizable other, calls into question G.H.'s identity and self-boundaries, appears as a threat that will undo human meaning, will contaminate her world's organization and order, her cleanness. It triggers human feelings, moral affections, dictated by order-words: 'but "rejection of cockroaches" was merely a set of words' (Lispector 1988: 70). They are looking at each other, but what does a barata see? The animal vision is seeing nothing, it's a gazeless eye, devoid of meaning, devoid of human consciousness. The object of the animal vision is sensation: 'a movement that glides from things that have no meaning by themselves to the world full of meaning implied by man giving each thing his own' (Bataille 1992: 21). The cockroach sees her not with the eyes but with the body, 'each eye itself looked like a cockroach … each eye reproduced the entire animal' (Lispector 1988: 48). The barata is faceless, a black hole of faciality. There is nothing to see, nothing to interpret, it escapes signification. The face is the head, the body: they are indistinguishable. It is an inhuman face,[16] an empty force, expressionless, a face before signification and her eyes are objects of tactile sensations, 'proprioceptive sensations' (Deleuze & Guattari 2003: 169). Her face is an empty landscape, a nakedness. 'The room with its secret cockroach has repelled me … I had been repelled by the sight of a nakedness as strong as a mirage's nakedness' (Lispector 1988: 41). As soon as the cockroach starts coming out from the inside of the wardrobe, G.H.'s fear transforms into 'the desire, justified or not, to kill' (Lispector 1988: 45). Levinas argues in *Totality and Infinity*:

> To kill is not to dominate but to annihilate, it is to renounce comprehension absolutely. Murder exercises power over what escapes power [...] I can wish to kill only an existent, which is absolutely independent, which exceeds my powers infinitely, and therefore does not oppose them but paralyses the very power of power. The Other is the sole being I can wish to kill. (Levinas 1979: 198)

However, G.H.'s desire to kill does not come from a sense of powerlessness towards the other, but from a deep (and threatening) intimacy with the barata, an intimacy that stems from a feeling she comes to realize only when she finds herself trapped and immobile from fear and repulsion: the attentiveness to living.

> I recognised too the attentiveness that I had experienced before, the attentiveness that never leaves me and that, in the final analysis may be

the thing that is most a part of my life – that perhaps is my very life itself. What is the only sense a cockroach has? Attentiveness to living inseparable from its body. (Lispector 1988: 43)

G.H.'s encounter with the barata is not an opening to humanity in the Levinasian sense (consolidating her human identity through otherness) but an opening to the animality, to an immanent immensity within her she never experienced before: 'I sensed with fright and dread, that that "I-being" came from a source much prior to any human source, and horribly much greater than any human one as well' (Lispector 1988: 50). She slams the door on the cockroach's protruding body. 'What had I done?' (Lispector 1988: 45). A wounded specimen of the cockroach species, a wounded specimen of the human race, an emptying out of her humanity. 'Could I have known right then that I wasn't referring to what I had done to the cockroach but instead to what I had done to myself?' (Lispector 1988: 45).

The seduction the barata exercises is a seduction of the unknowable. 'Since animality cannot be known, our representations of it must of necessity be false' (Mardsen 2004: 40). An unknowability that also reflects the extent to which G.H. is a stranger to herself, estranged from the animality inside her (as immediacy and immanence[17]), alienated from an attentiveness to living that passes through the body. 'In the presence of the living cockroach, the worst discovery was that the world is not human, and that we are not human' (Lispector 1988: 61). As Bataille remarks: 'The animal opens before me a depth that attracts me and is familiar to me. In a sense I know this depth, it is my own' (Bataille 1992: 22). Writing is impure for Cixous, precisely because it resides in this depth, 'it comes from deep inside' (Cixous 1993: 118), from this intimacy and affinity with the inhuman. Writing is a search for this lost intimacy, for the animal continuity[18] (in Bataille's sense) that we, as human discontinuous beings, have forever lost. It is through the lines of writing (for Bataille, through poetry) that we come closer to animality, to our ahuman part, since poetry and literature take us away from meaning (subjective consciousness) to meaninglessness (the limits of language), from knowledge (and its epistemological subject/object conditions) to participation, or what Deleuze calls becoming. 'It is this animality that is touched in the poetic – not as a symbol but as the eruption of vital force' (Mardsen 2004: 44).

Bataille makes it clear in the *Theory of Religion* that religion's resurgence is based on the human being's resistance to immanence. The notion of the impure comes to suppress the animality which we are part of, yet from which we strive to distinguish ourselves, so as to assert ourselves as distinct (that is, discontinuous) beings.

'But you shall not eat of the impure: which are the eagle, the griffin, and the hawk. And everything that crawls on the ground and has wings shall be impure and shall not be eaten'. I opened my mouth in fright: to ask for help? Why? Because I did not want to become impure like the cockroach? What ideal held me from the sensing of an idea? Why should I not make myself impure exactly as I was revealing my whole self? What was I afraid of? Being impure with what? Being impure with joy. (Lispector 1988: 64–65)

Being impure, unclean, immund (being out of this world) is joy or gives joy. What is forbidden, what the He-Bible forbids, what defines our humanity is the prohibition of jouissance, the prohibition of joy directly related to the flesh: eating the forbidden meat, becoming the impure flesh, tasting the living, getting defiled. 'The animal that eats another does not distinguish what it eats in the same way that a human being distinguishes an object. There is no opposition between the animals in question. On the contrary this act confirms the similarity between the eater and the eaten' (Mardsen 2004: 38). Such a similarity does not mean sameness but an immanent differentiating that escapes a huMANized conception of difference at the level of the concept (e.g. the rigid classification of the Mosaic code that requires a prior distinction between 'subject' and 'object', a metaphysical, hierarchical schema imposed upon nature[19]).

The desire for intimacy is the desire to surrender to immanence, to experience continuity with the world, the desire to become-animal, become-flesh. It is through vision and eating that G.H. surrenders to immanence and empties herself from humanity. 'One sees and one hears like one touches' (Levinas, in Oliver 2001: 206). Touching is a relationship: you cannot touch without being touched, without being affected. She becomes (with) what she sees. Seeing puts her in a series of becomings: becoming-cockroach, becoming-flesh, becoming living matter. A tactile looking that connects her with the world of pure matter, a looking 'so greatly disorganizing and disillusioning'(Lispector 1988: 5), a looking that exposes the truth of the flesh beyond the organization of the body (e.g. specimen/species).

But it was then that I saw the cockroach's face (…) it was a shapeless face (…) I looked at its mouth: there was the real mouth. I had never seen a cockroach's mouth. In fact I had never really seen a cockroach. I had only felt repugnance at their ancient, ever-presented existence. (…) And so I discovered that despite their compactness, they are made up of shell after shell, gray and thin, like the layers of an onion (…) I looked at it with that mouth of its, and its eyes: its eyes were black and radiant. (Lispector 1988: 47, 48)

The cockroach is exposed as a naked flesh, beyond repugnance and fear, outside human sentimentality and human representations. The barata's body in its nakedness, emptied of all that is external to the living, becomes a pure affirmation of material existence, an intensifying materiality. 'Exposed flesh is not transgression but a scandal' (Hardt 2002: 80). Impure flesh enacts its own logic of passion and invites G.H. to immerse with the impurity of the world, feel the joy of the impure, the joy of being released from the prison of separation, the joy of connecting with the flesh of the world. She abandons humanity to connect with the world. 'Abandon me! Incarnation is all about abandonment – abandonment to the flesh' (Hardt 2002: 78). The passion of G.H. demands from her to abandon her humanized feelings, her utilitarian human sentiments (of fear, hope, love).

> Hope in what? ... I had based an entire hope on becoming something I was not. The hope that for the first time I was going to abandon. In my life up to now had that hope being grounded in a truth? I now ... doubted. To know what I really had to hope for, would I have to pass through my truth? (Lispector 1988: 50)

By looking at the cockroach, touching the impure, the forbidden, G.H. abandons the truth of the Mosaic Law, she renounces divine separation, becomes the 'anomalous' and passes through her truth; that of the exposed flesh, naked matter. 'Flesh is the superficial depth' (Hardt 2002: 83) a matter/realisation of an inaccessible depth, of 'a source much prior to any human source' (Lispector 1988: 50). Divinity is no longer to be found in a transcendent supreme being but in the fully exposed flesh of the nailed Christ,[20] in the fully exposed flesh of the crushed cockroach.

> And so I discovered that despite their compactness, they are made up of shell after shell, gray and thin, like the layers of an onion, as though you could lift one layer up with your fingernail and there would always be another one underneath and another [...] And all covered with cilia ... and its eyes: The eyes of a girl about to be married. (Lispector 1988: 48)

'The exposure of the flesh is erotic' (Hardt 2002: 80). She saw *it* (*it* was a *she*) before her, face to face, fully exposed, open and wounded, dark and mysterious, squirting white matter, hard on the outside, soft with many layers and folds on the inside; a living flesh forming itself through contraction and expansion that likes to be touched and caressed on all sides.[21] It is inside out. She has never really seen it before. We have been taught humanized feelings of repugnance and fear. Anything that morphologically does not count as one (e.g. the territorialized concept of the Phallus) is the anomalous that disturbs our clear categories of comprehensibility.

They measure themselves against each other, they are both female: one is a woman G.H., the other is a barata, which is feminine (the archaic feminine, she embodies all history). They are looking at each other. But as we cannot know what an animal sees, we do not know what a woman sees, what is the feminine gaze. 'I don't know what a cockroach sees. But the two of us were looking at each other, and I also don't know what a woman sees' (Lispector 1988: 68). G.H. needs to exchange with her in the deepest sense,[22] she needs to taste it, to taste the impurity of the body, the white matter, the barata, the baratinha (small barata), the boca de baixo (mouth underneath, below), boca mijada (mouth covered with or filled with urine).[23] Touching with the mouth, tasting the living is a deadly disease: a *mal-de-amores* (sickness of lovers), a *mal-de-cristaos* (sickness of Christians) and mal-de-Venus (sickness of Venus).[24] Eroticism always entails a 'little death': a surrendering of our individual separateness, a momentary continuity, an inhuman act (Bataille 1986). She fears and craves for the infection: by getting diseased, getting nauseous she will vomit up the last human remnant: her desire for beauty and morality.[25] 'The first timid pleasure that I feel is being able to say that I have lost my fear for the ugly' (Lispector 1988: 13). 'But now I have a morality that dispenses with beauty. Beauty was a soft enticement to me, it was the way I, weak, and respectful, adorned the thing to be able to bear its core [...] I don't want a well-made face. I don't want the expressive. I want the materiality of things' (Lispector 1988: 150). Tasting the living is an act of passion, an act of love and that of a lover. In a dizzy spell, G.H. lets herself fall back into animality, into the world of the flesh and pus, the world of excreta and spurt. She tastes the living, the cockroach, the barata, the baratinha (vagina in Brazil) and moves down the pyramid of holiness, in the lowest animal strata (the crawling, creeping, swarming, teeming, bleeding, menstrual, feminine creatures of abomination). By tasting 'the imperfect, broken, bleeding specimen' (Douglas 1972: 50), she has escaped the eye of God. She is now sensed not perceived. G.H.: no longer her initials, the abbreviation of a name, but a becoming-demonic, becoming-woman, becoming-flesh becoming-cockroach, becoming-imperceptible in the outside-of-self plane.

> I, neutral cockroach body, I with a life that at last is eluding me because I finally see it outside myself – I am the cockroach, I am my leg, I am my hair, I am the section of brightest light on the wall plaster – I am every Hellish piece of myself. (Lispector 1988: 57)

Finally my love I fell[26]

I tremble and resist. To fall in love is an ahuman act: falling into the black holes of desubjectification, dehumanization. 'Dehumanization is as painful as losing everything, my love' (Lispector 1988: 66). But I had to institute immurement, to annihilate myself, to erase myself so as to be able to speak, to be able to say to you what cannot be said, to find the words, to find these other words I didn't know before, to unlie. 'How can I speak of a love that contains only what is felt?' (Lispector 1988: 126). It is difficult. To be able to use a truth means destroying the self. Our whole life is based on lying, on a blind faith in human sense[27] and an obstinate renunciation of everything that falls below our civilised level. But we have worked on the way, we have gone all the way down, my love, my oldest love, to 'the lowest and the deepest' and you kept holding my hand. 'Because it is an enormous task to belie and unlie – we might say everything that out of love and cowardice, out of love as cowardice we would never have said' (Cixous 1993: 48). Loving, like writing, is *not arriving*: it is letting go, letting it happen, letting it surpass myself[28]; a surpassing that does not exclude me. It is to reach the violent potential inside the self, since the tenderest caress is experienced as violence or a shock to our discontinuous, isolated human form: it dissolves the boundaries of our bodies.

Touch me, caress me. The lover, like the writer, knows well that the idea of self-sufficiency is a lie.

> Through language the idea that we can exist as self-sufficient is destroyed: 'being depends on the mediation of words, which cannot merely present it arbitrarily as "autonomous being", but which must present it profoundly as "being in relation"'. (Noys 2000: 14–15)

Our crimes are prompted by jouissance, Cixous writes, 'because we desire to live as we have never lived, totally nude' (Cixous 1993: 48). Stripping ourselves naked of civilisation, human values and human morality, being beyond the confines of the self. Making love, like writing, entails nakedness, dispossession, loss of control.

Writing, like loving,[29] is born once we lose the power to say 'I'. 'I' is merely one of the world's instantaneous spasms. If, according to Kafka, we need the kind of books that 'stab us and wound us, the ones that affect us like a disaster', because they destroy our 'I' viewpoint, likewise, we need the kinds of love that take us through Hell, 'the Hell that comes from love, the hell of love' (Lispector 1988: 126): the neuter of love that reinstates 'existence without being (human)',[30] a love that snatches language and experience from negativity and instrumentality, from hope; from a determination of love that is entirely human. 'What I thought I knew about love, that too I'm leaving behind, I almost no longer know what it is, I no longer remember [...] I have called my hopes for love "love"' (Lispector 1988: 79).

A hellish and tortuous love that elicits hatred since it evokes danger; 'I am just in love with the cockroach' (Lispector 1988: 107) and I have lost all my human baggage with my engraved name initials. 'Warm me with your plumbing, comprehend me for I do not comprehend myself' (Lispector 1988:107). Ahuman love invades me now. Not a love of redemption, or hope, neither a desire to love, or even worse, a desire to be loved, but a neutral love that renders 'hope' meaningless. A neutral love of the 'now', of the living matter: an attentiveness to the living. What comes out of the cockroach, what comes out of the womb is a nowness, the squirting of fluid, the expulsion of matter, a taste of living. 'The moment of living my love, was becoming so "now" that I was putting my mouth into the matter of life [...] Blessed be the fruit of your womb – I want nowness without decorating it with a future' (Lispector 1988: 71, 75). Love not as desire but as mere need, 'things need things' (Lispector 1988: 164), without decoration and fiction, without metaphor and metonymy, outside humanizing sentimentality.

> It's a new need on a level that I can only call neutral and terrible. It's a need with no pity for my needing and no pity for the cockroach's needing [...] The cockroach was touching me through with its black, faceted, neutral look...With disgust, with despair, with courage, I gave in. I had waited too long, and now I wanted to. (Lispector 1988: 79, 80)

It is by moving further from disgust and fear, passing through death, that we come to a recognition of love.

> I was much less than human...
> I finally extended beyond my own sensibility...
> The inhuman is our better part
> The world is interdepended with me and I am not understanding what I am saying, never!
> Only because of the cockroach do I know.
> But I know now
> There is something that must be said, that must be said
> I'm going to tell you that
> I love you
> (Lispector 1988: 61, 109, 173)

Notes

1   'The sight of her was a shock', the poet Ferreira Gullar remembered of their first meeting. 'Her green almond eyes, her high cheekbones, she looked like a she-wolf, a fascinating wolf...I thought that if I saw her again I would fall hopelessly in love with her' (Moser 2009: 2).

2   Deleuze prefers the word *style* than the term *écriture*, since the latter is linked to structuralism and is too language-centred. With the term 'style' (which can also be used in painting), Deleuze construes a materialist understanding of language and a materialist conception of the sign that opposes the binary logic of Saussurean semiology.

3   A paradox since representation belongs to the logic of the Same, and a logocentric thinking (of analogy, resemblance, identity, opposition).

4   My reading of the novel has been greatly informed by Helene Cixous' work on Clarice Lispector's literature, as well as, on her work on writing (Cixous 1990; 1993).

5   The subheading has been an appropriation of a phrase by Cixous: '...he gave me death. To start with' (Cixous 1993: 12).

6   'It is not an unconscious populated with Freudian scenes. True, it always takes place "behind something", as Clarice says. It is pre-logical, pre-discursive. It happens because there is, because there takes place' (Cixous 1989: xxxiv).

7   Here, and for the rest of the chapter, I am following Cixous's gesture
     addressing Clarice Lispector with her first name, in a poetic gesture of keeping
     intimacy with her writing (not the author as a dead fact) and including
     her as one of the characters along with G.H. in the novel, often in an
     undifferentiating way: is it the passion of G.H or the passion of C.L.?

8   I am using Cixous's translation as being more accurate and loyal to the
     original text, which is different from the one found in the published English
     version.

9   Naked human experience escapes discursive construction and signification. It
     is an affective experience, yet a-conceptual, a-signified that belongs to what
     Deleuze calls transcendental empiricism: it transcends the visible (in the sense
     of what is possible to be seen-as-understanding).

10   I borrowed the sentence from Cixous's book *Three Steps on The Ladder
     of Writing*, Trans. Sarah Cornell and Susan Sellers (New York: Columbia
     University Press, 1993), p. 58.

11   The animal encounter in this novel does not hold a symbolic character. The
     novel thus avoids repeating humanistic fantasies of otherness, and thus does
     not reproduce an existing social imaginary that fetishizes the other (either
     as being threatening or celebratory), that would perpetuate specific power
     dynamics on the level of meaning and representation.

12   A real immediate experience causes a sensory shock to thought because it
     transcends faculties of perception related to a linguistic understanding and
     feeling (a human seeing and feeling that can be linguistically 'translated' or
     mediated). Such an experiencing extends beyond the 'given' data of subjective
     affections and perceptions and affects the mind 'outside of all representations'
     (Deleuze 2004: 9). The signs the room emits are direct signs that cause
     'vibrations, rotations, whirlings, gravitations … that directly touch the mind'
     (Deleuze 2004: 9) and put human understanding in crisis.

13   '"Ef-face-ment" should always be spoken as the effacement of an original
     figure, were it not that such an effacement itself effaces itself' (Derrida 1974:
     8).

14   'The dash is the figuration of jump' (Cixous 1990: 74).

15   'Generally, this activation or actualization of metaphor consists in animating
     the inanimate, transferring it into the "psychic" order of things' (Derrida
     1974: 39).

16   'The inhuman in human beings: that is what the face is from the start. It is by
     nature a close-up, with its inanimate white surfaces, its shining black holes, its
     emptiness and boredom' (Deleuze & Guattari 2003: 171).

17   'I am able to say that the animal world is that of immanence and immediacy,
     for that world, which is closed to us, is so to the extent that we cannot discern
     in it an ability to transcend itself' (Bataille 1992: 23).

18   'To be fully "continuous" with our animality would be to abandon the
     cultivated discontinuity of both knowledge and human being' (Mardsen 2004:
     37).

19   'So the positing in the world of a supreme being, distinct and limited like a
     thing is first of all an impoverishment. There is doubtless in the invention of a
     supreme being, a determination to define a value that is greater than any other.
     But this desire to increase results in a diminution' (Bataille 1992: 34).

20 'Impure carnality, or rather the divine exposure of the flesh enacts its own logic of passions. This abandonment is the joy that Pasolini sees in the Christ's example' (Hardt 2002: 82).

21 The cockroach is thigmotropic. *Thigmotropism* (*thigmo* meaning touch in Greek) is when an organism, such as a plant, moves or grows with touch or contact stimuli (e.g. vines). Here I draw an analogy with Irigaray's descriptions of the female sex and feminine pleasure as being plural, deriving from the entire body (Luce Irigaray 1985). The cockroach (the barata/baratinha) stands also for the female genital in the Brazilian culture.

22 'Even when it is a woman who is becoming, she has to become-woman, and this becoming has nothing to do with a state she could claim as her own. To become is not to attain a form (identification, imitation, Mimesis) but to find the zone of proximity, indescernibility, or indifferentiation where one can no longer be distinguished from a woman, an animal, or a molecule – neither imprecise nor general, but unforeseen and nonpreexistent, singularised out of a population rather than determined in a form' (Deleuze 1997: 1).

23 These words are synonymous for vagina in everyday language in Brazilian culture. See Parker (2009: 43).

24 The word 'mal' in Portuguese carries a double meaning of both 'sickness' and 'evil'; see Parker (2009: 44).

25 'Morality, Fernando Pessoa wrote, is "the effort to elevate human life, to give it a human value"' (Moser 2009: 56).

26 This phrase is taken from Clarice Lispector's novel *The Passion According to G.H.*

27 Both as sense/sensation and reason/to make sense.

28 'Writing is inseparable from becoming: in writing one becomes-woman, becomes-animal or vegetable, becomes-molecule to the point of becoming-imperceptible' (Deleuze 1997: 1).

29 '(For Bataille) There is not an opposition between language and experience but a more disorientating experience of contamination' (Noys 2000: 50).

30 'The neuter has been often cited as the symbol of Blanchot's "existence without being"' (Bartoloni 2010: 4).

PART THREE

Ahumanity: A Liberation of Life

CHAPTER EIGHT

Suicide for Animals

Claire Colebrook

Art and writing have perhaps always been defined in opposition to suicide. The desire to live on, a commitment to survival, a passion for the eternal and perhaps a highly troubled relation to 'life itself' – demanding the maintenance of what is most fragile – characterize the artwork in its very historicity. Even if we accept the most literal, reductionist and artless inquiries into the essence of art – such as archaeological theories that art begins with a human desire to ward off death by creating figures of the present that will live on, or evolutionary postulates that art extrapolates cognitive features that have been selected for the organism's survival – and then consider high modernist celebrations of art as a loss of the organic body and individual self for the sake of a timeless matter in itself, it appears that art is human only in its curious relation to non-suicide. Art is not only an extension of capacities for living on, or an extrapolation of our tools oriented to fitness and self-maintenance (in which case art would be a sophisticated animal mechanism). On the contrary, it is only in the imagination of non-existence or a *virtual* suicide that something like art occurs.

Consider this in a quite literal and reductive manner before exploring what it might mean, today, in relation to what I will refer to as the artful war on animal suicide. First, according to some archaeologists, art occurs initially as a way of dealing with death: cave paintings are either monuments that allow the organic to live on, allow those left behind to ameliorate the horrors of absence, or even (as Stephen Mithen has more joyously argued) create a range of sensible exploration and sharing from which communities of cognizing and communicating individuals emerge. If material and animal existence simply *is* then it is the sense not of one's own self and world, but a world in one's absence that elicits a desire to write, to externalize and formalize an event or sense such that it survives beyond its present. Art begins as a warding off of death, which suggests that for all its lofty aspirations it is ultimately rather animalistic: tied to primitive desires for survival, self-maintenance and a governing of forces. But if this is so then it is precisely this aspect of animality – an expenditure of energy for the sake of living on – that will then create a curious counter-animality. In order to survive as an animal, the human produces a series of figures that will – far from furthering organic existence – produce an existence beyond the organism. So, we might say that it is because man is a suicidal animal, capable of acting beyond the interests and borders of his organic selfhood that he takes up the figuration of animality. From a cave painting of a bison to William Blake's image of the ghost of a flea (which I will examine later) every artistic image is at once animalistic and suicidal in a manner which creates something like a humanity that can only live on as other than animal through a suicidal war on animals.

There are instances of animal suicide, and perhaps human suicide occurs at the point at which we are most confronted with our animality. That is, it is precisely when we are, to use Heidegger's phrase, 'poor in world' that we might no longer live towards death. We might no longer recognize that we are constituted by a range of potentiality that at once precludes us from fulfilling all possibilities, but nevertheless opens us to a choice to take up this specific, decided and open future. Being human, at least traditionally, is defined as being able to liberate oneself from any determined end: as being self-creating, self-defining and thoroughly open to the world. It is perhaps when one encounters an irreducible non-freedom or a resistance to self-production that one decides to terminate life. This can take two forms: the obvious animality that would lead a human to terminate its own being would be a certain physical, material and inertial resistance; or, and perhaps this is suicide proper rather than a euthanasia that would end a life that is not sufficiently alive, one ends life precisely through a sense of the inescapability of freedom, of not being animal. John Milton expressed this second sense of despair at not being merely animal in *Paradise Lost* when Adam acknowledges that it is quite just to be cast out of paradise for failing to live up to the demands of a free rationality that ought essentially choose the good, but denies that it is just to grant such freedom to a living being. That Promethean despair of the pains of freedom that is repeated throughout Romanticism is coupled with the despair of the suicidal structure of the artwork. The freedom that places the human animal at odds with the earth both enables the creation of an artwork that – because it is freely created and not at one with nature – is also subject to conditions of decay, disappearance and even autoimmune disease. For art inscribes a border between the living on of the animal and the expenditure of a force beyond that animal's organic border. So, the human animal can only create art by sacrificing an element of its animal life to set itself apart, and yet it is that setting apart creativity of the human that also places the human in close relation to self-extinction.

If it is possible for the human animal to undertake a war upon itself, which in its most extreme form would lead to self-annihilation, this is only because humanity is necessarily a form of war against animality. This thematic has gained focus recently through both the global sense of possible human extinction that follows from the violence of/on animality and the exposition of that animal violence in a philosophy that is no longer sure of its own reason. Instead of the human and human art examining its violent presentation of animals, it is now necessary to see the human animal and the human/animal as tied to a violence intrinsic to presentation. I would like, therefore, to suggest a series of reversals.

First: it might appear that the human war on animality, or the use, consumption and terrorization of animals is an extension of human survival; surely we destroy animals in order to live on, and surely the animal, in turn, consumes the stored energy of plants in order to maintain its own living being. Accepting this picture would place the human above animals in a hierarchy of consumption and survival (and that hierarchy might be either a difference in degree or of kind, either a question of the human being's rationality as such, or simply humanity's increased power and potential). But the war on animality and the capacity to dominate animals is only possible through a war on the self: for there can only be a relation between human and animal if the human has already detached, englobed or organized itself *as thinking organism* in opposition to a world of animality that appears as an orb of life, as that towards which we might direct *either* violence or the attribution of rights. Rights, whether they be human or animal, or the right to live or die, are always the rights *of* this or that specified being, and a being can only be specified, if it is bounded in some manner. The human capacity to bear a relation to animality is possible only because the human can relate to itself, apprehend itself as higher than or other than animality; and this affection of itself is also, as Derrida has pointed out, a form of attack upon the self. Auto-immunity is that process whereby a living body maintains its own borders by closing off a full and absolute relation to the outside; one deadens oneself to the full intensity of life, marking out one's own proper being by taking what is other than the self as an allergen or irritant. Let us remark then that it is through killing, consuming, attacking and diminishing the animal that the human might mark itself off as other than animal, but that this war will necessarily attack and diminish the human animal's potentiality for thinking. Well before Derrida theorized the animal explicitly, he noted that Heidegger's assumption of the distinction between animal and human was a *dogma* (2005): a point at which thinking deadened or reified itself by swallowing a distinction it ought to have left open for question (Geschlecht).

Second reversal: it might seem that if humanity and animality are neither simple opposites nor happy co-habitants (and are instead produced through the war humanity rages on itself through its attack on animals), then we might at least say that it is through art – other than war – that humanity rises above animality. But this is not so. Why, we might ask, did Deleuze and Guattari tie writing and creation to becoming-animal? Is it really the case that art is that which constitutes our humanity in opposition to the animal? Is it not more likely that it is only through destroying the human – destroying the war we undertake on animals in order to separate, elevate and grant ourselves rights – that something like writing might occur? We need to annihilate man as a being who has the power to think and create, destroy the humanist notions that thinking and creation are expressions *of* some preceding subject; only then would we arrive at an art that is not determined in advance according to some pre-given figure of a proper humanity. Art is not that which elevates humanity above the animal; art occurs when the human animal attacks its own war on animals.

Third reversal: today theory is turning to animals, reviving itself through animals and it does so, happily, through two proper names, Deleuze and Derrida. Derrida, as I have already suggested, attacks the very notion of *the* animal, precisely because that category has already precluded any thought of the multitude of figures of life, potential and duration that would somehow save the human from the grips of subjectivism. For Derrida, then, we might say that the survival of writing occurs when the war between human and animal becomes a *perpetual peace of democratic writing*, when we do not yet know what counts as human or animal in advance. Derrida has aligned writing directly with democracy and justice precisely insofar as a literary writing would not be subtended by a subject of enunciation. That is: if the human who opposes himself to animals or who grants rights to animals can write in such a way that the text is no longer tied to a subject who speaks in order to predicate a world – if literature can 'say anything', having been released from the norms of an already given polity – then writing is democracy, an opening of auto-affection onto radical hetero-affection. In this case (despite what Derrida says manifestly about the avoidance of suicide) all writing is suicidal: for it is only if writing is no longer held close to the living subject and is released into an archive that is fragile and open to extinction that anything can be said at all. The condition for a text or work of art's survival is its detachment and release from its originating subject; a full mastery and self-governance would preclude the circulation and liberation of the work beyond its origin. Deleuze seems at first to be compatible with this liberation through writing, and it is perhaps the *becoming* of becoming-animal (which in turn is tied to writing) that would suggest, like Derrida that the war *on* animals comes to an end through art and literature. However, if there is a necessary death and suicide at the heart of Derridean writing, insofar as an archive can be effected only through incarnation beyond the living body, and if 'the animal' is for Derrida a category too tied to the self-sameness of the human that must be destroyed to release a text, for Deleuze writing must avoid suicide and embrace rather than deconstruct 'the' animal. It is not any specific animal, and not an act of imitation or empathy of a living animal but a trait – or that which has already been released from the animal's living body – that survives in writing. So, one does not paint the screaming animal, but the scream – not the devouring maw, but something like an animal devouring in the work (2005: 51–52). Far from seeking to uncover the nuance of any *actual* animal, and far from deconstructing the subject by problematizing its delimitation from those aspects of animality through which humanity would detach itself, becoming-animal is a path to the virtual: if it is possible for us to live in this world of humans and animals, this is only because there are virtual ideas or potentialities of humanity and animality. For Deleuze and Guattari that potentiality of the human – grounded in the figure of the bounded organism that maintains itself through common sense, good sense, labour and the repetition of the same – faces another potentiality in the anima

1. Animality is a different potentiality, or a different economy of potentiality; humanity understands and figures itself as the ground from which acts, accidents, events and predicates might be thought, while animality – and not the animal, or specific animals – is an explosive power. Whereas the human as a self-maintaining organism is seduced by the image of its own bodily borders into thinking of itself as an integrated being, the animal is pack-like, contagious and offers a release of predicates from a grounding body: but this is possible not if we transport ourselves into imitating or even feeling-with the animal, and certainly not by attributing rights or dignity to the animal. Such passages from human to animal would be ways of maintaining the human through animality: both by extending humanity's range to animals, and allowing humanity to elevate and congratulate itself from its moral capacity to empathize. To think of animality and art together, then, is for Deleuze counter suicidal: the destruction of the human that occurs in the passage to the animal is a release from the same dull round of human organization and an opening to figures and traits that insist of themselves. Animality in a certain sense *is* art. For Deleuze, the human ceases to be suicidal, and ceases to diminish and impoverish itself when it moves beyond man and animal towards a genuinely creative writing.

So, let us say that there appears to be a war between Deleuze and Derrida over animals: either writing is possible and necessary beyond the human-animal border, and is necessarily suicidal in its detachment from life (Derrida) *or* it is through a passage beyond the limit of the human to the threshold of animality that writing becomes non-suicidal. But let us make one final reversal of this war *between* Deleuze and Derrida *over* animals, and instead place them at war with themselves. That is, let us say that Deleuze's notion of a non-suicidal writing of becoming-animal, and of a creativity liberated from any pre-given ground, cannot avoid a certain death-trap of the human, and this because it seeks to avoid and ward off any bound or border that would impede and diminish its potentiality in advance. Has not man, at least in his aspiration to be god, not always resisted any essence that would determine in advance the trajectory of his becoming? Similarly, if Derrida begins writing and animality with the suicide of the human – for *the animal* is an insufficient concept to allow one to move beyond the human, and the human can only maintain itself through an archive that already bears the possibility of existing beyond its founding and intentional sense – he nevertheless recuperates the human, or destroys his own suicide. To define writing as democratic and oriented towards justice, precisely because the release and inhumanity of writing liberates it from a determining human ground, is to betray the suicidal dimension of writing: its capacity to *say nothing*, and to be animalistic in a manner that is, even on Derrida's own terms, *evil*. If we shift the war that is between Deleuze and Derrida to a war that occurs in any theory and its relation to art, we can see that what both these figures seek to discover, outside philosophy and man, already inhabits the suicidal art of the animal.

This war that is bound to the work of art is not *between* a humanity that would destroy itself for the sake of a writing that would live on beyond the human and an animality that liberates humanity from its enclosing circularity; it is a suicidal animal war. In order to make sense of this internal war, that is not a war on terror but a terror of war that cannot be contained in a figure, I want to look first at Derrida's concept of auto-affection, and then at Deleuze and Guattari's concept of becoming-animal. The first concept, auto-affection, accounts for the way in which the human encircles itself in order to face the world as a globe populated by animals over whom it has mastery. The second concept of becoming-animal accounts for a potential future in which this encircling has ceased, and has done so for the sake of a trait or singularity that does not maintain itself within itself. But in what sense could such a trait result in art, and how might such an art be *thought*? What I want to suggest is that Deleuze and Derrida as proper names marking out the borders of humanity and animality should be read *not* as opposed persons, as warring men representing two modalities of life: a humanity that regards itself as always already animal, and a humanity that bears the power to pass to an animality that is virtual, un-lived and never given. Rather the animal in art, as art, is a suicidal animal.

Writing, auto-affection and auto-immunity

The war on animals and the environment, or the englobing of the world as manipulable resource is only possible because man as a subject is an autonomous self apart from the world. This autonomy or distinction is only possible, though, if the self distinguishes itself; and this in turn is only possible through a prior war on the self. It is through some process of marking itself out, or what Derrida would refer to as auto-affection and auto-immunity (2002), that the self becomes distinct: englobing itself so that it can be other than a world it englobes. Passing from the transcendental necessity of this self-attack that marks out the autos, we could consider writing, or the force of tracing and marking that differentiates, as both that which enables a human distinction and threatens that distinct humanity with an internal condition that is not its own and that it does not master. By contrast Deleuze and Guattari do not, as Derrida does, use the concept of writing to name – even though it is not a name – the tracing out of a difference that would allow something like a self to come into being through affecting itself, marking itself, punctuating itself. Instead, Deleuze and Guattari regard writing, and writing in a properly productive creative mode as the criterion through which the self of self-affectation and self-englobing might be released from itself. This allows us to suggest a possible contrast between Derrida's diagnosis of an auto-affection that introduces an irreducible allergen into the self, and Deleuze and Guattari's notion that the sound through which I would hear myself speak is already a sound from elsewhere – the gnashing teeth of the animals (1987). If one could hear the gnawing away at the self that effects the self then one would be at once destroyed in one's self-englobing, self-encircling and lifeless mastery, and be taken by such a frenzy that one would need to write. Such a writing would have to avoid suicide. If writing were to become self-enclosed, bounded or circular, then the becoming would be cyclic: akin to the alcoholic's marking out of the limit at which he would have to stop drinking in order to be able to wake up tomorrow in order to start drinking again. In terms of writing, the criteria that enable it to avoid such circularity, according to Len Lawlor following Deleuze and Guattari (2007), is a distinction between form and function. In terms of writing one would extract traits. To give a concrete example from Deleuze (2000), we would favour those moments in Proust where love enables the narrator to be captured by a quality of skin of his beloved, or a musical phrase, producing an affect that opens the voice of the text to intensities that are not grounded on a bounded self, on a subject of enunciation, or an autonomous ground for whom a text, as form, would be nothing more than a vehicle for expression.

Writing is tied to becoming-animal precisely because this non-suicidal writing would not turn back upon the man who weighs himself down with the great corpus of literary works, works that are then the objects of veneration, exegesis, dutiful reading and veneration. A writing of *form* that directs becoming to the text as organism – a text that would master and produce all its internal relations – is surpassed by an animal writing. It is not writing about animals, but is animal rather than human in its release from self-englobing mastery; its effects, traits, pure predicates are released and created without determining in advance that they will return to maintain and ensure the maintenance of a subject. And such a writing and animality would also open a becoming-woman insofar as both woman and text are radical modes of disguise: if man is that subject who can produce a text as an organic form, it is because he can – like God – create that which is other than himself, a second nature that would reflect back to him his own divine being. But what if there were not a subject who preceded and underpinned textual becoming, just as if there were not man who preceded and mastered an object nature? What if what we know as the self were nothing other than all the traits, feints, occultations, dissimulations and simulations that pulse through time? That is, there is not a self who then writes, a subject who then plays the animal or takes on a sex: there are instead affects, intensities, openings of relations *from which* one might presuppose a subject who must have been – man as subject. But such a presupposition that would posit man as the author of a well-wrought text would be *ex post facto*, illegitimate and would also preclude the possibility of thinking of animality and woman not as medium through which a text is formed – woman as muse, or animal as fabled character.

Now it is with these two Deleuzo–Guattarian criteria of writing as non-suicidal and non-circular that I would like to pose two questions:

First, in dividing writing into a good function-oriented non-formal writing, a writing that would not be circular and self-enclosed, are we not repeating one of the most fundamental onto-theological humanist figures? God in Christian theology is a being who is not submitted to any determined or bounded form, whose act of creation is free and unnecessary, and whose essence is only to exist – not subject in advance to any determined form. And when secular humanism takes over this figure – a figure that reaches its height in modernism – it is the artist who, far from being enslaved to already existing forms and producing the same dull round is nothing other than the absent, divine and impersonal force that sends forth a text into the world, a text that is not to be read *back* as the signifier of some intent. In terms of globalism and the war on animality, could we not say that it is the attack on the self-enclosed circle – the animal that is subjected to instinct and self-sameness, *not yet opened to man's radical powers of open self-creation*, that allows for human speciesism? And could we not also say that woman, not as a given form but as a power of affectation – a breath, a sigh, an affect – has always been the good and proper form of the feminine, as opposed to a woman who would play at being man, taking on the self-affectations of subjectivity? When modernism and certain forms of post-structuralism hail woman as other than the man of philosophy do they not extend, rather than overcome, a commitment to the figure of man as the being who is never mired in his own substance, whose potentiality for self-creation through what is not himself frees him from mere life?

Second, on avoiding suicide and passing from Derrida to Deleuze, from writing as a quasi-transcendental to writing as the criterion that marks out form from function: could we not say both that writing is necessarily suicidal and necessarily formal? In order for a text to be produced, to have a force or affect beyond its origin, it must be written; it must be punctuated, differentiated and articulated in some manner that allows for its repetition and force. But the very writing that allows for the circulation and affecting power of a text is also what allows that text to be repeated in a dull, lifeless, circular, mechanistic and merely technical manner. And this is also to say that the force of functions – the sigh, caress, gnashing, frenzy or noise that would be other than the self-regarding voice of man – must nevertheless take on form. If writing is to function as the site of judgement, where a good writing of forceful affective creation is separated from a merely systemic, form-enslaved writing of self-maintenance, then one must have determined in advance what counts as a proper suicide. What must be killed off is the inert, the in-itself, the senseless and the uniform; what must be allowed to live on is that which creates without thought of itself. In many ways then it is the suicidal self – a subject who is not enslaved to living on – who produced the good and proper non-suicidal text: I abandon my Cartesian subjectivity for the sake of writing; I do not enclose myself within myself but freely sacrifice my bounded organic being for the sake of a becoming without end. Not only do such distinctions between a life that is capable of undoing itself and abandoning itself and a life that is merely itself rehearse a Hegelian logic of mastery through negation (and perhaps necessarily), we perhaps avoid confronting a transcendental suicide that it is the task of environmental philosophy to elucidate.

Our current global crisis is indeed one of suicide: so entranced have we been by our own autonomy that we have forgotten that we become who we are through a world and life that is not our own. Our self-maintenance and mastery is destroying the milieu in which we live and, in turn, the species that we are. But is this suicide an exception? And can it be avoided without other suicides? It would not be exceptional insofar as the story of life is one of a series of suicides: the metabolic processes that led to human existence were preceded by a series of environments that through time became extinguished, allowing for other milieus, eventually leading to the anthropocene era. To halt the accelerated suicide of our current milieu would perhaps require a strange (suicidal) war on the story of life. Man has so far – for his own organic and animal survival – been at war with the very milieu that is his life. Ending that war requires an attack on what he is, a suicide. Such a suicide would at once be in accord with all those processes of extinction that have led to radical evolutionary becomings, at the same time as a decision *to no longer be human* would be the most unnatural and suicidal of gestures.

We might also note, more narrowly in relation to the milieu we are inhabiting today, the strange occurrence of a double suicide. We are, after all, enjoying a time when philosophy or 'theory' itself is faced with its own demise when confronted with economic and rationalizing imperatives, a demise that is all the more threatening and imminent when we consider 'European' philosophy which had its heyday in the '80s and outside philosophy departments. It is possible to say that the living on of Deleuze, his intense marketability and citational frequency, occurs only when the corpus brings about its own death: Deleuze's creation of a vocabulary that would answer to the demands of a truly radical philosophy was the very medium that allowed that corpus to fall into the hands of a violent non-philosophy, such that it is the task of what survives of philosophy today to retrieve and save Deleuze from all the deaths he has suffered at the hands of those who use terms such as rhizome, line of flight, becoming-woman and deterritorialization as unthinking and impressionistic figures rather than concepts with a truly philosophical force. We are witnesses of a corpus that wanted to do philosophy by doing violence to its deepest propositional logic, but in so doing allowed itself to die at the hands of those who would take the linguistic means for achieving a higher philosophy as philosophy itself. But if there is a suicidal tendency in the very force that allowed Deleuze to have a philosophical life, insofar as the circulation and living on of the body of Deleuze's work was accompanied by a necessary loss in its critical intensity, we could also say that this is coupled with a positive sense of suicide: the crucial threshold is not between the organism of self-maintenance and its own death, but between a life that can liberate itself from survival and take the risk of creating what may not have an after-life. But a mirroring point can be made about Derrida, Derridean theory, and what remains and survives of his philosophy in the wake of Deleuze. I mentioned earlier in this essay that Derrida tied writing at once to animal suicide – a gnawing in the text that does not open out to a future of sense, hope and survival – *and* to a democracy, deconstruction and justice that can 'say anything' insofar as text detaches itself from any living body. This allows us to think of Deleuze and Derrida as warring potentials: the artwork as suicidally animalistic, a machine that lives without a sense of survival or justice or *world*, and of art as so animalistic, so productive of traits and functions that it destroys the human and thereby ends the war on animals, the war on the globe, the war heading to extinction.

I referred earlier to Blake's illuminated print of the ghost of the flea. Now there is always something of the animal/human hand at work in Blake. Both Derrida and Deleuze refer to the war of the hand: for Derrida it is the human, all too human, distinction between the human hand that gestures and gives, and the animal hand that takes that cannot be sustained. And it is the violation of the distinction that occurs in a certain violence in the work, as the eye that views the engraving can feel the resistance of the hand to the matters that would release the sense of the expressed. The hand that writes is at once a hand opened to the infinity of sense, to a potentiality of being read, repeated, carried on through time, *and* a hand subjected to the singularities of matter, both the force of the matters that take on the grip and grasp of the hand, and the subjection of those matters to a time when it is no longer possible to mark the difference between an act of the hand and a radical passivity of hyle.

If there is something that answers to what Agamben refers to as the 'anthropological machine', (2004) whereby man has to mark and re-mark his distance from his own animality, then there is also an animal machine whereby the very medium or machine through which such distancing takes place operates with its own logic and potentiality. This was how Blake placed the flea within his semi-Leibnizian universe; perhaps everything that lives is holy and has its own grasp of the infinite, in its own partial, dim and confused manner, but perhaps there are those aspects of the infinite that are also holy in their rigid atomization, in their distance from all memory, living on and sense. Perhaps it's the gesture of accepting a certain absence of living on and openness that takes the human beyond its self-maintenance, and the animal beyond the sense of its proper world. So there is a necessary animal suicide of the human hand, where intentionality, gesture and the creation of a monument for the future has to pass into brute force, risking its demise and corruption. And there is also a human suicide of the animal, where the bringing into being of a world beyond the humanity of sense, recognition and communality must depend on a matter that, in its sensibility, resists sense. This concluding note allows us to ask why Blake felt it worthwhile not just to give form to the flea, but to the ghost of the flea – a flea that appears on stage as a dramatis personae, as a flea acting the flea, becoming-flea. Fleas are parasites and signs, signs of disease, filth and an imperative for extermination. On the one hand, we can see Blake's ghost-flea as a figure of human suicide: destroy the human organism, tear its folded human world apart and open oneself to the infinite. Indeed, it's the war of the printing press – man's own hand – that destroys what Blake refers to as the slothful vegetating man; and this then opens the Spinozist sense of a world that would have been invisible and poisonous to the human organism but an emblem of immortality for a life beyond the human.

> 09 This Wine-press is call'd War on Earth, it is the Printing-Press
> 10 Of Los; and here he lays his words in order above the mortal brain
> 11 As cogs are formd in a wheel to turn the cogs of the adverse wheel.
> 12 Timbrels & violins sport round the Wine-presses; the little Seed;
> 13 The sportive Root. the Earth-worm, the gold Beetle: the wise Emmet;
> 14 Dance round the Wine-presses of Luvah: the Centipede is there:
> 15 The ground Spider with many eyes: the Mole clothed in velvet
> 16 The ambitious Spider in his sullen web; the lucky golden Spinner;
> 17 The Earwig armd: the tender Maggot emblem of immortality:
> 18 The Flea: Louse: Bug: the Tape-Worm: all the Armies of Disease:
> 19 Visible or invisible to the slothful vegetating Man.
> 20 The slow Slug: the Grasshopper that sings & laughs & drinks:
> 21 Winter comes, he folds his slender bones without a murmur.
> 22 The cruel Scorpion is there: the Gnat: Wasp: Hornet & the Honey Bee:
> 23 The Toad & venomous Newt; the Serpent clothd in gems & gold:
> 24 They throw off their gorgeous raiment: they rejoice with loud jubilee
> 25 Around the Wine-presses of Luvah. naked & drunk with wine.
>
> (9–24, Blake, *Milton*: 27)

On the other hand, Blake presents the flea's ghost, not the flea itself but an animal that is barely animal, placing itself on the human stage. In his prophecies that double the book of genesis, Blake describes the human skeleton becoming englobed with flesh, and focuses on the brain as the englobing globe, the organ that will close vitality into the same dull round:

02 7. From the caverns of his jointed Spine,
03 Down sunk with fright a red
04 Round globe hot burning deep
05 Deep down into the Abyss;
06 Panting: Conglobing, Trembling
07 Shooting out ten thousand branches
08 Around his solid bones.
09 And a second Age passed over,
10 And a state of dismal woe (Blake, *Urizen*: 11).

In his picture of the flea, Blake presents an exoskeleton, as though the human animal has been unfolded, to escape its organic animality. Blake learned to depict human figures through the classical methods of studying anatomy, and through the copying of effigies in Westminster Abbey: man begins with the skeletal structure, after which it is his flesh that encloses him into his own view of the world. Blake's flea kills off man's animality, the living organic flesh, to produce a pure figure – the parasite of the skin unfolds to reveal line, staging, strutting, framing and display. Animality, or organic being, is destroyed to reveal a ghost that is both pure performance – vaudevillian – and pure outline. And it is this outline or figuration that liberates form from figure or figure from form that allows the living flesh to pass over into this monumental inscription – the life of which is unreadable and unliveable.

CHAPTER NINE

Dark Pedagogy

Jason Wallin

A thirteenth-century Hessian chronicle documents the capture and presentation of a wolf-child to a local lord (Steel 2012). Snatched by wolves at age three and nurtured as a member of the pack, the account reports that the child walked on all fours, could leap great heights, and possessed an appetite for raw meat. Bound with wood and forced upright 'in human likeness', the wolf-child was hence consigned as a spectacle to the court of Henry, Prince of Hesse (Steel 2012: 11). While Steel admits that the account of the Hessean 'wolf-child' constitutes an anomaly within medieval textuality, it is no doubt familiar for both its conceptualization of non-normal life as *disability* and its eschewal of ontological difference for the *image of man*. Here, the binding of the wolf-child's spine to force it erect has special significance in relation to what it means to be *human*, for from Plato onwards, the *human* is marked by its deterritorialization from the mutability of the earth. Herein, Plato's allegory of the cave posits the dwelling place of animals as imperfect and substandard, for in turning towards the truth, the philosopher-priest must first break from the fetid and dark holes of the ground. Delinked from the miasma of the ground and born into occularity, the *human's* gaze is transcendently elevated towards heaven. Renouncing quadrepedal life and its intimate connection with the earth, the deterritorialization of the human promulgates a dual *telos* (Lewis and Khan 2010; Steel 2012). First, the human achieves 'distance' from the earth by being remade as an occular being. In this image, the relation and hierarchy of bodily organs become anthropocentrically overdetermined. As Steel articulates from Ovid's *Metamorphoses*, what distinguishes man from beast is that '...our faces [are] set not to gaze down at the dirt beneath our feet but upward toward the sky' (Steel 2012: 20). Second, as an organism hence elevated above the material entrapments of the earth, the human is recast in a position of dominance over the mutable. This is the founding of a hierarchy in which nonhuman life becomes both *for us* and dependent *upon us*. In this double *teloi*, animality becomes something to overcome and like the Hessean wolf-child, to be fashioned in an image given anthropocentrically, if not as an identifiable human, than as an 'Oedipalized' pet for the pleasure of the royal court.

While the chronicle of the Hessean wolf-child might be familiar for the manner in which it articulates the capture of difference in impelled resemblance to *human life*, it is not without its resistance. Having never lost the capacity for human speech, the chronicle describes that the wolf-child frequently remarked on his preference to live amongst the wolves. As Steel (2012) writes, the wolf-child hence 'assimilates poorly to human society not because he became irreparably animalized, but because he would *prefer* to be among wolves' (2012: 17, *emphasis added*). This detail of the chronicle exposes the anthropocentric construction of disability. That is, disability becomes relative to both the wolf-child's willing escape from a human image of life and its desire for the affects and potentials of non-human filiation. In alignment with the presumed dominance of human life over all others, the counter-actualization of orthodox moral, communal and subjective formations can only ever be treated as abnormal, or rather, as potential modes of being to overcome. This ontological privileging suggests that animality must always be on its way to becoming-human, if not in resemblance than in meaning for us as moral, developmental or cultural indices. For the Hessean wolf-child, the body is impelled into conformity to the human's bipedal distance and transcendent gaze away from the mutable ground of the earth. It is further subjectivized through the 'refinement' of its desires coextensive to the moral, perspectival and 'normative' models of human life projected upon it. In this image, to become alongside 'non-Oedipalized' animals is to compose something queer or horrific. Such counter-actualizations of the human image fail to be thought as ethical experiments in how a life might go, and are framed instead as failures to realize oneself as fully human. Yet, it is from this image of the human that the wolf-child willingly recedes. In a seventeenth-century retelling of the Hessean chronicle, the wolf-child chooses death in isolation over integration into human community (Steel 2012).

This chapter will attempt to break from the anthropocentric image of life inhering the educational project by creating new conditions for thinking an anti-speciesist pedagogy. Such a pedagogy, I will argue, is reliant on the creation of new images and machines of disidentification through which pedagogy too might recede from the presumption that there is but one life – and that it is a *human one*. Such a task is crucial insofar as it might be ventured that the biopedagogical 'refinement' of the wolf-child's desires share with contemporary education a founding investment in the production of a molar human subject, or rather, a subject imagined and selected in resemblance with the anthropocentric root of contemporary schooling. Extending through the Platonic aspiration for transcendence over animal life and the Enlightenment escape of 'the rational subject' from the material entrapments of the earth, education since industrialization has accelerated the anthropocentric conceit that the world is *as it is for us* (Thacker 2011). This conceit is produced in several ways, not the least of which is via the representational presumption that the world reflects our knowledge of it, or rather, that the world conforms to an anthropocentric image in which life itself is continually captured as an object of meaning *established in advance* of its difference. This mode of capture is implicated with two anthropocentric legacies in education. The first pertains to the obfuscation of ecology under the transcendent emplacement of epistemological constants reified by contemporary calls for the standardization of schools and the implicate logics of imitation and resemblance advanced therein. What Nietzsche (2000) dubs the *illusion of transcendence* or the presumption of a *higher* and *immutable* truth existing above material reality becomes intimate to the keen hierarchical division of ontological substances perpetuated in contemporary educational thought. Delinked from the geo-pedagogical question of how knowledge is composed in the first place, or rather, how knowledge is always-already implicate with a virtual problematic field, the transcendent illusion of education purports to a regular and stable image of reality as the highest function of what it means to be 'learned'. From kindergarten onwards, the formal school aims to refine the desires of the student away from material life and towards the transcendent, to turn away from both the animal and child's mutable relation with the earth and to overcome it by selecting only those desires that desire transcendence and mastery over both self and world. It is in this image that the labour of the school is often marked by a radical disconnection from the morphological potential of social ecologies, reducing the potential connective and affective powers of institutional desiring-production to the homogeneity of factory routine. That the *ready-made* territories of curricular standardization and highly regulated factory routines of formal schooling obfuscate the affective potentials for material connection inhering educational labour perpetuates the notion that mastery of the world through learning refers to the world *itself*, as if horrors did not exist recalcitrant to the transcendent striation of the world according to *higher* principles of Truth, law and teleological promise (Nietzsche 2000). It is this horror that new teachers invariably face when they enter into the complex 'geo-pedagogical' lived-curriculum of the school (Aoki 2005). Teaching, they quickly realize, has much less to do with clinging to the transcendent than it does with the necessity of modulating one's affective powers in relation with *other* bodies. This is, of course, a corollary to Deleuze's (1994) pedagogical lesson on learning to swim. It is not sufficient, Deleuze argues, that the swimmer represent the *official* or transcendent *techniques* taught to them poolside. The swimmer must be prepared to deterritorialize such *official gestures* in order to produce viable connections with the virtual problematic field 'posed' by the conditions of the water's 'body'. Recalcitrant to the highly territorialized and patterned image of the standardized curriculum and its implicate break from material relations then, Deleuze's pedagogical lesson insists upon a style of learning born from a break in the repetition and expectation of *constants*, or rather, of the becoming-other of identitarian resemblance by producing 'good connections' with the virtual problematic field of the milieu.

From its industrial conceptualization, the school has taken as its task the refinement of the subject's desiring-production towards the discovery of constants, rules and axioms. It is through such a 'discovery curriculum' or rather, by learning what everyone already knows, that one achieves mastery over the world. Acquiescing to the illusion of transcendence and hence, a 'subjectivation in the transcendent', human and inhuman life are divided. Here, Plato's eschatological image of the Great Chain of Being assumes renewed significance in the modern school. Through functions of ranking, division or segmentary molar cutting, even the youngest children are oriented to recognize themselves in the identitarian 'face of man'. This is to say that where school presumes in advance the production of molar social subjects, its pedagogy functions to produce matrices of recognition that inform upon the subject a *faciality* that overcodes the body with surface signs of class, species, race, gender and history (MacCormack 2004). It is in this image that the subject itself is produced, circuiting the body's affective potentials to a molar grid which selects in advance the terms upon which one might become recognizable *as a rational and civilized subject* (*bios*). This pedagogical function has its corollary in the popular fairy-tale cliché where the *inhuman* face of the animal is 'positively' transformed into the image of *Prince Charming*, or otherwise, where the unformed head (in Pinocchio, for example) is seen as a transitory phase on its way to actualization in an orthodox image of childhood (Genosko 2002). And so it goes with Jonathan Levine's (2013) zombie-romance *Warm Bodies*, where the symbiotically dishevelled *meat-head* of the zombie is rehabilitated through its normative *becoming-human*, or rather, via the rehabilitation of its 'inhuman life' (*zoë*) upon the orthodox face of the gendered, racialized, and historicized *human being* (*bios*). Akin to the 'biopedagogy' levied against the Hessian wolf-child, whose body is subjected to the image of the *human face, faciality* functions as an abstract-machine for organizing the 'educated' body by means of an expansionist, imperialist and colonizing *limit-face*. This is to say that *faciality* limits *potentials* for expression and the creation of hitherto unnamed connections according to prior regimes of signification, presupposing in advance the ideal form *life* should assume.

Today, it might be advanced that the processes of education have become so enamoured of the *face of man* and its 'illusory beautiful life' that the foundation by which life is ascribed to being is made to extend from the *face of man* as its arboreal root (Colebrook 2011: 36). Herein, the school curriculum and its organization of disciplinary study produces an archive of human superiority by overcoding life in its image or rather, by making life relevant to its discovery *for* humans. If not in the form of historical or scientific triumph, education today lauds a new circuit of *faciality* via neo-liberal subjectivization where 'one' continually finds their own reflection in things, as if beneath the world, a unified and 'natural' human '*I*' insisted as a prime manifestor of meaning-making. Attempts to escape the *face* or those dominant screens of signification through which the subject is produced lie at the heart of an educational problematic against which are mobilized the resources of ubiquitous surveillance and standardized controls repressing the differentials of ontological organization into resemblance with the face of the rational and unified human. This is to say, following Agamben's (2004) modern conceptualization of the 'anthropological machine', that the school functions to repress the 'nonhuman within the human', or rather, to discipline the *animality* of the human into the shape of a recognizable biopolitical subject subjectable to established modes of control and desire (2004: 37).

The school's anthropocentric territorialization of life in the identitarian image of *human life* might otherwise be known through the degraded status of animals in the material practices of the institution. In the United States alone, an estimated 20 million animals per year are killed for the purpose of dissection in biology class laboratories. Implicate with mass industry, many of the animals used in such school dissection labs are bred for the express purpose that their deaths will function in service to the knowledge and experience of the student. Such precedent for the *utility* of animal life in secondary classrooms is corollary to the multi-million-dollar enterprise of animal research in universities, which report continual increases in animal 'biomedical' experimentation, stress testing, vivisection and genetic modification. In each instance, the animal is thought as a sacrificial vehicle *for us*. In less overt ways, the conceptualization of the animal as an object *for us* insists as a 'hidden' supplement throughout the curriculum. For example, insofar as the study of home economics is influenced by livestock industry lobbyists, the animal as a literal object of consumption is normalized apart from ethical consideration. Elsewhere, the animal is almost completely banished from history as anything other than a vanishing mediator of human progress. And where animals do insist within the educational imagination, they assume a degraded, Oedipalized status through which they become domesticated classroom-pets or banal markers of school identity. Following Deleuze's critique, it is this domesticated animal, made either *for us* or as a recognizable familial object, that constitutes the most revulsive conceptualization of the animal, for where the animal is *only* as it is *for us*, its difference is nullified (Deleuze & Parnet 2010). Such a conceptualization, it seems, is *unthinkable* in education. It is at this juncture that we might ask what the animal – and in particular a non-Oedipal animal – *means* for educational thought. That is, where education itself stems from an anthropocentric arboreal root in its task of producing *human subjects*, the animal, its affectations and powers to act are always-already covered over.

Territory

The *covering-over* of the animal and animal life in education is not simply a matter of epistemological concern. Rather, where schooling in general takes as its task the regulation and reproduction of life in the image of a citizen adapted to dominant modes of desiring-production and orthodoxies of identitarian resemblance, its stakes are inherently ontological. What then, are the stakes of thinking alongside the animal in education? To begin, we will return to Deleuze for whom the animal is *not* the domesticated animal adapted to the habits of the household and the routines that produce them. For Deleuze, the difference of the animal is intimate to the way in which it does not conform to, but rather, produces *a* world. Through the emission and reception of signs, Deleuze avers, an animal marks out a territory. A bird produces a territory with its song, a wolf by its markings, a gibbon by flashing the red of its chest. This is to say that a territory does not exist in advance, but rather, *must first be created* – and from what is a territory created but the decoded body of the earth *not yet* accorded shape or measure? That a territory must *first be made* marks a 'fundamental' challenge to anthropocentric thought in education, for where schooling posits a territorial habitus in advance of students, the animal's material relationship to the earth insists that territory neither is *primary* nor permanent. It must be made and remade in relation to the territories that abut and intersect it. Yet, Deleuze's conceptualization of the animal goes further still, for there are certain animals that *are always on the move* through which their material folding and delinking with the earth are intimate to the imbricated material practices of territorialization, deterritorialization and reterritorialization (Deleuze & Guattari 1994). For example, where a wolf deterritorializes their 'habit', their departing establishes a vector of reterritorialization elsewhere (Deleuze & Parnet 2010).

To think in place of the animal, or rather, through the animal's material practices of folding and delinking with a milieu might mean to question how territories and the habits of behaviour that sustain them are created *in the first place*. For educational thought, this approach necessitates the question of *how things got to be as they are* and further, *how* the material repetition of the territory informs upon the kinds of subjects 'thinkable' institutionally. It is this latter question that is intimate to Guattari's experiment in rethinking the organization of the clinic at La Borde (Dosse 2010). That is, what becomes crucial for Guattari in his internal revolution of the clinic is the revolutionary modulation of institutional territories in a manner capable of freeing the subject into new forms of enunciation and group-subject identification. Key to this modulation is the ecological rethinking of the institution in a manner distinct from the *official group-subject* positions (doctors, nurses, cooks, patients, etc.) produced from the perspective of an external and hierarchical organizing metric reinforced by university training, 'psychopharmacological' approaches to patient treatment and the degraded status of the patient as an 'object' of rehabilitation (Guattari 2009). More simply, Guattari's (2000) work at La Borde posits the *unthought* affective power of the institution's territory, or rather, its connective assemblage of groups, subject, objects and spaces in ways capable of liberating institutional life or otherwise obstructing it altogether.[1] Herein, Guattari's reconceptualization of the institution as a material ecology that can be *remade* in support of new subject and group relations posits the importance of territory, or rather of breaking with territories in order to escape the 'deathly repetition of everyday life' (2000: 149). A central problem of education, Guattari & Rolnik (2008) argue, might be articulated along these very lines, for what remains characteristic of the formal educational project but its emphasis on empty forms of repetition indifferent to becoming. What remains largely unthinkable in education is the very notion that territories must *be made in the first place*, and in their making, are demonstrative that the territory (what is) is always suffused with potentials for counter-actualization (what might be). The Hessian wolf-child's desire to be with the pack marks one such counter-actualization, where the territory and sign-markers of the state's biopedagogy are rejected for another style of living altogether. What is at stake in this unthinkable desire is not simply its renunciation of the human, but rather, the signs through which the anthropocentric territorialization of life is reproduced. That is, what does the dissensus of the wolf-child corrupt but the normalized subjectivity of the state and its reification in the Oedipal image of the heteronormative social connection (Guattari 2000)? For educational thought to move alongside this counter-actualization would necessitate a breach from the transcendent. It is in this manner that the archi-textures that have hitherto constituted the 'ground' of educational thought might be rethought as but a *single* image of how a pedagogical life might go.

World

What does the animal do, Deleuze insists, but create *a* world (Deleuze & Parnet, 2010)? For Deleuze & Guattari (1986), this is what the animal shares with the artist, the writer and philosopher. That is, through the creation of a unique syntax or rather, singular qualities for affecting and being affected, both the animal and the artist produce *a* world distinct from the world *in general*. For animals such as the tick, *a* world of signs and affects can be extremely limited. Drawing on the biological theory of Jacob von Uexküll, for example, Deleuze & Guattari (1987) describe the world of the tick in terms of only *three affects*: sensitivity to light, the smell of mammals and of burrowing at the point of easiest access to the host's skin. This might be put differently to contend that both the tick *and* its world *are* its powers to affect and be affected. It is this singular capacity to affect and be affected that Deleuze & Guattari (1986) speculatively extends to the artist, author or philosopher who in adopting a unique style or approach is able to produce *a* world that counter-actualizes dominant patterns of perception and sense making. This is not to presume that the human can think *in place* of the animal, but rather, to will the disidentification of the world *as given* through the creation of originary affective corridors. Such 'disorienting effects' are intimate to the diagrammatic works of von Uexküll, whose own work is replete with speculative diagrams regarding non-human experiences of the human world (Agamben 2004: 45). The effects of these diagrams gesture towards a vehement anti-humanism in which the *human world* is apprehended from an alien vantage, palpating an ecosophical dissensus against the image of a single *human* world. For what von Uexküll's (2010) diagrams suggest is that there might *always-already* be an alien gaze troubling the orthodox *image of the world* given *for humans*. To rejoin Deleuze (2000), it is this very disruption of orthodox sensibility or *common sense* that inheres the work of the artist, author or philosopher malcontent to the representation of the world as it is given *for us*. For what attracts Deleuze to the potential of art is not simply its ability to multiply the *given* but rather to palpate new conditions for thought and action in a manner capable of dilating an account of ontological difference (Deleuze 2000). In an ostensible attempt to maintain the force of non-identification and alterity, Deleuze shows preference for the alien life of the tick, lice and flea. For it is via this alien life that the most familiar coordinates of the *human* – particularly the image of the human 'bounded', unified and organized into patterns of desiring-production – might be put into question.

The stakes of such ontological dilation are paramount in education, which for all intents and purposes functions as an anthropocentric machine of coding, albeit inexactly, the desiring-flows of the classroom towards homogeneous and regulated outcomes. Such outcomes presuppose the *face of man*, or rather, that the subject will become in the image of a molar, identitarian subject for whom reality will be operationalized by the potentials ascribed to it biopolitically and economically. That is, through the accrual of debt and the fettering of biopolitical life to the desiring-machines of corporate banking, the institutional selection of desire correspondent to an image of the *good citizen* and the 'refinement' of will in concert with institutional capital, the subject is *always-already* thought along a line predestined to its realization in a *human-all-too-human* image of life radically divorced from ecosophical implication (Holland 2012). This general problematic is exemplified by Deleuze & Guattari's (1987) critique of Freud's clinical work with Sergei Pankejeff (Wolf Man), whose articulation of a dream in which he is pursued by wolves is recoded upon the Oedipal, or familial (mommy-daddy-me) mytheme. Rather than acknowledging the non-human intensities or inhuman assemblage that populates Pankejeff's dream of a wolf-pack, Freud reterritorializes the enunciation upon the familial order, hence delimiting the patient's enunciation by colonizing it within a signifying regime regulated by the transcendent mytheme of Oedipus Rex. This superegoic overcoding does not amount to a cure. Rather, as Guattari would remark on Freud's treatment of Little Hans, signs of pathological fear would emerge only after the commencement of face-to-face treatment (Guattari 1972). The policing force of the superego had effectively made the patient worse. Where the territories of the educational project continue to appeal to an anthropocentric or otherwise anthropomorphized image of life, the detection of either *alter life-forms* or *life* prior to its formation as *human life* become largely negated. In this overcoding, contemporary educational thought becomes complicit with a necrophilosophical drive through which life is made to reflect in already-constituted life-forms (MacCormack 2012: 117). This drive is not simply manifest in the formal practices of the schoolhouse, but is inherent to the very modes of research used to think the educational project. Where critical theory and autobiography (the 'egology' of identity) might *begin* by mapping life upon prior interpretive systems for example, life is *already* drawn into correspondence with a mortified 'epistemic state' through which it is made to 'count' representationally (MacCormack 2012: 116). Today, it seems that there is little that escapes the state of the self-reflexive 'I' and further, the identitarian categories through which the subject is biopolitically 'counted' (race, gender, sex, religion, family, etc.). Everything 'counted' is made to return to these indices. The problem of this approach is relatively straightforward. Where *we already know what things mean*, the potential of commencing a politicized ethics of *life itself* becomes epistemologically overdetermined. In this necrotic scenario, the terms upon which life can be thought are already constituted. Further, where life is continually made to 'count' representationally, the singular, the inhuman and non-representational become problematic – but from the perspective of the index that they flee and are subsequently reterritorialized. Here, *life itself* is rendered equivalent to what *already* counts as life and more specifically, to an image of life marked by anthropocentric privilege and the hysterical reclamation of identitarian fundaments extinguished by postmodernity.

Swarm

Beneath Sunnydale High School, the setting of Joss Whedon's popular *Buffy the Vampire Slayer*, exists the *hellmouth*. From its gaping maw, all manner of demonic and other-worldly forces issue forth as forces of contamination, putrefaction and morphological becoming. Beyond a convenient plot device, that Whedon envisions the hellmouth beneath Sunnydale High School articulates two kinds of knotted forces at work in schooling: the molar regulation of institutional time, space and identity and the molecular forces of dissensus and disidentification that threaten to queer the school's machines of social production. That the hellmouth figures as a literal break in the school's foundation is corollary to its revolutionary force, which aims at producing all kinds of non-normative and inhuman becomings-animal recalcitrant to their repetition in the *face of man*. Herein, beneath the striated architectonics of Sunnydale High, the *hellmouth* palpates an *unthought* swarm-ontology or rather, an 'ungrounding' of the human as the primary life-form of the school and its processes.

This notion of 'ungrounding' appears in the thought of Agamben (1998), for whom the alien-animal intensities of '*raw life*' already occupy the 'social' – in albeit submitted status to the meaningful life of the biopolitical citizen (*bios*). Zoë nevertheless marks an 'outside' to representation insofar as its drives neither imitate nor labour in an image of molar life, unified being or stable identity. Rather, *zoë* figures as a transversal force or *inhuman* potential for becoming (Braidotti 2011). Such transversal force constitutes a key focus in Reynolds's (2002) alter-genealogy of sixteenth-century European criminal culture, through which he demonstrates how socially transgressive performances of *demonic, monstrous*, and *animal-becomings* functioned as social conductors for the internal critique of state hegemony and Christian eschatology by dilating the bounded metaphysical image of *human life* upon a queer ontology *unthinkable* by the regulatory body of the state or moral machines of the church. As Reynolds documents, the anti-theatricalist movement was born not out of an anxiety that public performance would inspire people to become demons, animals or monsters in a literal sense, but rather, that they would come to produce the countercultural and non-conformist affects of the theatre *by other means*, harnessing molecular flows of becoming as a means to critique the biopolitical ensconcement and repetition of *life* in highly patterned modes of enunciation. Herein, *zoë*'s expressive force is coextensive to what might be called the *nomadic subject* or the potential transgression of the subject's bounded metaphysical image by carrying it beyond the threshold state of *being-human*. Such a transgression inheres Deleuze & Parnet's (2008) fascination with the 'swarm-ontology' of lice and fleas, the organization and challenge of which mark a becoming in *A Thousand Plateaus*, where Deleuzeguattari (1987) write not as individual, 'unified' authors, but as a *pack* or *swarm* machine short-circuiting the representational impulse to reinscribe the text within a matrix of authorial convention and identification. Perhaps more radically, the swarm-machine composed in *A Thousand Plateaus* ungrounds Deleuze and Guattari's *proper philosophical names* across a multiplicity of potential personae and untimely, *inhuman* arrangements.

To think in terms of this 'swarm ontology' might entail revolutionizing aspects of orthodox schooling and its bourgeois organization of the social by assuming the individual as its basic unit (expressed as the numerical equivalent to 'one'). Tied to the representation of the unified and 'bounded body', the vaunted celebration of the uncontaminated human marks a failure to think in terms of the swarm's non-identity or the assertion that *we have never been humans proper* by fact of our constitution by microbial and amoebic intelligences that are not *our own*. Ansell-Pearson dubs this 'the filthy lesson of symbiosis', where life thought as a molecular multiplicity no longer functions 'in accordance with the superior laws of race or blood, genus or species' (1999: 182–183). That humans share with other life-forms, from the orangutan to the pumpkin, significant similarities in genetic makeup attests that to be *human* is to think only a single scale of ontology grounded in the transcendent illusion of anthropocentrism (Hroch 2013). For education, 'swarm ontology' might mean rethinking the life of the school as less the site of 'egological' cultivation than the task of creating ecosophical modes of pedagogy capable of attending to the ways in which education remains deeply complicit in naturalizing speciesist relations to the world. This necessitates that pedagogy become capable of modulating scales and durations of experience non-resemblant with *'common sense'* (that which everyone already knows). This is to say that pedagogy's *becoming-animal* might entail being 'always on the lookout' for the singular, or rather, for the molecular flows of the classroom capable of participating in the dehabituation of life from its rigidified entrapment and repetition (Deleuze and Parnet 2010). This ecosophical rethinking of ontological scale is more than simply an appeal to 'multiply perspectives'. Rather, it is, as it was for Deleuzeguattari's *pack* writing-machine, the creation of a new plane for political and ethical experimentation. That 'swarm ontology' already detects the queer symbiosis of human/inhuman assemblages suggests a turning from the transcendent towards the material connection of life forces and their potential to constitute an ecosophical ethics that begins by displacing the anthropocentric conceit of a 'unified' and 'uncontaminated' *world-for-us*.

Burrow

The territory of the animal does not simply extend along a horizontal plane, but enters into conspiracy with the earth in order to produce all manner of subterranean passage from the fox's den to the 'subcities' of the mantis shrimp and ant. The animal's subterranean world enters into fidelity with the planet in distinction to the *human's* orientation to the transcendent, which ultimately favours the presence of *logos* to the subterranean warren of the animal. For while the *illusion of transcendence* is bound to its realization in 'ideal truths', there persists in the act of burrowing a recession from presence toward secrecy – from arborescence to rhizomatics. Put differently, the *burrow* produces a new kind of territory that Deleuzeguattari (1987) dub *holey space*, a concept for thinking on the material perforation of social space and as a process of communicating new kinds of material affiliations that break away from foundations. That holey space is a concept nearly unthinkable in schooling is a product of the mechanisms of surveillance under which education transpires and for which certain attributes and desires are selected and regulated. Where pedagogy might attend to molecular *life* or rather, breaches from the image of the world *as it is given*, there is a precursor to *holy space*. This might happen rarely, when a class is caught in an intensity or attraction that creates, however temporarily, a singularity that breaks from the planned curriculum, the normative chronometrics of the school, or the general regulation of affects into what Guattari calls 'redundancies of images and behavior' (2000: 61). To think the *burrow* as a *holey space*, or of *burrowing* as the process of creating it, subverts education's teleological aim of moving towards the realization of 'ideal forms' and the submission of life to a single point of view through the establishment of an anthropocentric colonial optics. That is, *holey space* conspires to both secrecy (*where we are not*) and the creation of original percepts from beneath the ground and in the composition of subterranean rhizomatic passages. Such *burrowing* is oblique to the bureaucratic organization of curriculum, for what is *burrowing* but a becoming-animal through the creation of connections and cartographies that resist the metaphysics of presence of rather, the image of the world as it is *given*. It is this very mode of becoming that inheres the Deleuzeguattarian (1983; 1987) project, born as it is through the connection of 'bastard' thinkers, or otherwise subterranean philosophical impulses that produce new conditions for philosophical thought-action. Beneath the ground of *philosophy proper*, Deleuze demonstrates, exist all variety of darkened passages subtending and betraying the coded territories and habits above. If such a becoming-animal could be thought for education, it would entail a pedagogical approach born first from the betrayal of representation or fidelity to practices of tracing *decalcomania*) and repetition proscribed by *given* educational territories – *what we ought to learn* and *how we ought to learn it*.

That the *burrow* punctuates the territory, forcing it into secret nuptials with unregistered forces suggests that astride the *official enunciations* of the institution might subtend all manner of *unthought* connections and compositions through which different ecologies or cartographic diagrams of the world might be forged. For like the child who unearths a rock to find beneath a writhing assemblage of life-forms and receding clandestine tunnels, a pedagogy committed to unmaking the *face of man* might begin with the acknowledgement that those foundations and structures that maintain an image of the world as it is *for us* fail grievously to account for the impersonal worlds of 'stranger strangers' and their ambivalence for the world of the human (Morton 2010; Thacker 2011). For a pedagogy interested in habilitating a renewed connection to the environment, such 'dark ecology' is itself a mode of dehabituation for its introjection of percepts and affections *too weird* to be absorbed into the anthropocentric schemas of orthodox schooling, necessitating the opening of schematic territories *from within* and *beneath* on behalf of searching out new ethical relations to *life* that do not reflect in the image of the human, but its hallucinatory undoing for the purpose of defraying the speciesist, colonial and narcissistic practices that are the legacy of anthropocentrism. For against the metaphysics of presence particular to the Western *logos*, the *burrowed holey space* of the animal is closer to logocentrism's ancient twin, *loxos* (a place of ambush). This fidelity is articulated in Hesiod's creation myth *Theogeny*, where *loxos* (ambush) thwarts the defilement of the Earth (Gaia) by ambushing and castrating the unwelcome suitor Ouranos (Heaven) (Lambert 2005). Hidden from heaven (the transcendent powers of Ouranos), *loxos* constitutes the staging point for the emergence of a 'new race of barbarians' insubordinately poised to contravene the power of Empire (Hardt & Negri 2001: 217). In this sense, *loxos* marks a conspiracy with the Earth to ward against overcoding from above, a problematic given contemporary urgency when one considers the ways in which *life itself* is reduced to its use-value for human infrastructures, and further, the manner in which education continues to produce an image of thought that posits a human face on the world, rendering *life* equivalent to those meanings, desires and teloi suited to the perpetuation of normalized subjectivities, orthodox patterns of human/inhuman relations, and the reification of anthropocentrism as '*common sense*'. These modes of capture found the modern factory-school, which is fundamentally oriented to the 'refinement' of raw life (*zoë*) into highly regulated patterns of organization. In a vision of schooling as prescient today as at the turn of the twentieth century, Cubberly writes that 'our schools are, in a sense, factories in which raw materials (*zoë*) are to be shaped and fashioned into products to meet the various demands of life' (1916: 338). Herein, life is already life as it is *for us*, or rather, as demand defined anthropocentrically.

Black

The chronicle of the Hessean wolf child with which this chapter began bears upon the 'anthropocentric machine' of schooling, for at their 'root', both the 'biopedagogy' of the wolf-child's 'refinement' and the general idea of education are predicated upon the production of what it means to be *human* (Agamben 2004). There is little doubt that formalized schooling has and continues to mobilize a hidden curriculum oriented to the extreme blinkering of ontology according to a privileged anthropocentric image as the ground of difference. Such an image of thought inheres the influential Enlightenment writings of Rousseau, whose romantic image of 'pedagogy proper' is fundamentally recalcitrant to the horrors of 'mixing', 'disfigurement' and 'deformity' characterized by the threat of the inhuman (Lewis & Khan 2010: ix). For what pedagogy must aspire to, Rousseau agues in the pedagogical treatise *Emile*, is the purity of proper human development as it is ostensibly inclined to individual, civil and democratic ideals. It is in this 'founding mythology' for pedagogical thought that schooling becomes linked to an ontological caesura dividing the human from the inhuman, or rather, the transcendent from the material (1979: 75). This marks a general cutting-off from both the materialisms of non-Oedipal animals and, further, an ecosophical pedagogy that takes seriously the violent environmental consequences of institutionalized speciesism, racism and coloniality. Our attention must extend beyond such bad pedagogical practices as the anti-materialist abstraction of the periodic table, the archival production of the human face in the art studio, or dissection of non-human life in the biology laboratory. While such practices certainly require renewal, this renewal must emerge alongside a revolution of the anthropocentric image of thought subtending the educational project and the implicitly violent relations to other beings it produces. Herein, the decolonization of education must begin by revolutionizing the *human-all-too-human* molar face it presumes as its model. Further, this attempt at decoloniality must figure in the general 'freeing' of *life itself* from the idea that *life* is predestined to repeat in molar forms. To rejoin Spinoza (1985), *we do not yet know what a body can do.* Relations being external to their terms, we do not know in advance the connections, relations or forms of desiring-production with which a body will assemble.

While the question of how we might begin to think a world that is not *our own* seems a ludicrous project for the fact of education's anthropocentric founding, that education *must* attend to such a question is pressing as increasing evidence points to the immanent collapse of the anthropocene (Colebrook 2010). That the 'human' must become something else to survive is a moot point, as is the obsolescent conceit that the world is *as it is for us.* Today, all kinds of animal and inhuman life, from the bioactive leachates of plastics to the mountain pine beetle point to the faltering myth that 'we' are in control. For while talk of ecological sustainability maintains the primacy of the human by making 'sustainability' equivalent to the survival of the human species (and its select anthropomorphized others), what such discourse fails to recognize is that *life will go on*, with impersonal ambivalence for human concern or nostalgia. Not even the images of the posthuman cyborg, vampires or wolfmen and their quasi-maintenance of the human will occupy this most *impersonal* plane of mineral, vestigial and alien microbial life (Thacker 2011). The pedagogical problematic raised here queries how human life might be thought at the moment when the bounded image of human life reaches its terminal point. And yet education labours on in seeming denial that its founding presumption, the organization of human life, has reached a terminus – now succeeded by the belief in the ideal of immortality and a wholly transcendent world that we might no longer have to believe in this one. This is, of course, a pedagogical failure insofar as belief in this world, or rather, the creation of *a* world, necessitates thinking in terms of an immanent ethics capable of creating alternative ontological diagrams to the organization of human above inhuman life. That education and the diagrams for thinking life are implicit in the production of conditions upon which violence against animal and nonhuman life is normalized is cause for pessimism aimed at the manner by which we come to understand and reflect ourselves as *human* in the first place. Where pedagogy can be thought through the dark ecologies of defraying territories, scales of existence, contaminant swarms and the *holey space* of the burrow, it might begin to loosen the habitual territories and their repetitive tracing that constitutes the bureaucratic plan of the school. For what the lesson of 'dark ecology' suggests is that pedagogy might best begin by jettisoning the false-optimism of transcendence for the horror of a world that gazes impersonally on every celebration of the self or historicization of the world from the perspective of a single species.

Anti-Speciesist pedagogy: A dark educational ecology

For pedagogy to be rethought as *anti-speciesist* necessitates the operationalization of an ethical anti-correlationism, or rather, a recalcitrance to the habit of presuming that the world exists only insofar as humans exist to produce it (Harman 2009). That correlationism denies the autonomy of *things* by reducing matter to the necrospectives of anthropocentric meaning is to negate the 'dark and concealed reality' or accursed share of *things* as they always-already recede from the machines of anthropocentric capture intimate to educational production (2009: 205). The affirmation of this 'dark ecology' necessitates no less than the systematic overturning of the anthropocentric horizon that is the presupposed *telos* of education. Such a revolution would entail the eschewal of transcendent values, categorical representations and circuits of identification that not only fulminate the *face of man*, but regulate forces of experimentation and speculation in its image. To think a 'dark ecology' for pedagogy is to orient education to that *accursed share* that is neither wholly captured nor negated by the representation of reality given anthropocentrically. This is to exhaust the imperial 'desire to dominate the earth's life-forms' intimate to the anthropocentric episteme of modern education, for alike Joanna Macy's advocacy for Nuclear Guardianship, pedagogy thought astride dark ecology entails the rejection of the imperial desire to flee the earth for some transcendent ideal, palpating instead an ethical duty towards both the *excessive materiality* of the planet and its consequential mutation as a result of our living upon it (Morton 2007: 157). To think pedagogy as a duty to such *excessive materiality* would necessitate dilating the task of education upon its consequences for non-human life while ceding the vaunted status of knowledge production and human consciousness as incommensurate with the 'whole of reality'.

This is not to suggest that *there is always more to learn*, but that our learning always falls short of apprehending the unfathomable thought of the 'radical other' and its singular modes of producing *a* world. Herein, the task of pedagogy might entail the continual disjunction of life from epistemological exhaustion through the introjection of thought that renders education's already constituted circuits of production *out-of-step* with the material realities they naïvely seek to represent. Such might be the case when history is rethought in *geological* not genealogical terms, when science is brought to bear upon its speculative and fictional probe-heads, or when art is reborn through grotesque impersonal affects that betray the sentimental and romantic aesthetics of 'easy life' (Gough 2004; Lambert 2005; Morton 2007).

Pedagogy must be made adequate to the ecological challenges of the present, and not simply for the sake of anthropocentric *self-preservation*. That schooling continues to produce oppressive and imperial relations with non-human life under the alibi of educational stewardship or the romantic image of non-human dependency necessitates the creation of thought capable of short-circuiting the image of education as an unquestionable transcendent 'good'. Thought astride dark ecology, pedagogy might hence break the repetition of anthropocentric nostalgias by resituating the educational event in relation to an immanent ethics. In place of *egology* or the production of 'educated citizens', an *ecological* nuptials and expanded 'subjectivity'. This is to say that education must be made adequate to the creation of relations 'good' for their enhancement of *life itself*, where life does not aspire to the image of the human subject that might *then* be taken as an indexical model for difference. In practical terms, 'dark ecology' already betrays the presumed 'good' of education by insisting that the 'good' can only be assessed through the material relations and kinds of objects education is capable of producing – and not simply *for* the human. Not what education *can do* in its limited sense of accreditation or accumulation then, but what qualities of arrangement it is capable of assuming with ahuman ecologies. This might suggest for pedagogy a renewed point of reference in a speculative world *without humans*, or rather, *a* world where the human constitutes but one species amongst many. It also suggests the cultivation of care towards what is 'nonidentical with us' (Morton 2007: 185). This is not to glorify the ruin of the species, but rather, the repetition of its arboreal *teloi*. In breaking the repetition of anthropocentric auto-glorification, pedagogy might hence be recommended as a project of humility whose aim is no longer the self-reflection of *humility as a human quality*, but as a condition of immanence where the human is no longer projected into a position of assumed superiority *over* the world, but implicated with the material ecologies of *this* planet (MacCormack 2013). This means, in part, mobilizing an active refusal to 'transcend' the death of this planet in lieu affirming the dark side of our interconnection with it (Morton 2007).

The corruption of educational thought organized from the perspective of a single species might defray the molar subjectifying processes of schooling and its lock-down of desiring-production by positing an alternative 'ground' to the face of man that is presumed as its arboreal foundation. This would entail breaking from the correlationist conceit that the world is *as it is for us* by making the ontological consequences of educational thought and practice intimate to the very task of education. Put differently, the image of thought produced by education must become an integral part of the school curriculum as a means both to address the onto-materialism of thought and to renew a belief in this world by reconnecting education to both social and ecological spheres. It is crucial that the material influence of educational production be detected and further, given a broader range of expression and influence capable of producing new conditions for thought and action in the world. Following, the conceptualization of the school as a segmental preparatory space distinct from social and ecological spheres must be overturned through the active material reconnection of pedagogy with *this* world and its immanent challenges as a means to break from the transcendent image of life implicate to education's reification of imperialism. Concomitantly, the analysis of educational systems requires reconceptualization such that the 'school' is no longer pathologized as a social space somehow removed from broader social and ecological problems, but rather, seen as both symptomatic of such spheres and as a fulcrum for the creation of new ways of living.

An anti-speciesist turn in education capable of bringing about new relations between human and non-human life will ultimately rely upon micro-practices in the everyday. At their best, such pedagogical micro-practices will defer the imposition of an organizing metric for desiring-production by actualizing lines of flight for every presumed model of how life *ought* to be arranged. This means, above all, that education must first become immanent to the embedded ecologies of the classroom and not, as education's bureaucratic image would have it, the transcendent curriculum as plan, the external chronometric control of classroom life, or the segmentary treatment of subject areas where new conditions of thought might otherwise be cultivated. Pedagogy must aim to function affirmatively where vectors of difference emerge in the daily life of the classroom. This is to begin to treat desire and desiring-production as a force without image and hence, as a force of potential connection and experimentation without resemblance. By delinking desire from the school's habitual forms of production (this is how desire *ought* to be circuited), pedagogy might palpate the question of why *this* (set of relations) and not *something else?* It is here that pedagogy becomes political in a manner that does not aspire to the image of the political citizen, but rather, the dilation of the political subject upon unthought dark ecologies concomitant with, yet unequal to the rendered territories of both the *polis* and its presumed subject.

Notes

1. Mobilizing transversal thinking against the overstratified routinization of the clinical model, Guattari would rethink the institution by drawing clinical staff into a direct and non-hierarchical relationship with patients. Waging a critique of the institution from within, Guattari and Oury would help produce a transversal cartography dubbed 'the grid' (la grille), a rolling system of work rotation in which medical and non-medical clinical personnel and patients would work in heterogeneous groups to perform clinical duties. 'The grid' at La Borde would draw new group-subject cartographies by modulating universes of reference.

CHAPTER TEN

Self-Harm, Human Harm?

Ruth McPhee

The term 'self-harm' and the conceptual associations that this term carries are social and political constructs. The subjective category of the 'self-harmer', the wounded or scarred body, and the emotional embodied states associated with these experiences are at once overdetermined and inadequately recognized. Layers of cultural meanings have built up around them in accordance with normative ideologies from various discourses that regulate thought about illness, sanity, suffering, addiction, corporality and gender. This layering of signification has often resulted in the imposition of rigid boundaries that function to channel theories and representations of self-mutilation into pre-existing models and to exclude any less deterministic understandings. This chapter intends to unpick some of these socially constructed meanings, to explore how the self-mutilated body can be understood as a becoming-ahuman, and to offer some possible alternative perspectives in order to rethink this body, its experiences, and its relationship to signification anew. These considerations are inherently and necessarily ethical, for they concern the very definitions of what is human, how we approach the question of alterity and how we may regard the pleasure and pain of others.

Before proceeding any further, some clarification of terminology may be helpful. 'Self-harm' is generally understood as referring to deliberate and conscious acts such as cutting or burning one's own skin, superficially and more seriously; this is the phrase most prominently used within popular culture, particularly within the United Kingdom. Gloria Babiker and Lois Arnold discuss potential difficulties of definition in their *The Language of Injury: Comprehending Self-Mutilation* and suggest that 'self-harm' is too broad a categorization, referring as it does to a wider spectrum of self-destructive behaviour that also includes suicide (this is problematic for reasons that shall be elaborated upon later). Their conclusion is that 'self-mutilation' and 'self-injury' may be the most appropriate terms: the former being preferred by many of the individuals who do it, and the latter most accurately describing the 'spoiling' of the skin or actual damage done to the body (Babiker & Arnold 1997: x). More recent accounts within psychiatry and medical discourse have also favoured the use of the term 'self-harm' for a broader range of behaviours, including those with suicidal intent, and self-injury or self-mutilation to refer to non-lethal but deliberately injurious acts towards the self. In this chapter, my concern is with these non-suicidal forms, and in particular those which result in visible damage to the body in the form of marks such as cuts, burns, scabs or scars. The visibility of this damage is, in some cases, intentional, and plays a significant role in the meanings and experiences associated with these practices, both for the subjects themselves and within the social sphere. Armando Favazza's fascinating work in *Bodies Under Siege*, one of the most sustained and influential explorations of self-mutilation as a cultural phenomenon as well as a psychiatric one, is also suggestive about debates around definition. Favazza distinguishes between cultural forms of self-mutilation (such as certain tribal initiations) and what he terms 'pathological self-mutilation' that is associated with mental distress or illness. Here he discusses a variety of clinical cases covering a huge range of behaviours that include more common incidents such as inflicting cuts and patients sticking needles into their flesh, to those which do more permanent damage such as eye gouging and genital mutilation. Favazza's book is illuminating not only for the vast ranges of experiences included, which gives an insight into just how disparate these practices may be, but also because by including culturally accepted (or even demanded) self-injurious acts he crucially emphasizes that perceptions of normality and abnormality, sanity and insanity, with regard to the body and what is done with it or to it are always socio-culturally contingent, even when it comes to the seemingly finite limits of corporeal pain and harm. However, in maintaining to some extent the distinction between cultural and pathological self-mutilation, he fails to move away entirely from constructions that accord with more normative ideals. One of the central aims of this chapter will be to examine and challenge the theoretical and representational norms that have congealed around self-harm and that have served to conceptualize it primarily in relation to mental illness, perversion and self-destruction, situating the self-mutilated body as exterior to the realm of the proper and coherent 'human'. The process of challenging these deterministic norms requires an open address to questions of identity, the possibility of ethical encounters in the face of otherness and the transformative and generative potential of signifying corporeality.

Whilst there has been an increase in cultural depictions of self-mutilation in recent years as well as in psychiatric and medical explorations of the subject, within wider society it still retains its status as taboo and for most who practice it remains secretive and intensely personal. For those who witness it, responses range from perplexity to disgust to outrage, and are frequently accompanied by attempts to arrest, control or explain such behaviour. In many cases the extremity of the reaction to the idea or sight of the self-mutilated body with its cuts, scabs and bruises far outstrips the damage that has been done. A sense of disproportion surrounds self-harm; attitudes towards it simultaneously posit and respond to these wounded bodies as objectified spectacles to be apprehended through the gaze of cultural normativity and held up as 'damaged', to be figuratively and literally probed by institutional discourses that regulate the body and the subject. This disproportion is congruent both with the overdetermined cultural status of self-harm, and with the lack of desire to truly engage with or ethically address this embodied subject within a social order that places the integrity and coherence of the human body and mind above all other concerns. The ability to act with deliberate intention and self-determination is central to humanist understandings of the subject's place in the world; a part of the consternation and horror that self-mutilation evokes may be attributed to its perceived status as intentionality and deliberation gone awry, put to transgressive use that denies and mortifies the insistence of easily definable boundaries of sanity/insanity and pleasure/pain, whilst all the while attesting to the insistence of the body and skin in the realms of desire, openings and sensation. Thus both the acts themselves and the corporeal marks that function as persistent echoes of these acts are regarded as an affront to propriety and human identity.

When addressing the ways in which the self-mutilated body has been positioned as ahuman theoretically and in a more everyday context, there are two registers to consider, distinct yet remaining irrevocably interconnected. Firstly, the visceral and often involuntary response to the sight of wounded skin and flesh, to the visible marks on the body that evoke the vulnerability of the self and force a typically unwanted confrontation with the other who is at once too familiar and too alien. Secondly, the socio-cultural norms that govern the body and its relation to meaning-making; these norms can be detected in more 'intellectual' and reasoned responses to self-mutilation but also play a constitutive role in visceral, unthinking reactions in that they structure what is felt within the arena of abjection. Kristeva describes the encounter with abjection thus:

> A massive and sudden emergence of uncanniness, which, familiar as it might have been in an opaque and forgotten life, now harries me as radically separate, loathsome. Not me. Not that. But not nothing, either. A 'something' that I do not recognise as a thing. A weight of meaninglessness, about which there is nothing insignificant, and which crushes me. (Kristeva 1982: 2)

The self-mutilated body, with its wounds and scabs, with its blood and pus and unnatural openings, exists within this border space of simultaneously self and other, too much meaning and not enough meaning, its abject state 'disturbs identity, system, order' (Kristeva 1982: 4) and invokes an involuntary eruption of horror, repugnance and nausea from the spectator looking on. This response can also be situated in the context of the social significance placed upon the skin, the part of the body that is most frequently and most visibly affected. Skin, too, has become highly discursively determined in terms of how the subject conceives of themselves and their relationship with others and with the rest of the world, and is loaded with meanings pertaining to signs of identity and varying degrees of humanness: 'Skin is the site of encounter between the enfleshed self and society...Skin is a marked surface inscribed with texts of race, gender, sexuality, class and age' (MacCormack 2012: 22). Each of these aspects of identity organizes the be-skinned entity into a hierarchical strata that places them in closer or further proximity from the image of the ideal and flawless human espoused within humanist thought; then, within this overall schema into additional compartments of 'value' based upon socio-cultural notions of beauty and desirability, morality and propriety. The reconfiguration, typically labelled as damage, of this privileged organ and its always already designated social significance further accounts for the violent reactions towards self-injury as the desired spectacle of smooth and 'perfect' human surface is disturbed. The skin is already regulated according to particular norms, yet the skin of the self-harmer may perversely augment, nullify or actively refuse these norms. If the abject defies the oppositional structures that organize the social world into self/other, centre/margin, proper/improper, then skin itself occupies a categorically problematic and thus potentially enabling position as a border membrane:

> The information provided by the surface of the skin is both endogenous and exogenous, active and passive, receptive and expressive, the only sense able to provide the 'double sensation.'...the subject utilizes one part of the body to touch another, thus exhibiting the interchangeability of active and passive sensations, of those positions of subject and object, mind and body. (Grosz 1994: 35–36)

Skin, then, may maintain constraining conceptions of the subject and identity but may also function in some circumstances as a site of excessive disruption from which to challenge normative regulatory ideas about the body. Grosz's comments here also serve as a reminder that the appearance of self-injured skin, whilst crucial for a consideration of how it is culturally regarded, is only one aspect of this debate. The sensations involved with the processes of self-mutilation must also play a role in the dynamics between these acts and meaning-making; this shall be returned to shortly. Therefore, the body and particularly the skin of the self-harmer provides the means for calling attention to and disturbing symbolic structures of the subject that have long been held in place by cultural and political discourses. Just as Freud turned his attention to the 'problem' of masochism, a phenomenon that he regarded as seemingly 'incomprehensible' because of its apparently contradictory nature combining pleasure and unpleasure (Freud 1961: 155), so many theoretical accounts of and cultural attitudes towards self-injury have approached it as an enigma that must be unravelled and reconstructed in a more explicable way: an unacceptable conundrum to be solved through the rational application of psychiatry, medicine or similar institutional practices. Like masochism, self-harm emerges as a paradox that seems antithetical to the human instincts of self-preservation and pain-avoidance that are often assumed as self-evident. The primary drive behind the majority of existing conceptualizations has been to situate self-mutilatory practices within narratives that render them coherent within established frames of human understanding, thus sublimating the 'problem' of self-harm and its potential as a disruptive force into normative modes of psychical and physical activity. This urge towards the apparent imperative to explain and control self-harm has resulted in its co-option by various fields of discourse: psychiatry, literature, feminism, the media, amongst others, all desiring to dilute or deny the visceral disorder that it insists upon. This process renders the subject in question as an ahuman object, a 'self-harmer' (or the more specific label used particularly in the United States of America, 'cutter'), that needs to be studied, explained and 'cured'. Self-harm has thus been compartmentalized into a narrow selection of narratives recognizable within dominant modes of discourse, each imposing a restrictive framework of assumed meaning around it by (sometimes well-intentioned, sometimes less so) writers, doctors and theorists.

Two central assumptions that have emerged in popular culture are, firstly, the dismissive utterance that self-injury is 'just attention-seeking' and secondly, the almost diametrically opposed belief that it foretells of suicidal intent. Both of these ideas seem to be supported by testimonies given by self-identified 'cutters' in Marilee Strong's book *A Bright Red Scream*, a fascinating collection of interviews and descriptions about self-mutilation. However, whilst Strong offers some insightful and empathic discussion of these accounts, the compulsion remains in her work to organize them into discernible trajectories that can be traced back to emotional or psychological trauma, or traced forward to suicide or recovery. The acts themselves are placed within a determining chronology that disavows their elements of immediacy and rupture. The (mis)understanding of self-injury as 'attention-seeking' is congruent with its perceived association with an infantile, pre-linguistic state: expressing distress through the body is seen to indicate the inability to communicate via the 'civilized' and approved method of social language. This also situates such subjects as exterior to the realm of humanity that is governed by and reliant upon these rigid structures of language and meaning-making, thus, 'pre-linguistic' becomes equitable to 'pre-human'. Although within dominant modes of thought this exclusion would be considered negative and inextricably associated with the failure to adequately socialize, in fact it is in this position of refusal and exteriority that the radical and disruptive potential of self-mutilation may lie. The complex dynamics between self-injury and language, or more accurately self-injury and signification, will be elaborated upon later in this chapter. For now, the second and equally problematic tendency identified earlier needs addressing: the assumption that situates self-mutilatory acts within the negativity of suicidal desire. This constructs these smaller acts of injury as meaningful as a microcosm of or precursor to the broader desire for an absolute nullification of the body and self. Favazza states that until very recently, 'in both professional and popular thought, self-mutilation was regarded generally as a type of suicidal behaviour' (Favazza 1996: 232). Whilst this perception may have lessened within medical and psychiatric disciplines, in popular culture this association arguably remains dominant (for example, the character of Daisy in James Mangold's 1999 film *Girl, Interrupted*). The compulsive urge to connect even superficial instances of cutting that may do little or no lasting damage with the much more serious wish to end one's life may seem peculiar given that it manifests a sort of cultural desire towards suicide. However, this explanation serves to assign a specific intention and to absorb these acts into a goal-orientated structure that whilst nihilistic, accords nonetheless with an emphasis on aim over process, the end as opposed to the immediate. The assumed future act of suicide is used to explain what otherwise appear as random present acts of cutting, burning or ingesting (and certain types of self-harm in particular seem to adhere to this narrative, for example the flesh wounds inflicted by the 'cutter' seem to foretell of wrist-slashing, or the swallowing of toxins providing a preamble to the fatal overdose). However, the processual and repeated nature of self-harming ultimately renders this narrative obsolete: to the outside (and non-'expert') viewer, the failure of the final and finite act to materialize only seems to exacerbate the sense of horror and incomprehension that is evoked. Favazza observes that the activities and injuries of the 'self-harmer' are often regarded as even more shocking, disgusting and baffling than suicide, because from an external point of view they may seem utterly pointless. The suicidal subject attains an ultimate point of finality: their action is goal-orientated and thus more comprehensible. The self-harming subject, however, remains 'very much alive and able to haunt us in the flesh' (Favazza 1996: 288–289). This description of the self-mutilated body as transgressive spectre is reminiscent of Kristeva's description of the abject as 'death infecting life' (1984: 4). The self-harmer appears as an offensive stain, disrupting socially established meanings of corporeal identity and acting as an eruption of visible suffering that exceeds understanding. This calls to mind the eponymous protagonist of 'The Hunger Artist' in the short story by Kafka, a writer who as Favazza says, 'perhaps more than any other, has succeeded in developing self-mutilation as a most peculiar and penetrating literary genre' (1996: 18). A circus performer finds that his once-admired ability to fast for days falls from favour but still refuses to eat, sinking lower and lower in the dirty straw of his cage and remaining for weeks as a living cadaver that refuses to recover or to perish quickly and decently. 'A small impediment, a smaller and smaller impediment ... ' (Kafka 2000: 313). This imagery is imprinted onto the mind of the reader, lingering, haunting yet too-tangible.

In the instances in which self-harm is associated in any way with more positive types of representation, it is within what could be described as therapeutic or redemptive narratives, seen in popular culture in films like *Secretary* (Steven Shainberg, 2002), as well as in psychiatric texts such as those by Strong or Babiker and Arnold. These may appear to provide an alternative mode of understanding to the juvenile/suicidal dichotomy, but in fact function according to a comparable rhetoric of pathology and goal-oriented finality that similarly works to reaffirm the position of a 'proper' human subject. Within such understandings, the psychical and physical experiences associated with self-mutilation are contextualized in terms of a necessary suffering taking place within an overall schema of self-healing and recovery. Karl Menninger was the first to suggest self-injury as a form of self-healing and although this observation was not heeded for several decades (as Favazza notes, 1996: 232), it has gradually become another pervasive cultural understanding. The initial diagnosis of self-destruction must be made in order that the idealized progression from unhealthy and abject thing to healthy subject with a healed body and mind can be tracked, and the effectiveness of social institutions such as psychiatry, or in the case of *Secretary* love and marriage, witnessed and confirmed, delivering the organism back to humanity by ironically being offended at its refusal of the perceived base zero of the life drive of its animal definition. Again, the positions of centre and margin are reestablished and the social order is shored up against the dysfunctional otherness that threatens to puncture it.

To situate these discursively constructed narratives philosophically, and to begin to move beyond them, the ethical context of self-mutilation must be established. I will draw here upon two texts that offer rumination upon the relationship of the self to the other and on the concept of the human: Lyotard's short discussion of the photographs of female hysterics taken at the Salpêtrière hospital in the late nineteenth century in 'Speech Snapshot', and Judith Butler's book *Precarious Life*, written in the aftermath of 9/11 and in response to the polemical 'us/them' rhetoric that subsequently emerged in the United States and elsewhere. The notion of automatic empathy invoked by the visible suffering of another is one of the great myths of humanism; as Butler argues, this notion is demonstrably dependent on the extent to which this 'another' is perceived as a kindred type of human and is thus identifiable, and to what extent they appear as an unfamiliar alterity:

> Some lives are grievable, and others are not; the differential allocation of grievability that decides what kind of subject is and must be grieved, and which kind of subject must not, operates to produce and maintain certain

exclusionary conceptions of who is normatively human: what counts as a
liveable life and a grievable death? (Butler 2004: xiv–xv)

This articulates nicely the societal paradox of regarding the suffering of
others when this suffering is by no means seen as 'equal' in every case,
suggesting the discomforting but accurate proposition that only the 'human'
can suffer in a way that is deserving of attention or care. It can thus be
asked to what extent the empathy extended to those who self-mutilate is
dependent upon their lives being understood as adequately 'liveable' and
their suffering appropriately 'grievable'; is this only the case insofar as
the visibility of their experiences accords with culturally recognized and
approved narratives of infantile tendencies, suicidal intent or redemptive self-
healing? The notion of some kind of shared human state has been robustly
and necessarily criticized by theorists of the posthuman, the inhuman, the
non-human and, when considering the suffering of another, corporeal or
psychical, the inadequacy of the humanist model is thrown sharply into
relief. Susan Sontag states, 'No "we" should be taken for granted when
the subject is looking at other people's pain' (Sontag 2003: 6). Although
for the self-harmer themselves, actions, experiences and meanings may be
private and unique, it is clear that their place within the discursive terrain
of the social world unavoidably results in institutional and intersubjective
responses. Therefore, as Butler and Sontag prompt, it is vital to engage with
the various players in this dynamic and to enquire who or what is looking
as well as who is being looked at and how these looks might be mobilized
in such a way that normative dichotomies are disturbed.

Yet, again assumptions are manifest here, and in this ethical context
further questions must be raised – why is empathy necessarily presumed to
be the desired reaction to self-harm? It may be appropriate in some cases
but ineffectual, unasked for or simply irrelevant in others. Lyotard reminds
us of the need for an 'opening up' of the realm of interpretation through
questioning, rather than closing it off through prescriptive construction. In
reference to the Salpêtrière photographs he states:

So this is what you imagine: perhaps they have a soul, perhaps they hear
the question; but it is not your question and you do not hear their reply;
in principle you admit that the cries, contractions, fits and hallucinations
observed during the attacks are, in some sense, replies; so you give
yourself three things to construct – the language they speak with their
bodies, the question to which their 'attacks' respond and the nature of
what is questioning them. (Lyotard 1993: 130)

The problem that Lyotard draws attention to here is the same compulsion to
assign meaning from an external position, to talk about or to talk to rather
than to talk with, or to simply let be. This is the process of construction
he speaks of, a process that involves the 'language of prescriptions, not

questions' (Lyotard 1993: 131). I argued earlier that there is a strong cultural association of self-mutilation with the infantile, pre-linguistic state: raw wounds on arms and legs are regarded as an ahuman and primitive cry that exists outside the symbolic domain of accepted language, the 'Bright Red Scream' of Strong's title. As with Charcot's hysterics, forever captured as a spectacle to be examined and interpreted over and over, the discursive drive is to stabilize and explain these infantilized 'creatures'. If they cannot speak for themselves appropriately or understandably then others will speak for them or more accurately over them, 'translating' their perceived cries for attention or help into a more socially coherent language, delivering their perversion of animal life into human discourse.

The as-yet unspoken element looming at the intersection of hysteria and self-harm is of course gender and cultural conceptions of femininity. Like the female hysterics at Salpêtrière, the specifically corporeal and spectacular nature of these bodies is not neutral but caught up in a network of cultural ideas about how the female body should look, function and behave. Sustained studies demonstrate that those who self-injure are not just female, may be a variety of ages and ethnicities and from a variety of backgrounds; nonetheless, a 'typical' model of the self-harmer and specifically the 'cutter' has emerged within both popular culture and medical discourse and has proved remarkably persistent:

> A cutter profile was created by the first confluence of psychiatric interest in a 'delicate' form of self-mutilation: the delicate cutter is typically a white, adolescent girl...The white, suburban, attractive teenage girl persists as the face of self-mutilation. (Brickman 2004: 87)

Looking only to cinema here, this 'delicate cutter' is much in evidence in Western representations of self-harm, with *Girl, Interrupted*, *Secretary*, and *Thirteen* (Catherine Hardwicke, 2003) providing just a few recent examples. As Brickman argues through her article, the tendency is also prevalent in television, fiction, magazines and psychiatric literature. This 'typical' profile has served to privilege a certain form of self-harm (cutting) over others, whilst perpetuating the institutional structures that have situated women and girls as objects of scrutiny to be categorized and regulated by phallologocentric discourses such as medicine, psychiatry and art. In perspectives on hysteria and self-mutilation, femininity is constructed as equitable to pathology, an unhealthy relationship to one's own body and an inability to adequately enter social systems of language. This final point indicates the conflation of conceptual norms that position women as uncivilized, infantile and primitive with self-mutilation as ahuman and abject. The construction of the typical female cutter and their subjective position is also reliant on normative ideas about femininity in relation to beauty and the skin. If skin is imbued with meanings relating to its status as border between self and world/interior and exterior, as psychically invested surface of self-image and projected identificatory surface of the other, these meanings are also determined dependent on normative ideas about gender. Brickman argues that in order to accord with cultural standards of beauty, young female skin is required to appear as flawless and unmarked; such skin is coded as uniquely precious and thus the violation of it is regarded as particularly noteworthy and grotesque (Brickman 2004: 98). The perception of the female body and norms surrounding femininity and its relationship to signification are at stake here; however, specifically feminist responses to self-mutilation often remain prescriptive and condemnatory, another example of the co-option of these practices into a pointed political narrative. Louise J. Kaplan includes 'Mutilations' within her Female Perversions, placing this within the broader context of her thesis that patriarchy gives rise to various self-destructive pathologies for women and arguing that these behaviours result from 'a childhood of deprivation and trauma' and anxieties about gender identity and the body within patriarchy:

> Because the self-mutilator did not feel secure within her body in childhood, to her the expectable adolescent anxieties coalesce into an unsupportable mutilation anxiety. Her active and defiant gestures of self-mutilation are most directly a means of avoiding a passively suffered mutilation but also a method of forestalling final gender identity and denying that the illusions and hopes and dreams that made life endurable are lost forever. (Kaplan 1991: 364)

Although Kaplan allows for the possibility of self-injury as an active form of behaviour, she also conceptualizes it as entirely reactionary and overwhelmingly negative. The familiar associations are manifested again: of self-mutilation with arrested emotional development and a childlike psychical state, and with something inherently feminine and self-destructive that occludes the position of other gendered or non-gendered self-mutilatory identities. Most problematically, these practices are once again funnelled into a single and closed system of understanding which denies the vast range of different experiences and meanings that may actually be involved. The assumed alignment of self-harm with the female and with stereotypical femininity is perhaps reflective of women's socio-historical position as less-human object to the dominant and privileged male subject, an oppositional logic that remains to a large extent within contemporary societies as women continue to be measured in relation to the idealized standards of patriarchy. Women have, therefore, long been situated in closer proximity to the abject, the primitive and the ahuman. A Möbius strip-like logic is apparent here in which the default model of the self-harmer is assumed to be female because of these existing conceptualizations of gender, whilst simultaneously the notion of self-harm gains a particular social significance through its association with the state of femaleness. It is clear that gender has a part to play in these experiences and meanings, but to focus on this aspect alone is to ignore the broader question of the ahumanism of this particular kind of marked body.

Thus, the connection between self-mutilatory practices and the construction of meaning is a crucial area of consideration but is far from straightforward and often resists the social and political spaces allowed for it within culture. Insofar as it is possible to link self-harm to the process of meaning-making, it is not a type of meaning that is stable, unified or easily grasped. The sensations and significations connected with cutting, for example, are multiple and constantly shifting; to suggest just a few from this myriad selection, we might think of the sensation of cutting itself, those feelings associated with seeing skin part and blood well up (release, relief, eroticism, aesthetic appreciation), and later, the sight of the scabbing and the healing, the formation of a scar which changes its tone and texture as the weeks and months pass. Beyond this, contextual experiences such as associated music or locations, favoured instruments for carrying out the injuries, the feel of clothing over the wound or the insistent sensation of pulling that the movement of limbs can evoke. To conceive of one signifying framework that could account for all these processes and more – these physical and psychical sensations too numerous to list – is to remain bound to a repressive and institutionalized discourse that seeks to co-opt and control any body that refuses to adhere to the standardized codes of the human. The entry into language is regarded as instrumental to the processes of subjectivation and becoming 'properly' human, the underlying assumption to these accounts is that to be accepted as human (with all the rights, identities and intersubjectivities that this entails) is, to a large extent, reliant upon one's ability to exist within the peculiarly human symbolic world of intelligible shared systems of signification. Language, then, is associated with the social domain and structuring of the human. In this context, it is interesting to note that some of the writers of the less prescriptive accounts of self-harm discussed in this chapter make use of the term 'language' in the titles and the arguments of their books (for example, Strong's text is subtitled *Self Mutilation and the Language of Pain*, whilst Babiker and Arnold's *The Language of Injury* is equally as direct). This suggests that self-mutilation calls for a rethinking of more traditional theoretical models of language and the subject, one that offers less rigid boundaries and a much broader understanding of how signification may be manifested and experienced. Kristeva's *Revolution in Poetic Language* provides an invaluable starting point for this project, and in particular for an alternative philosophy of language in relation to the corporeal.

Kristeva argues that the codifying philosophies of language which dominate Western theory (linguistic, structuralist, psychoanalytic, and so on) have functioned as ossifying and possessive structures, acting as 'agents of totality' that withdraw the body from direct experience and repress the processual nature of subjectivity (Kristeva 1984: 14). The social mechanism and the way that language has been used and understood within it work to repress the generation of significance and once again to promote the normalizing image of the 'proper' social being or what Kristeva describes as 'the thinking subject, the Cartesian subject who defines his being through thought or language' (1984: 14). This mechanism and the disciplines that manifest and perpetuate it are to be emphatically understood as ideological structures of control that limit the subject and restrict the processes of signification; this, for Kristeva, is the symbolic modality of language and constitutes one part of the signifying process. The self-harming 'narratives' discussed earlier in this chapter may be regarded as strategies of symbolic language that aim to stratify the subject and their relation to their own bodies and the bodies of others within the constraints of dominant ideologies. Yet, there is more to the signifying process than this, although it has infrequently been recognized in dominant theories. Kristeva asserts that we must also look to the semiotic modality of signification, associated in her theory with non-verbal systems such as music, kinesis and gesture, and experienced more immediately, more viscerally. Although the subject and the processes of signification which constitute subjectivity and intersubjectivity arise from the dialectic between these two modalities, symbolic language has repeatedly been privileged over the semiotic chora, resulting in the undermining of corporeal experience and the denial of its role in the creation of meaning (Kristeva 1984: 24). Kristeva describes the chora as:

> Not yet a position that represents something for someone (i.e. it is not a sign); nor is it a position that represents someone for another position (i.e. it is not yet a signifier); it is, however, generated in order to attain to this signifying position. Neither model nor copy, the chora precedes and underlies figuration and thus specularization. (Kristeva 1984: 26)

Humanism aligns with, and indeed has been instrumental in privileging, the symbolic modality. It prizes the singular, the individual and the stable; it insists upon fixity through limited and proscribed forms of communication and signification. The chora consists instead of process and multiplicity, refusing to settle into any one pattern of identity or meaning. It is, therefore, antithetical to normative humanist models in terms of corporeality, subjectivity and their relationship to generative significance. Within the semiotic modality, it is not possible to speak from any single authoritarian position, and for this reason it is through the semiotic that revolutions against the dominant may be articulated or expressed. Here, too, lies the ethical potential of the semiotic as it offers an alternative to the restrictive symbolic framework within which one perspective may silence another. Self-mutilation, its processes and its marks, can be seen to belong to the modality of the semiotic chora as opposed to symbolic language. It moves towards signification but does not act as a singular sign that can be easily read or identified, instead manifesting a process that is inextricable from embodiment and that opens out into a multiplicity of potential meanings, preceding and exceeding the symbolic language that strives to structure and control it. When Grosz describes the 'landscape' of the skin as comprising 'the articulation of orifices, erotogenic rims, cuts on the body's surface, loci of exchange between inside and outside' (Grosz 1994: 36), recognizable within this description are both Kristeva's semiotic chora, which maps and remaps the body in a constant and never complete process of resignification, and the modified body of the self-mutilating subject with its cuts, ridged scars and newly created areas of erotic investment. Wounds manifest themselves as novel and self-determined openings, bruises create new spectrums of colour, scar tissue that is devoid of feeling may serve to heighten sensation when the surrounding skin is touched: these areas upon the evolving landscape of the body provide a redistribution of intensities that is not constrained by socially designated investments in specific body parts or corporeal acts.

So, the processes of self-injury and the transformation that they effect on the body of the subject are part of this generation of signification. But the actual sensation of pain is also crucial here, as a wilful inversion of Elaine's Scarry's thesis in the fascinating and unsurpassed *The Body in Pain* suggests. Scarry's concern is the question of how physical suffering may structure the subject's experience of the world around them and their position within it, with one of her central claims being that physical pain carries with it the ability to 'utterly nullify the claims of the world' (Scarry 1985: 33). The attention and perspective of the subject in pain shrinks inward from the expanse of their surroundings to the focussed and inescapable demands of the body, and inward further still to the specific point of injury. The body becomes the world, the wound the locus of this world. Everything else becomes meaningless, exterior to the senses. A crucial part of this process of 'unmaking the world' as conventionally or symbolically understood is the capability of physical pain to dismantle language. This results in 'the twofold denial of the human, both the particular human being hurt and the collective human present in the products of civilisation' (Scarry 1985: 43). In the examples that Scarry explores, the enforced removal of the tortured subject's linguistic capability by the torturer is regarded as absolutely central to the process of dehumanization inherent in this violent act. This refers not only to speech, but to the internal ability to organize one's thoughts along linguistic lines. To deny a subject language is to deny them the very position of subjectivity, to remove them from language is to remove their humanity. Further, the very idea of 'civilization' is threatened through the destruction of one of its most potent signifiers, according with the presupposition of a particular relationship to language that being human necessitates. Whilst Scarry's focus on torture and the conflicts of war mean that she frames this idea of the loss of language and the loss of this particular idea of the 'human' within a highly negative framework, taking her discussion of the 'unmaking of the world' in conjunction with Kristeva's concept of semiotic signification allows for a recasting of the effects of physical pain in a different light. If the definition of 'the human' as it stands in our social world is inherently problematic, might the deliberate infliction of physical pain upon the self serve to 'unmake the world' in a more active sense, to move towards the disintegration of the rigid structures of order and meaning that have, after all, worked to codify identity and subjectivity according to an exclusionary schema? This is not to advocate or glorify self-mutilation as a specific strategy of political resistance, but to posit it as a potential site within which the subject may present a challenge to the symbolic and begin to generate meaning in a different way, a way that is entirely embodied, indifferent to or defiant of the designated uses and appearances of the flesh, and that eludes any fixed experience and interpretation. Only through the process of unmaking the human expression of the world, through the 'rupture and articulations' (Kristeva 1984: 26) of the semiotic order, might the possibility of different systems of signification and subjectivity emerge. And just as the chora catalyses a constant and never-ending process of making and remaking, over and over, so the ruptures articulated upon the skin through self-mutilation insist upon the opening up not just of the body, but of meaning-making itself as a practice of expansion and multiplicity. The corporeality of self-mutilation materializes excess and disruption, through this calling for a dismantling and recreation of the social world and our place within it.

CHAPTER ELEVEN

After Life

Patricia MacCormack

Ahuman ethics occupy an ecosophical terrain of thought coalescent as material, affective and activist. Ahuman ethics operate via an ecological consistency. The difficult conundrum of ethical address to alterities, while resisting holding any one organism as inherently posthuman, inhuman, ahuman, animal, other (whatever any of these words may mean) or even reducible in reference to itself, is a difficulty which both shows the need for and catalyses creativity in reference to rethinking lives. Guattari states, 'The ecosophical perspective does not totally exclude a definition of unifying objects ... but it will no longer be a question of depending on reductionist, stereotypical order-words' (2000: 34). Encounters with ahuman conceptuae (concepts, personae and their co-emergence, including with their own selves, inter- and intra-connectivities) are events of joy and necessity. Encounters with animals or ourselves as animals (defined as either resonant with or as failed humans) take those same terms in order to reduce manufacturing of continuous power machines. What ahumanism is or could be is, finally, what essentials urge its conceptuae, what wrongs are redirected through encounters, what paths created, what thought opened and what outside glimpsed. For oppressive machines, the ahuman aberrant is required to isomorphically raise the status of the majoritarian, and the future hurtling posthuman's future is only as a cog in that operation of ascension. Ecosophical and eco-minoritarian elements of ahuman theories seek to alter this monodirectional system. However, if they do so, would we still be the 'humans (however "post" or "a") connected with or acting like ... ', and would it, as it has been argued, ultimately benefit us too, be *good for us*? The question is, are we ready to give up all human referents? This kind of utilitarian imperative, noble and radical though it is, changes the relations but perhaps never entirely allows escape from persistent terms, or terminologies, even while we grapple with learning to speak silently and think otherwise. Without being pessimistic, is it viable or even possible to ask if we can ever enter into entirely posthuman, inhuman, ahuman becomings? When the human becoming-imperceptible politic dissipates the human into collective molecular assemblages with environment and cosmos, when I becomes we, is it not still *our* task, and *our* multiplicities, and *our* assemblages because primarily our ecological and philosophical disasters we seek to rectify and our being (whatever that may be) we seek to undo and reform?[1] Are any ethical experiments fatally human projects of cosmic connectivity? As categories melt, entities hybridize, what will be recognizable as human? Is this aspiration for the answer being 'nothing' in its actualization something towards which ahuman life is authentically capable? I do not mean to raise demands for pay offs or results, antagonistic to becomings and the opening for new potentialities, but thinking the unthinkable has varyingly easier and more perplexing ways to move towards next steps in new ethical relations. This chapter will attempt to show that, like the other examples of ahuman life *The Animal Catalyst* has offered, there is one example of a response belonging to the easier way. That is, an openness to the very viability of the continuation of what was formerly called the human – the cessation of the reproduction of human life.

Extinction is activism in three ways. The first is imaginatively expressing and accounting for the life we live even though it was not chosen. It validates the inevitability of life and may lead to decisions that give that life its freedom through its perpetuation or extinguishment.[2] The second, more extreme form of activism, comes from the decision which acknowledges life is inevitable and beyond the control of that emergent life, but this life may control its finitude, through suicide.[3] Nonetheless 'this death always comes from without, even at the moment when it constitutes the most personal possibility' (Deleuze 1994: 113). Suicide is a recombining of chaos potentials that results in waves of particle affects which precede and exceed the tentative myth of absence/presence but that comes from a certain will to a new occupation of cosmic consistency. Vitalistic suicide is not a cop out, nor is living necessarily a choice to be a certain kind of subject. Life continues after suicide through affect. The first two elements are entwined in that to die is to die actively, to live to affect others for the express purpose of affecting others so they may live vitalistically, Blanchot's passivity that is active love without condition or mastery: 'it is in *friendship* that I can respond, a friendship unshared, without reciprocity, friendship for that which has passed, leaving no trace. This is passivity's response to the un-presence of the unknown' (Blanchot 1995: 27). Coming from these elements, the third is accepting that choosing not to reproduce entails vigilance for immanent lives. It opposes hedonism which would privilege our lives, as the last generation, as free to do what we wish and decimate what is left, just as postmodernity does not replace the single subject with multiplicity as being and doing anything without purposeful acknowledgement of affectivity. All three projects enrich life. They emerge based on necessity; neither the move after the next nor the entire narrative can be predicted in advance. Problems for the far future are complaints (not unviable but also not productive) which reduce the life of the open future and so limit the expressivity of imaginings of openings. Are the pragmatics of concerns over what will happen a few activist moves down towards extinction so different from contemporary concerns over impending deaths by dissymmetry of resources and war in the world and its presumed futures? Guattari states, 'In the final account, the ecosophical problematic is that of the production of human existence itself in new historical contexts' (2000: 34). Guattari advocates the philosopher as futurist, and futurity as the jubilant purpose of rethinking subjectivity and relationality. It would be a mistake to understand the cessation of the human as a denial of futurity. The future is not discontinued as a result of human disappearance, it is the very definition of what an imperceptible, cosmic, immanent future can be because it is future without thinking in advance as a thinking human. In order to be accountable ahumans, near futures, tactical little goals and strategic unification of issues in order to increase the expressivity of other lives are nodular moments towards the ultimate creative future of joy, which the human cannot think and to which, if the future is the real goal of ahumanism, even while it attests to the present being the location of that goal and its activisms, the human cannot belong. Jeffrey McKee claims the ultimate casualty of human expansive population growth is biodiversity itself, 'both extinction and population growth are natural phenomena. What is unnatural is the magnitude of both trends in today's world. And what is unusual is that one species has a choice to alter the course of things to come' (2003: 171). This emphasizes that diversity is the greatest sacrifice, structures of multiplicity, connectivity and immanence are the main casualties of human population and while the structure itself is destroyed, ethical interaction is impossible between individual lives. Extinction means nothing in ethical consideration when single, real lives in their unique emergence and duration are the crux of relational considerations between lives. Doug Cocks states, 'Extinction of the individual, the species or the ecosystem occurs when it has no pre-programmed response rule for an eventuating environment or cannot devise such a rule…a problem to be solved [assimilation]…to be dealt with [accommodation]' (2003: 230). Programming and resolution are notoriously human compulsions. From a humanist perspective, they are viable as much for the power they produce as for the benefits they afford. Humans may be most adept ethically at accommodation of this world through our absence. Because humans invented the concept of species itself (leading to speciesism and denying lives or the dead) they must be the species to change the becomings to come. These must not include our own becomings beyond the becoming-imperceptible. Perhaps a perversely literal interpretation of Deleuze and Guattari's call to becoming-imperceptible is to define imperceptibility as absolute absence. Perceptible by whom is the question that leads to those who perceive often being victims of perception as an encounter with affects produced by the entity perceived. The affects of human existence are immeasurable. Measure adheres to value both as quantity and quality: 'The question is not how many people the Earth or the universe can support, but rather, which people it can support, which existences. Number here, immediately converts its magnitude into moral magnitude: the size of humanity becomes indissociable from its dignity' (Jean-Luc Nancy 2000: 180).

Reproduction, or rather the repudiation of reproduction, underpins posthuman theory. Serres states:

> The perpetrators of bloody domination may well have been thrilled to find this world and seize the laws of determination, theirs, the same as theirs, those of extermination…Then Mars rules the world, he cuts the bodies into atomized pieces and lets them fall…law in the sense of dominant legislation…the law is the plague…Reason is the fall. The reiterated cause is death. Repetition is redundancy. And identity is death. (2000: 109)

Ahuman theory deals explicitly with the death of identity, because the demand for identity, to be identified by the identity which one has been proscribed and which one must accept to register as an identity, is where lives emerge as the cells of signifying systems. Of extinction and ethicists at the end of the world, John Leslie critiques Emotivists, Prescriptivists, Relativists (but somehow not himself as a Utilitarian) for seeking a complete and accurate version of reality, querying 'how one could ever say humbly that one's own present ethical standards, even if fully self-consistent, may be mistaken' (1998: 160). While he argues against privileging Cartesian life as subjectivity over lived-life, this emphasis on a subjective ethical map as consistent requires a consistent subjectivity first. Both Leslie and prescriptivism then mistake morality for ethics.

Dominant systems need repetition both to maintain their power and to make alterations which would disprove their claimed logic quietly without being perceived as rupturing their own operations. The bodies which populate *The Animal Catalyst* antagonize reproduction, and in their audacious celebratory existences they deny the phantasy of reproduction constituting life. How can we consider absence and cessation without sacrifice? Can the end of the human without replacement be a creative, jubilant, affirmation of 'life', where life is defined as affect and thus the ambition towards the cessation of the human in existence a celebration of the capacity for other lives to express opened through the removal of human affectivity? Of life, Spinoza and death, Gatens and Lloyd state:

> To understand our eternity – which in our less enlightened state we conceptualise through the illusion of a continued existence after death – we are to engage, Spinoza tells us, in an exercise of 'feigning'. We are to consider the mind, that is, as if it were beginning to exist, and now beginning to understand itself as eternal. Despite the contradiction which

reason can discern in the exercise, it is harmless, he assures us, provided we know what we are doing. The fictions of the wise allow glimpses of the deep truths which elude reason operating without imagination. (Gatens & Lloyd 1999: 38)

While explicators of Spinoza would operate under the consensus that will and appetite strive towards joy which is averse to death and which makes suicide unthinkable as irrational, I wish to adapt this idea another way. Spinoza states of death: '*A free man thinks of nothing less than of death, and his wisdom is a meditation on life*' (1994: 151 original emphasis). Wisdom comes from reason as imagination. Spinoza urges us to think the eternity of our lives while aware this is both fallacious and makes us irrational. However, as rationality in Spinoza is borne of self-preservation – the will to continue through which essence is found – knowing the impossible, the event which repudiates our existence, our rationality and our preservation while simultaneously refusing it by exchanging it for the concept of eternity without us, creates an intra-affective ethics, a molecular terrain of disagreement and conscious incommensurability which itself sustains us. Spinoza's request for self-understanding as meditation on the mind's eternity posits the self and mind as continuously germinal, a perpetual beginning which unravels via the multiple trajectories within the mind's multiple intra-affects and their collisions and mutations with the affects of others. The will has no absolute beginning, nor established stasis, nor perceptible end. We know all three things while knowing our claim to know them is feigned. Life is this way understood as the infinite beginnings which teeter upon potentialization at each constellation of interaction and relation. If what we claim to know as 'human' life were sought to cease, this does not necessarily conform to what Spinoza defines as suicide or even death. The gradual cessation of human life on Earth and in the Universe is the beginning of the contemplation of the eternity of life affects, of the life of all ecosophical cosmic interaction. This can be understood in the renegotiation of what is meant by a will, an appetite, a self, or rather, where we draw the lines between different incarnations of these. Already the self is made up of multiple interactive affective selves (what, in many philosophies after Leibniz, Deleuze and Serres, could be called the soul), while the cosmos is a singular consistency. If each entity aspires to greater perfection, thus greater joy, if human life was an element of the cosmos which facilitated lesser or greater perfection, we must ask to what extent the cessation of human life would increase joy? Of course this is an unanswerable question. But my point here is that contemplating the cessation of human occupation of Earth and space is the opposite of being against a meditation on life. Just as we can never know what the lives to come will be, yet we think them, or we can never know our own life after death, while knowing there is no hermeneutic absolute concept of either, forsaking the repetition and reproduction of the human cannot know its effect but can encounter life as the ultimate unthinkable outside, and the freedom of man which Spinoza celebrates becomes freedom of life itself without man. The lesser man, the bound man, is the man led only by affect (as reactive) or opinion, the greater man by reason (Spinoza 1994: 151) which is consciousness as imagination.

The perpetuation of human life as human subjectivity is arguably an *a priori* presumption, a reaction to predetermined culture, against a vitalistic, entirely unique event, and borne of the opinion that one should perpetuate the species which requires the species precede the qualities which would presumably be used to vindicate its perpetuation. Put simply, joy at the celebration of life must ethically define life as a connective consistency, not my, one or human life. Nancy states, 'The speaker speaks for the world, which means the speaker speaks to it, on behalf of it, in order to make it "a world"' (2000: 3). Ahuman theory consistently seeks the silencing of what is understood as human speech emergent through logic, power and signification. Human speech makes the world according to the human, tells the world what it is and speaks for the world, that is, to other humans and to the gods of human speech – religion, science, capital, the family (of man). Silencing human speech opens a harmonious cacophony of polyvocalities imperceptible to human understanding, just as human speech has the detrimental effect of silencing unheard, unthought expression.

Human life has demarcated itself as an object, demarcated the world into objects and by this operation, facilitates, vindicates and perpetuates its own object-ness. Its object-ness is its subjectivity, its subjectivity the impossibility for other life to be. Our access to the life of other life as it lives and perceives rather than as our object is irreducibly absent. Human knowledge of life sacrifices that life, conceptually and actually. 'The sacrificer needs the sacrifice in order to separate himself from the world of things and the victim could not be separated from it in turn if the sacrifice was not already separated in advance' (Bataille 1992: 44). Most importantly 'this is a monologue and the victim can neither understand nor reply' (Bataille 1992: 44). The sacrificer gives other life its value through withdrawing it from a world in which the sacrificer is sovereign ruler as a result of the lament that the sacrificer has lost intimacy as life. The world of gods and the divine in this instance occupies the place which excesses of signification, capital and power have evacuated. The further estranged from life the human becomes, the more non-human elements and actual lives we humans drag with us in order to rectify this estrangement. The sacred and the divine are worlds which the human has created because this world is both too much and not enough. Nature is the jubilant infinite beyond what we can perceive or encounter, and excised though we attempt to be from it, we are a result of it, subjects to a sovereign with no intent, design or flexing of might. Nature is not eco-privileging. It is every connectivity potential in the world, the world and cosmos themselves, and each life in its most unassuming and barest living. We have separated ourselves from nature and claimed to have redeemed it by making it 'better' through manipulating those particles of chaos which antagonize will or control over destiny. In this sense modern (and postmodern) science, law and state are no different in our investment in them to the need for oracles and fate. 'Nature is reduced to human nature, which is reduced to either history or reason. The world has disappeared ... Curiously, reason acquires in the legal sphere a status quite similar to the one it had acquired in the sciences: the laws are always on its side because it founds law' (Serres 2002: 35). In contemporary desires to rectify some of what we have perpetrated, to turn our address to ecological and environmental issues, welfare and the redistribution of freedom we still fail to allow natural law (which we still define as external to the human, yet only we demarcate, separate and define externality) to govern, because natural law must be resonant with human logic. For the human, a law of nature is unthinkable. Nature itself in its current conception is a phantasy precisely because it is inconceivable, as Serres states: the world does not exist. What could be more simple, in order to allow the world to exist, then, than leaving it be? 'Issues', 'welfare' and 'nature' continue to dismember the world into pieces which are consumable but which fail to sufficiently (and efficiently) understand the connectivity that is all the world and in which human connections are few but their encroachments and effects are innumerable both immanently and continuously. Abolitionist ahuman ethics are only truly possible if we are not here.

Ahuman ethics seek new silences through which to speak and hear. If, simultaneous with the most desperate attempts to host the world more than we parasite from it while we remain, we can celebrate the death of the human – as subjectivity and ultimately as extinct – we are operating in the most creative of new spaces, the spaces in the world but which we never accessed. 'Go look for death' writes Serres, 'down in this world you allow yourself a thousand peaceful acts: to sleep, dream, talk, on and on, relax your attention' (2002: 111). Serres shows that death offers the world's spaces we choose to refuse, and which language conceals. Far from the violent destruction perpetuated through human regimes – Serres' Order of Mars – this death – the sacrifice to Venus in and from nature – makes the world strange, subtle, incandescently beautiful. It is harmonious with our new senses and posthuman ethical modes of perception. Civilization chases off death, but death opens up and occupies remote and strange worlds, 'everyone considers these worlds dangerous, but what they actually call for is simple presence' (Serres 2002: 113). Serres' worlds to which death leads us teach us other worlds are the opposite of the sacred worlds through which the sacrifice assures the stubborn and fearful human subject. Human extinction differs from sacrifice: we are not being sacrificed by nature in order to save it in the same way we as humans unethically sacrifice other lives to save ourselves from imminent death as annihilation. Nature does not want to sacrifice us. Investing nature with a destructive will overvalues our absence and once again returns us to the legislator and signifier of things. Conceiving human absence as sacrifice is an insipid response that claims we

give a gift of the most valuable element in nature – humans – in order to save
the nature we have manipulated. Human sacrifice is another manipulation.
Sacrifice of others or ourselves is life lived in death. Death in nature which
opens other worlds is the simple presence of life living. The absence of the
human is the most vital living yet to be accomplished: it is life lived as life.
Our accursed share is a life lived in horror at and refusal of our absence,
whereas

> life that is good is interested only in death, which, in exchange, shapes it.
> Once past the other worlds that stimulate our own, we will cast off anew
> towards death, our origin, to be reborn ... we have all become astronauts,
> completely deterritorialized: not as in the past a foreigner could be when
> abroad, but with respect to all humankind. (Serres 2002: 114, 120)

In this sense through the worlds death opens we apprehend the gravity of
the actions perpetrated upon lives to create the nation of the dead while
gifting ourselves actual life. Ethically, this new life lived in the worlds to
which our finitude introduces us makes us live differently, life configured in
wondrous unthought of ways which benefit nature through our becoming
more hospitable, less parasitic, more creative and productive in our
connections and the opportunities of expressivity we encounter from a
world territorialized constantly anew. The cosmic both extricates us from
the world we know and the knowledge that destroys the world while also
placing us inextricably within that world – the world become the encounter
with outside as we dream, sleep and imagine. Through managing what we
have done to the earth while we live, in an attempt to further its freedom for
expressivity, not with guilt but joy, allows us accountability with immanence
and futurity rather than a constant address to the past. 'Never forget the place
from which you depart, but leave it behind and join the universal. Love the
bond that unites your plot of earth with the Earth, the bond that makes kin
and stranger resemble each other' (Serres 2002: 50). Resemblance without
homogenization, land without sovereign and love without structuring
relation or condition are subtle, gracious interactions with the earth,
earths, ordinary emergences of and from the earth. Earth is matter itself, its
constellations, lives and relations unthinkable but everywhere and everyday
in the sense that they are constantly surprising without reason, and unique
without name. It is clear these new worlds are without much, even without
anything, certainly without humans, and so teeming with everything beyond
human comprehension. Everything the earth is left without in the cessation
of life as human and human lives converts to the within, a wholeness that
liberates becomings while the human is left behind, in time and purpose, in
signifying slaughter and actual destruction in its maintenance. Consistently
we see an earth emerge via the 'not' and the 'without', the very antithesis
of lack and irresolvable with lament. When all is lost to the human an
overwhelming everything arrives and the things we can do for the earth will

further this everything. Life as present to itself resolves any hint of absence in becoming-imperceptible, it is secret life.

> The secret is elevated from a finite content to the infinite form of secrecy. This is the point at which the secret attains absolute imperceptibility, instead of being linked to a whole interplay of relative perceptions and reactions...a nonlocalizable *something* that has happened. (Deleuze & Guattari 1987: 288)

What can we do now in and for the world? It must be a secret form of activism because it operates via tactics of unknowability, unpredictability and actions that take aim without a project, though its connectivities and hoped-for affects are contemplative, thoughtful and openings created beneficial. Secret humans are vitalistic in our repudiation of imperceptibility as absence. Ethical imperceptibility limits diminishment of the expressivity of the earth – we live a quiet undetectable life – and produces joyous openings for the earth's expressivity – a secret making things happen.

Ecosophy requires humans

> to bring into being other worlds beyond those of purely abstract information, to engender Universes of reference and existential Territories where singularity and finitude are taken into account by the multivalent logic of mental ecologies and by the group Eros principle of social ecology; to dare to confront the vertiginous Cosmos so as to make it inhabitable; these are the tangled paths of the tri-ecological vision. (Guattari 2000: 67)

Love is the catalyst for the posthuman ethical force. The ultimate love may be the acknowledgement that, while the tenets of the secret society's tactics are incremental, adaptive and thoughtful relations with the outside which are known only in small advance and thus not mapped in a project towards finitude, making the Cosmos inhabitable takes first the refusal of the privilege of 'the' human and in unpredictable developments, inhabitability of the Earth contingent on human extinction. In attempts to be hosts, we are actually being incidentally gifted the role of parasite towards joyous affects – our expressivity is challenged and extended while we launch upon the creation and habitation of other worlds within, and thus our pleasures are taken from these worlds and their affects independent of our detrimental diminishing force. For Deleuze and Guattari, like Nietzsche, Blake and Crowley, the basest level of human subjectivity that is ripe for becomings is the germinal, larval child, yet to be quickened into any position and who has their body stolen from them first. If, then, we were to explain to a child, with their strange machines of connection and comprehension, ahuman ethics inspired by Spinoza and developed by twentieth and twenty-first century theory, we could simply state these ethics are indescribable relations and connectivities seeking, in secret and silence and invisibility, and never arriving at the sought. They are instigated by the life we must immanently live in order to respect the death that we perpetrate. We thank as making our living joyous, the opening of all other organisms and their relations. Joy and thought become entwined. For Spinoza thought is a thing's power to increase, that is, to alter, transform, develop and expand, so the differentiation of the thing directly correlates with its liberty. Ethics as a system of relation makes each thing's essence come from preservation irreducibly independent from confirmation of similarity to itself at each moment. The gift of liberty is allowing the power of the other to expand towards unknown futures. To diminish the other's capacity to multiply and extend its capacities is, in Spinoza, hate. Hate is a form of pleasure – 'he who conceives the object of his hate is destroyed will feel pleasure' (1957: 41). Thus all force, both love and hate, is desire. And all force is affect.[4] But further, ahuman ethics are based on the premise that all conception is hateful ethics: in a deliberate truncated reading of Spinoza's claim ahuman theory acknowledges that 'he who conceives the object destroys the object', imposing a claim upon a body conditional on monodirectional exertions of perception as conception, limiting expressivity without limit. Ethical encounters are different to Kant's morality of benevolent totalizing ascension without qualification for which aesthetics (and thereby a certain definition of representation and perception) is responsible. The distance, even though unknowable, between things by which Kant and Hegel operate, even taking into account Hegel's criticism of Kant's claim that natural beauty is co-equivalent with the spiritual and artistic, is closed with Spinoza's intimacy of organisms liberated or oppressed by expression of the other by the self and the openings to joy which seek to expand through thought without knowledge. Serres opposes perception as a war waged against creation as an act of love: 'The text on perception ends with conception' (Serres 2000: 38–39). Further to this, Spinoza says *the world would be much happier if men were as fully able to keep silence as they are to speak* (1957: 30 original emphasis). Expressing entities (bodies, forces, connective planes) in inextricable proximity involves a threefold ethical consideration – the critique of the detrimental effect a claim to knowledge of another body perpetrates; address as creative expressivity opening the capacity for the other to express; acknowledgement and celebration of the difficult new a-system of bio-relations as an ongoing, irresolvable but ethical for being so, interactive, mediative project of desire. Fèlix Guattari calls this *'sense without signification'* (2011: 59), a language of sensation between.

Ahuman ethics are the between, the third in a relation between one, two and many. They activate as passage. They are the desire that we are. They come from and teach us how to love.

Who is love? Look at him well. He is a relation; he is the intermediary, he is the passage again, the pass; he is what passes, quasi object, the quasi-subject ... Who is love? He is the third man [sic], the son of lack and of passage, pass and lack ... love is the third; it is third, between two. It is exactly the included third. (Serres 2000: 241–242)

The cessation of reproduction may seem unthinkable, even mad. But life itself cannot exist in the perpetuation of human subjectivity – for formerly human life nor for any other. Many arguments may be made for the idiocy of suggesting extinction, both practical and moral, and many suggestions made for how we can continue sustainably. These questions return indeterminably all worlds to us, to our thought, our practices, our legislations and ultimately suggesting the world belongs to us, whether as desecrators or custodians. Is this love for an imperceptible unknowable other? Love the passage moves the world through relations which are defined by love itself; nothing exists except in its relationality. All life lacks in solitude. Without relation, within self and with external forces, life lacks. Humans continue to show their want for interaction with non-humans. Want is monodirectional; love is gracious acknowledgement of the relations we have made and those we must inevitably continue to make. Love will not cease at human absence, just as life has not ceased in post-subjectivity theory. The millions of considerations of what will happen are for our secret projects which are based on need as they arrive. If the question of human extinction seems ridiculous, the very least we can offer as an act of love is an ethical address to the purpose of why we see its need to continue. Questions are secret, because the answers exist only in the creation of new questions. Ahuman ethical questions shift from 'what am I?', 'why am I?' and open up the infinite thought found in the gracious, quiet, secret and effulgent query 'what is love?'.

Notes

1 Baofu sees the future of the human when identified as post-modern post-human extinction with a new transcendental humanism: The spread of floating consciousness across the cosmos without biochemical constitution, and the emergence of hyper-spatial consciousness in multiple dimensions of space-time in this world. But he retains the idea of the *'mastering* of complexity in the cosmos' and *'understanding* and *manipulating* complexity' (245, my emphasis).
2 This is the system underpinning the political agenda of the Voluntary Human Extinction Movement. www.vhemt.org
3 The positive elements of suicide as vitalism are becoming increasingly present in writings which explore both the suicide of many philosophers and also the fallacy of suicide as a result of, and inextricable with, despair. See, for example, Braidotti (2006: 233–234), Weinstone (102) Colombat (1996) on Deleuze's suicide. Suicide is also one of the four stations of The Church of Euthanasia's manifesto, the others being sodomy (or any non-reproductive sex), abortion and euthanasia (although each has deep complexities). See thechurchofeuthenasia.org

4 Seigworth points to the mistranslation of affect, which, in most English editions of Spinoza translations, is 'emotion'. He describes the failure of singular emotion to account for *affectio* and *affectus* and then the soul, which, from two to three become 'multitudinous affectivity' (160) as described by Deleuze. Spinoza defines desire (from which all affects come) as already at least three by which all other emotions arise (1957: 37). It is clear Seigworth, Deleuze and Spinoza each account for desire as expressivity, power, passion and action while attending to its inexhaustible and mysterious multiplicity and mobility.

BIBLIOGRAPHY

Introduction

Deleuze, Gilles (1988), *Spinoza: Practical Philosophy*, trans. Robert Hurley, San Francisco: City Lights Books.
Deleuze, Gilles and Félix Guattari (1987), *A Thousand Plateaus: Capitalism and Schizophrenia*, trans. Brian Massumi, London: The Althone Press.
——— (1994), *What Is Philosophy?* trans. Hugh Tomlinson and Graham Burchell, New York: Columbia University Press.
Francione, Gary L. (2007) 'Reflections on Animals, Property and the Law and Rain Without Thunder' 10 *Law and Contemporary Problems* 9: 36
Guattari, Félix (1996), *Soft Subversions*, trans. David L. Sweet and Chet Wiener, New York: Semiotext(e).
——— (2011), *The Machinic Unconscious*, trans. Taylor Adkins, New York: Semiotext(e).
Lyotard, Jean François (1988), *The Differend: Phrases in Dispute*, trans. Georges Van Den Abbeele, Minneapolis: University of Minnesota Press.
Serres, Michel (1995), *Genesis*, trans. Genevieve James and James Nielson, Ann Arbor: University of Michigan Press.
——— (2002), *The Natural Contract*, trans. Elizabeth MacArthur and William Paulson, Ann Arbor: The University of Michigan Press.
——— (2007), *The Parasite*, trans. Lawrence Schehr, Minneapolis: University of Minnesota Press.

Chapter 1

Adams, Carol J. (1994), *Neither Man nor Beast: Feminism and the Defense of Animals*, New York: Continuum.
Adams, Carol J. (2000), *The Sexual Politics of Meat: A Feminist-Vegetarian Critical Theory*, New York: Continuum.
Davis, Karen (2005), *The Holocaust and the Henmaid's Tale: A Case for Comparing Atrocities*, New York: Lantern Books.
De Angelis, Richard (2005), 'Of Mice and Vermin: Animals as Absent Referent in Art Spiegelman's *Maus*', *International Journal of Comic Art* 7:1, 230–249.
Derrida, Jacques (2002), 'The Animal that Therefore I Am (More to Follow)', *Critical Inquiry* 28: 369–418.
Dunayer, Joan (2001), *Animal Equality: Language and Liberation*, Derwood, MD: Royce.

Gourevitch, Philip (1998), *We Wish to Inform You that Tomorrow We Will Be Killed with Our Families: Stories from Rwanda*, New York: Farrar, Straus and Giroux.

Harrison, Robert Pogue (2005), *The Dominion of the Dead*, Chicago: University of Chicago Press.

Kappeler, Suzanne (1995), 'Speciesism, Racism, Nationalism ... or the Power of Scientific Subjectivity.' In Carol J. Adams and Josephine Donovan, eds., *Animals and Women: Feminist Theoretical Explorations*, Durham, NC: Duke University Press.

Kuper, Leo (1983), *Genocide: Its Political Use in the Twentieth Century*, New Haven, CT: Yale University Press.

Mason, Jim (1997), *An Unnatural Order: Why We Are Destroying the Planet and Each Other*, New York: Continuum

Patterson, Charles (2002), *Eternal Treblinka: Our Treatment of Animals and the Holocaust*, New York: Lantern Books.

Power, Samantha (2002), *'A Problem from Hell': America and the Age of Genocide*, New York: HarperPerennial.

Quine, Willard Van Orman (1960), *Word and Object*, Cambridge, MA: MIT Press.

Santa Ana, Otto (2002), *Brown Tide Rising: Metaphors of Latinos in Contemporary American Public Discourse*, Austin: University of Texas Press.

Sax, Boria (2000), *Animals in the Third Reich: Pets, Scapegoats, and the Holocaust*, New York: Continuum.

Spiegelman, Art (1986), *Maus: A Survivor's Tale. Book 1, My Father Bleeds History*, New York: Pantheon.

Thomas, Keith (1983), *Man and the Natural World*, New York: Pantheon

Chapter 2

Ash, Kyle (2005), 'International Animal Rights: Speciesism and Exclusionary Human Dignity', *Animal Law* 11: 195–212.

Balluch, Martin and Eberhart Faber (2007), 'Trial on Personhood for Chimp Hiasl', *Altrex* 4:24, 335–342.

Bevilaqua, Ciméa Barbato (2013), 'Chimpanzees in Court: What Difference Does It Make?.' In Yoriko Otomo and Edward Mussawir, eds., *Law and the Question of the Animal: A Critical Jurisprudence*, London: Routledge, 71–88.

Bryant, Taimie L. (2006), 'Animals Unmodified: Defining Animals/Defining Human Obligations to Animals', *U. Chi. Legal F* 137: 153–155.

——— (2007a), 'Sacrificing the Sacrifice of Animals: Legal Personhood for Animals, The Status of Animals as Property, and the Presumed Primacy of Humans', *Rutgers Law Journal* 39: 247–330.

——— (2007b), 'Similarity or Difference as a Basis for Justice: Must Animals Be Like Humans to Be Legally Protected from Humans?', *Law and Contemporary Problems* 70:1, 207–254.

Cavalieri, Paola and Peter Singer, eds. (1993), *The Great Ape Project: Equality beyond humanity*, London: Macmillan.

D'Arcy, Stephen (2007), 'Deliberative Democracy, Direct Action, and Animal Advocacy', *Journal for Critical Animal Studies* 5:2, 1–16.

Deely, John. (2005), *Basics of Semiotics* (Fourth edition) (Tartu: Tartu University Press).
DeKoven, Marianne and Michael Lundblad, eds. (2012), *Species Matters: Humane Advocacy and Cultural Theory*, New York: Columbia University Press.
Derrida, Jacques (1991), '"*Eating Well*," or the Calculation of the Subject: An Interview with Jacques Derrida.' In Jacques Derrida, Eduardo Cadava, Peter Connor and Jean-Luc Nancy, eds., *Who Comes after the Subject?* trans. Avital Ronell, London: Routledge, 96–119.
———— (1992), 'Force of Law: The Mystical Foundation of Authority.' In Drucilla Cornell and Rosenfeld Michel, eds., *Deconstruction and the Possibility of Justice*, trans. Mary Quaintance, Oxon: Psychology Press.
Diamond, Cora (2004), 'Eating Meat and Eating People.' In Cass R. Sunstein and Martha C. Nussbaum, eds., *Animal Rights: Current Debates and New Directions*, New York: Oxford University Press.
Doyle, Michelle A. (1996), 'CEASE v. New England Aquarium: Standing to Challenge Marine Mammal Permits', *Ocean and Coastal Law Journal* 2:1, 189–204.
Dunayer, Joan (2004), *Speciesism*, Lexington: Royce Publishing.
———— (2007), 'Advancing Animal Rights: A Response to Jeff Perz's Anti-Speciesism, Critique of Gray Francione's Work and Discussion of My Book *Speciesism*', *Journal of Animal Law* 3: 17.
Dundas, Paul (2002), *Jains*, Oxon: Psychology Press.
Favre, David (2004a), 'A New Property Status for Animals: Equitable Self-Ownership.' In Cass R. Sunstein and Martha C. Nussbaum, eds., *Animal Rights: Current Debates and New Directions*, New York: Oxford University Press.
———— (2004b), 'Integrating Animal Interests into Our Legal System', *Animal Law* 10: 87–97.
———— (2010a), 'Living Property: A New Status for Animals Within the Legal System', *Marquette Law Review* 93: 1021–1071.
———— (2010b), 'Wildlife Jurisprudence', *Journal of Environmental Law & Litigation* 25:2, 459–510.
Francione, Gary (1996), *Rain Without Thunder: The Ideology of the Animal Rights Movement*, Philadelphia: Temple University Press.
———— (2000), *Introduction to Animal Rights: Your Child or the Dog?*, Philadelphia: Temple University Press.
———— (2007), 'Reflections on "Animals, Property, and the Law" and "Rain Without Thunder"', *Law and Contemporary Problems* 70:1, 9–57.
———— (2008), *Animals as Persons: Essays on the Abolition of Animal Exploitation*, New York: Columbia University Press.
Gray, John. (2013), *The Silence of the Animals: On Progress and Other Modern Myths*, London: Allen Lane Publishers.
Gordilho, Heron J. S. (2010), 'Sentencia Habeas Corpus n. 833085–3/2005. The 9th Criminal Court of the State of Bahia (Brazil). Case Suiça vs. Zoological Garden of the City of Salvador' Found at: http://www.derechoanimal.info/eng/page/1465/sentencia-habeas-corpus-n-833085-3or2005-the-9th-criminal-court-of-the-state-of-bahia- (accessed 7 September 2013).
Halliday, Paul D. (2010), *Habeas Corpus: From England to Empire*, Cambridge, Mass.: Belknap Press.
Haraway, Donna (2008), *When Species Meet*, Minneapolis: University of Minnesota Press.

Hribal, Jason (2010), *Fear of the Animal Planet: The Hidden History of Animal Resistance*, Petrolia: CounterPunch.

Humphrey, Mathew, and Marc Stears (2006), 'Animal Rights Protest and the Challenge to Deliberative Democracy', *Economy and Society* 35:3, 400–422.

Jensen, Derrick (2006), *Endgame, Vol. I: The Problem of Civilization*, New York: Seven Stories Press.

Kafka, Franz, and Willa Muir (1952), *Selected Short Stories*, Vol. 283, New York: Modern Library.

Kant, Immanuel (1996), *The Metaphysics of Morals*, trans. Mary Gregor, Cambridge: Cambridge University Press.

Kelch, Thomas G. (2011), *Globalization and Animal Law: Comparative Law, International Law and International Trade*, Vol. 32. Dordrecht: Kluwer.

Kuhn, Thomas (1962), *The Structure of Scientific Revolutions*, Chicago: University of Chicago Press.

Latour, Bruno (2005), *Reassembling the Social: An Introduction to Actor-Network-Theory*, Oxford: Oxford University Press.

Ledingham, Katie (Review of) 'Wolfe, Cary 2012 Before the Law: Humans and Other Animals in a Biopolitical Frame' http://societyandspace.com/reviews/reviews-archive/wolfe-cary-2012-before-the-law-reviewed-by/ (accessed November 29, 2013).

Mussawir, Ed (2013), 'The Jurisprudential Meaning of the Animal.' In Yoriko Otomo and Mussawir Edward, eds., *Law and the Question of the Animal: A Critical Jurisprudence*, London: Routledge, 89–101.

Müllerová, Hana (2012) 'Animals Finally above Objects and Stricter Criminalization of Cruelty: Some Insights in Czech Animal Legislation' la web center de los animales con derecho pp. 1–7 (February, 2012). http://www.derechoanimal.info/images/pdf/MULLEROVA-Legal-protection-of-animals-in-the-Czech-Republic.pdf (accessed November 28, 2013).

Nattrass, Kate M. (2004), 'Und Die Tiere Constitutional Protection for Germany's Animals', *Animal Law* 10: 283–312.

Nietzsche, Friedrich (1980), *Sämtliche Werke: Kritische Studienausgabe*, vol. 2, ed. Giorgio Colliand and Mazzino Montinari, Berlin: de Gruyter.

——— (1982), *Daybreak: Thoughts on the Prejudices of Morality*, trans. R. J. Hollingdale, Cambridge: Cambridge University Press.

Pettman, Dominic (2011), *Human Error: Species-Being and Media Machines*, Minneapolis: University of Minnesota Press.

Philippopoulos-Mihalopoulos, Andreas (2009), *The Successful Failing of Legal Theory (Decolonisation of Legal Knowledge)*. London: Routledge.

——— (2012) 'Mapping the Lawscape: Spatial Law and the Body' In Z. Bankowski, M. Del Mar and P. Maharg, eds., *Beyond Text in Legal Education*, Edinburgh: Edinburgh University Press.

Planck, Max (1950), *Scientific Autobiography and Other Papers*, trans. F. Gaynor, New York: Scientific Library.

Rachels, James (2004), 'Drawing the Line.' In Cass R. Sunstein, and Martha C. Nussbaum, eds., *Animal Rights: Current Debates and New Directions*, New York: Oxford University Press, 162–174.

Ridler, Victoria (2013), 'Dressing the Sow and the Legal Subjectivization of the Non-human Animal.' In Yoriko Otomo, and Mussawir Edward, eds., *Law and the Question of the Animal: A Critical Jurisprudence*, London: Routledge, 102–115.

Roberts-Miller, Patricia (2002), 'John Quincy Adams' Amistad Argument: The Problem of Outrage: Or, the Constraints of Decorum', *Rhetoric Society Quarterly* 32:2, 5–25.

Sax, Boria (2002), *Animals in the Third Reich: Pets, scapegoats and the Holocaust*, London: Continuum.

Senatori, Megan A, and Pamela D. Frash (2010), 'Future of Animal Law: Moving Beyond Preaching to the Choir', *Journal of Legal Education*, 60: 209–236.

Shakespeare, William (1974), *The Riverside Shakespeare*. Vol. 2. Houghton Mifflin: New York.

Stone, Christopher D. (2010), *Should Trees Have Standing? Law, Morality and the Environment*, Oxford: Oxford University Press.

Szasz, Thomas (1973), *The Second Sin*, Flushing, MI: Anchor.

Vehkavaara, Tommi (2002), 'Why and How to Naturalize Semiotic Concepts for Biosemiotics', *Sign Systems Studies* 293–313.

Wagman, Bruce A., and Matthew Liebman (2011), *Worldview of Animal Law*, Durham: Carolina Academic Press.

Wise, Steven M. (1995), 'How Nonhuman Animals Were Trapped in a Nonexistent Universe', *Animal Law* 1: 15–46.

——— (1998), 'Hardly a Revolution – The Eligibility of Nonhuman Animals for Dignity – Rights in a Liberal Democracy', *Vermont Law Review* 22: 794–915.

——— (2000), *Rattling the Cage: Toward Legal Rights for Animals*, New York: Basic Books.

——— (2011), 'Legal Personhood and the Nonhuman Rights Project' *17 Animal Law 1* (2011) 2–3.

——— (2003), *Drawing the line: Science and the Case for Animal Rights*, New York: Basic Books.

——— (2004), 'Animal Rights, One Step at a Time.' In Cass R. Sunstein and Martha C. Nussbaum, eds., *Animal Rights: Current Debates and New Directions*, New York: Oxford University Press.

——— (2006a), *Though the Heavens May Fall: The Landmark Trial that Led to the End of Human Slavery*, Cambridge, MA: Da Capo Press.

——— (2006b), 'The Entitlement of Chimpanzees to the Common Law Writs of *Habeas Corpus* and *de Homine Replegiando*', *Golden Gate University Law Review* 37: 219–280.

——— (2010), 'Legal Personhood and the Nonhuman Rights Project', *Animal Law*, 17: 1–11.

Wolfe, Cary (2012), *Before the Law: Humans and Other Animals in a Biopolitical Frame*, Chicago: University of Chicago Press.

Chapter 3

Baird Callicott, J. (2001), 'Introduction to Environmental Ethics.' In Michael E. Zimmerman et al.,eds., *Environmental Philosophy: From Animal Rights to Radical Ecology*, Upper Saddle River, NJ: Prentice Hall.

Benton, Ted (2003), 'Earth Others', *Radical Philosophy* 118: 38–41.
Birch, Charles (2011), 'The Postmodern Challenge to Biology.' In Charles Jencks, ed., *The Post-Modern Reader*, Chichester: John Wiley.
Calarco, Matthew (2008), *Zoographies: The Question of the Animal from Heidegger to Derrida*, New York: Columbia University Press.
Curtis, Neal (2006), 'Justice.', *Theory Culture Society*, 23:2–3 (May 2006): 454–455.
Derrida, Jacques (1995), *The Gift of Death*, trans. David Wills, Chicago: University of Chicago Press.
——— (2001), 'Force of Law: On the Mystical Foundation of Authority.' Trans. Gil Anidjar. In Gil Anidjar, ed., *Acts of Religion*, London: Routledge.
——— (2003), *Philosophy in a Time of Terror: Dialogues with Jürgen Habermas and Jacques Derrida*, trans. Giovanna Borradori, Chicago: University of Chicago Press.
——— (2005), *Rogues: Two Essays on Reason*, trans. Pascale-Anne Brault and Michael Naas, Stanford: Stanford University Press.
——— (2008), *The Animal That Therefore I Am*, trans. David Wills, New York: Fordham University Press.
Diamond, Cora (2001), 'Injustice and Animals.' In Carl Elliott, ed., *Slow Cures and Bad Philosophers: Essays on Wittgenstein, Medicine and Bioethics*, Durham and London: Duke University Press.
Koch, Andrew M. (2007), *Poststructuralism and the Politics of Method*, Lanham, MD: Lexington.
Morton, Timothy (2007), *Ecology Without Nature: Rethinking Environmental Aesthetics*. Cambridge, MA and London: Harvard University Press.
Morton, T. (2012), *The Ecological Thought*, Cambridge, MA and London: Harvard University Press.
Plumwood, Val (1993), *Feminism and the Mastery of Nature*, London and New York: Routledge.
——— (2002), *Environmental Culture: The Ecological Crisis of Reason*, London and New York: Routledge.
Rawles, Kate (2007), 'Love a Duck! Emotions, Animals and Environmental Ethics.' In Hon-Lam Li and Anthony Yeung, eds., *New Essays in Applied Ethics: Animal Rights, Personhood and the Ethics of Killing*, Basingstoke: Palgrave Macmillan.
Singer, Peter (1977), *Animal Liberation: Towards an End to Man's Inhumanity to Animals*, London: Jonathan Cape.
Soper, Kate (2011), 'Martian Poet', *Radical Philosophy* 165: 55–57.
Sterba, James P. (2006), 'Justice.' In Andrew Dobson and Eckersley Robyn, eds., *Political Theory and the Ecological Challenge*, Cambridge: Cambridge University Press.
Thomson, Alex (2005), *Deconstruction and Democracy: Derrida's Politics of Friendship*, London: Continuum.
Weil, Simone (2005), 'Human Responsibility.' In Siân Miles, ed., *Simone Weil: An Anthology*, London: Penguin.
Wirzba, Norman (2008), 'Timothy Morton, Ecology Without Nature', *Journal for the Study of Religion, Nature and Culture* 2:4, 258–259.
Wolfe, Cary (2003), *Animal Rites: American Culture, the Discourse of Species and Posthumanist Theory*, London and Chicago: University of Chicago Press.

—— (2009), 'Humanist and Posthumanist Speciesism.' In Paola Cavalieri, ed., *The Death of the Animal: A Dialogue*, New York: Columbia University Press.

Chapter 4

Bains, Paul (2006), *The Primacy of Semiosis. An Ontology of Relations*, Toronto: University of Toronto Press.

Braidotti, Rosi (2006), 'Post Human, All too Human: Towards a New Process Ontology', *Theory, Culture, Society* 23: 197–208.

Dekoven, Marianne (2009), 'Guest Column: Why Animals Now?', *PMLA* 124: 2, 361–369.

Deleuze, Gilles (1968), *Spinoza et le problème de l'expression*, Paris: Minuit.

——(1969), *Logique du sens*, Paris: Minuit.

—— (1985), *Cinéma 2. L'Image-temps*, Paris: Minuit.

—— (1989), *Cinema 2, The Time-Image*, trans. Hugh Tomlinson and Robert Galeta, Minneapolis: University of Minnesota Press.

——(1990), *Expressionism in Philosophy: Spinoza*, trans. Martin Joughin, New York: Zone Books.

——(1990), *The Logic of Sense*, trans. Mark Lester with Charles J. Stivale, New York: Columbia University Press.

—— (1993), *Critique et clinique*. Paris: Minuit.

—— (1997), *L'Abécédaire de Gilles Deleuze*, dir. Pierre-André Boutang, Paris: Editions Montparnasse; Zone 1 DVD;

——(1997), *Essays Critical and Clinical*, trans. Daniel W. Smith and Michael A. Greco, Minneapolis: University of Minnesota Press.

Deleuze, Gilles and Félix Guattari (1980), *Mille Plateaux*, Paris: Minuit

——(1987), *A Thousand Plateaus*, trans. Brian Massumi, Minneapolis: University of Minnesota Press.

—— (1991), *Qu'est-ce que la philosophie?*, Paris: Minuit.

——(1994), *What Is Philosophy?*, Trans. Hugh Tomlinson and Graham Burchell, New York: Columbia University Press.

—— (1977), *Dialogues*, Paris: Flammarion; (1997) *Dialogues II*; (1987), *Dialogues*; (2002), *Dialogues II*, trans. Hugh Tomlinson and Barbara Habberjam, New York: Columbia University Press.

Deleuze, Gilles 'A as in Animal', http://www.youtube.com/watch?v=L_ZWwLKHQnU (accessed 8 March 2011).

Gane, Nicholas and Donna Haraway (2006), 'When We Have Never Been Human, What Is to Be Done?: Interview with Donna Haraway', *Theory, Culture, Society* 23: 135–158.

Haraway, Donna (2008), *When Species Meet*, Minneapolis: University of Minnesota Press, http://striphas.blogspot.com/2006/09/becoming-intense-becoming-haraway.html. Accessed 12 April 2012.

Lorimer, Jamie (2010), 'Ladies and Gentlemen, Behold the Enemy!', *Environment and Planning D: Society and Space* 28: 40–42.

Massumi, Brian (2002), *Parables for the Virtual: Movement, Affect, Sensation*, Durham, NC: Duke University Press.

Seigworth, Gregory J. (2005), 'From Affection to Soul.' In Charles J. Stivale ed.,
    Gilles Deleuze: Key Concepts, Chesham UK: Acumen, and Montreal: McGill
    Queens University Press.
Striphas, Ted (2006), 'Becoming Intense, Becoming Haraway.' 7 September
    (accessed 31/5/2011)
Turner, Lynn (2008), '"Stop Looking for Some Singe Defining Difference": The
    Ongoing *Arkhe* of Donna Haraway.' *Parallax* 14:3, 142–145.
Van Dooren, Thom (2009), 'Thinking with Dogs: A Review of Donna Haraway's
    When Species Meet', *Subjectivity* 28: 357–361.
Von Uexküll, Jacob (1957), 'A Stroll through the Worlds of Animals and Men',
    In Schiller, Claire, trans. and ed. *Instinctive Behaviour: The Development of a
    Modern Concept*, New York: International Universities Press.
Weisberg, Zipporah (2009), 'The Broken Promises of Monsters: Haraway, Animals
    and the Humanist Legacy', *Journal for Critical Animal Values* 7:2, 21–61.
Williams, Jeffrey J. (2009), 'Donna Haraway's Critters.' *The Chronicle of
    Higher Education* 18 October, http://chronicle.com/article/A-Theory-of-
    Critters-/48802/ Accessed 24 September 2011.
Williams, Linda (2009), 'Haraway Contra Deleuze and Guattari: The Question of
    the Animals.' *Communication, Politics & Culture* 42:1, 42–54.
Zourabichvili, François (1994), *Deleuze. Une philosophie de l'événement*, Paris:
    Presses universitaires de France.

Chapter 5

Adair, Gilbert (2000), 'Introduction.' In Raymond Queneau, ed., *Zazie in the
    Métro*, trans. Barbara Wright, New York & London: Penguin Books.
Barthes, Roland (1972), 'Zazie and Literature.' In Barthes, Roland, ed. *Critical
    Essays*, trans. Richard Howard, Evanston IL: Northwestern University Press.
Chtcheglov, Ivan (1989), 'Formulary for a New Urbanism.' In Knapp Ken, ed.,
    Situationist International Anthology, Berkeley, CA: Bureau of Public Secrets.
Debord, Guy (1989a), 'Introduction to a Critique of Urban Geography.' In Knapp
    Ken, ed., *Situationist International Anthology*, Berkeley, CA: Bureau of Public
    Secrets.
——— (1989b), 'Theory of the Dérive.' In Knapp Ken, ed., *Situationist
    International Anthology*, Berkeley, CA: Bureau of Public Secrets.
Deleuze, Gilles (1989), *Cinema 2: The Time Image*, trans. Hugh Tomlinson and
    Roberta Galeta, Minneapolis: University of Minnesota Press.
Deleuze, Gilles and Félix Guattari (1986), *Kafka: Toward a Minor Literature*, trans.
    Dana Polan, Minneapolis: University of Minnesota Press.
——— (1987), *A Thousand Plateaus: Capitalism and Schizophrenia*, trans. Brian
    Massumi, Minneapolis: University of Minnesota Press.
Gobert, David L. (1986), 'The Essential Character in Queneau's *Zazie Dans Le
    Métro*', *Symposium* 40:2, 91–106.
Queneau, Raymond. (1981), *Exercises in Style*, trans. Barbara Wright, New York:
    New Directions.
——— (2000), *Zazie in the Métro*, trans. Barbara Wright, New York & London:
    Penguin Books.

Chapter 6

Abbott, Mathew (2011), 'The Animal for Which Animality is an Issue: Nietzsche, Agamben and the Anthropological Machine', *Angelaki: Journal of the Theoretical Humanities* 16:4, 87–99.

Abraham, Nicholas and Maria Torok (1986), *The Wolf Man's Magic Word: A Cryptonomy*, trans. Nicholas Rand, Minneapolis: University of Minnesota Press.

Agamben, Giorgio (1998), *Homo Sacer and Bare Life*, trans. David Heller-Roazen, Stanford: Stanford University Press.

Balzac, Honoré de (1977), *The Wild Ass's Skin*, trans. Herbert J. Hunt, London: Penguin Books.

Baring-Gould, Sabine (1995), *The Book of Werewolves*, London: Senate.

Beckett, Samuel (2010), 'Texts for Nothing.' In *Texts for Nothing and Other Prose 1950–1976*, ed. Mark Nixon London: Faber and Faber.

Borges, Jorge Luis (1998), 'The Garden of Forking Paths.' In trans. Andrew Hurley. *Collected Fictions*, London: Allen Lane.

Brassier, Ray (2007), 'The Truth of Extinction.' In *Nihil Unbound: Enlightenment and Extinction*, London: Palgrave, pp. 205–239.

Broglio, Ron (2011), *Surface Encounters: Thinking with Animals and Art*, Minneapolis, University of Minnesota Press.

Deleuze, Gilles and Félix Guattari (1988), *A Thousand Plateaus: Capitalism and Schizophrenia*, trans. Brain Massumi, London: Athlone Press.

Derrida, Jacques (1989), *Of Spirit: Heidegger and the Question*, trans. Geoff Bennington and Rachel Bowlby, Chicago: University of Chicago Press.

——— (1994), *Specters of Marx: The State of Debt, the Work of Mourning & the New International*, trans. Peggy Kamuf, London: Routledge.

——— (2002), 'The Animal that Therefore I am Not (More to Follow)', trans. David Wills. *Critical Inquiry*, 28:2, 372–375.

——— (2009), *The Beast and the Sovereign, Volume 1*, trans. Geoffrey Bennington, Chicago: University of Chicago Press.

Freud, Sigmund (2010), *The 'Wolfman': From the History of an Infantile Neurosis*, trans. Louise Adey Huish, London: Penguin.

Gualandi, Alberto (2009), 'Errancies of the Human: French philosophies of Nature and the Overturning of the Copernican Revolution.' In Damian Veal, ed. *Collapse V*, Falmouth: Urbanomic.

Hardt, Michael andAntonio Negri, (2000), *Empire*, Cambridge: Harvard University Press.

Hell, Julia (2010), 'Imperial Ruin Gazers, or Why did Scipio Weep?.' In Julia Hell and Andreas Schönle, eds., *Ruins of Modernity*, Durham: Duke University Press.

Ingold, Tim (2010), 'Ways of Mind-walking, Reading, Writing, Painting', *Visual Studies* 25:1, 15–23.

Land, Nick (1992), *The Thirst for Annihilation: Georges Bataille and Virulent Nihilism*, London: Routledge.

Lippit, Akira Mizuta (2000), *Electric Animal: Towards a Rhetoric of Wildlife*, Minneapolis: University of Minnesota Press.

Lovecraft, H.P. (2008), 'At the Mountains of Madness.' In *Necronomicon: The Best Weird Tales of H.P. Lovecraft – Commemorative Edition*, ed. Stephen Jones. London: Gollanz, pp. 422–503.

Meillassoux, Quentin (2008), *After Finitude: An Essay on the Necessity of Contingency*, trans. Ray Brassier, London: Continuum.

Métraux, Alfred (1972), *Voodoo in Haiti*, trans. Hugo Charteris, Schocken Books: New York.

Negarestani, Reza (2008), *Cyclonopedia: Complicity with Anonymous Materials*, Melbourne: Re.press.

Nietzsche, Friedrich (2006), *Thus Spoke Zarathustra*, trans. Adrian del Caro, Cambridge: Cambridge University Press.

Rossello, Diego H (2012), 'Hobbes and Wolf Man: Melancholy and Animality in the Origins of Modern Sovereignty', *New Literary History*, 43:2, Spring, 255–279.

Rousseau, Jean-Jacques (1953), *The Confessions*, trans. J.M Cohen. London: Penguin.

Shukin, Nicole (2009), *Animal Capital: Rendering Life in Biopolitical Times*, Minneapolis: University of Minnesota Press.

Solnit, Rebecca (2007), *Wanderlust: A History of Walking*, London: Verso.

Thacker, Eugene (2011), *In the Dust of This Planet: Horror of Philosophy Vol. 1*, Washington: Zero Books.

Wolfe, Cary (2013), *Before the Law: Humans and Other Animals in a Biopolitical Frame*, Chicago: University of Chicago Press.

Woodward, Ben (2013), *On an Ungrounded Earth: Towards a New Geophilosophy*, Brooklyn: Punctum Books.

Benjamin, Walter (1998), *The Origin of German Tragic Drama*, trans. John Osborne, London: Verso.

Filmography

Encounters at the End of the World (Werner Herzog, 2007).

Evil Dead II (Sam Raimi, 1987).

In the Mouth of Madness (John Carpenter, 1994).

Chapter 7

Bartoloni, Paolo (2010), 'Blanchot and Ambiguity', *CLCWeb: Comparative Literature and Culture* 12.4. <http://dx.doi.org/10.7771/1481?4374.1675>

Bataille, Georges (1986), *Erotism – Death and Sensuality*, trans. M. Dalwood, San, Francisco: City Lights Books.

——— (1989), *The Tears of Eros*, trans. Peter Connor, San, Francisco: City Lights Books.

——— (1992), *Theory of Religion*, trans. Robert Hurley, New York: Zone Books.

Bergo, Bettina (2005), 'The Trace in Derrida and Levinas.' *Canadian Philosophical Association*, London, Ontario, https://www.academia.edu/1705190/The_Trace_in_Derrida_and_Levinas.

Cixous, Hélène (1989), 'Preface' in Clarice Lispector, *The Stream of Life*, trans. Elizabeth Lowe, Minneapolis: University of Minnesota Press.

——— (1990), *Reading with Clarice Lispector*, trans. Verena Andermatt Conley, Minneapolis: University of Minnesota Press.

——— (1993), *Three Steps on The Ladder of Writing*, trans. Sarah Cornell and Susan Sellers, New York: Columbia University Press.

Deleuze, Gilles (1995), *Negotiations*, trans. Martin Joughin, New York: Columbia University Press.

———— (1997), *Essays Critical and Clinical*, trans. Daniel W. Smith, Minneapolis: University of Minnesota Press.

———— (2000), *Proust and Signs*, trans. Richard Howard, Minneapolis: University of Minnesota Press.

———— (2004), *Difference and Repetition*, trans. Paul Patton, London: Continuum.

———— (2006), *Two Regimes of Madness*, trans. Ames Hodges and Mike Taromina, New York & Los Angeles: Semiotext(e).

Deleuze, Gilles and Félix Guattari (1994), *What Is Philosophy?* trans. Hugh Tomlinson and Graham Burchell, New York: Columbia University Press.

———— (2003), *A Thousand Plateaus – Capitalism and Schizophrenia*, trans. Brian Massumi, London & New York: Continuum.

Derrida, Jacques (1974), 'White Mythology: Metaphor in the Text of Philosophy', *New Literary History* 6:1, *On Metaphor*: Autumn, 5–74.

———— (1992), *Acts of Literature*, trans. Derek Attridge, New York, London: Routledge.

Dimoula, Kiki (2012), *The Brazen Plagiarism-Selected Poems*, trans. Cecile Inglessis Margellos and Rika Lesser, New Haven & London: Yale University Press.

Douglas, Mary (1972), 'Deciphering a Meal', *Daedalus* 101:1, *Myth, Symbol, and Culture*, Winter, 61–81.

Hardt, Michael (2002), 'Exposure: Pasolini in the Flesh.' In Brian, Massumi ed., *A Shock to Thought-Expressionism after Deleuze and Guattari*, London, New York: Routledge.

Irigaray, Luce (1985), *This Sex which Is not One*, trans.Carolyn Burke: Cornell University Press.

Kafka, Frantz (1978), *Letters to Friends Family and Editors*, trans. Richard and Clare Winston, New York: Schocken.

Levinas, Emmanuel (1979), *Totality and Infinity: An Essay on Exteriority*, trans. Alphonsos Lingis, The Hague, Boston, London: Martinus Nijhoff Publishers.

Lispector, Clarice (1988), *The Passion According to G.H.*, trans. Ronald W. Sousa, Minneapolis: University of Minnesota Press.

Lispector, Clarice (2012), *The Hour of the Star*, trans. Giovanni Pontiero, New York: New Directions.

———— (1992), *A Breath of Life*, trans. Johnny Lorenz, New York: New Directions.

Mardsen, Jill (2004), 'Bataille and the Poetic Fallacy of Animality.' In Peter Atterton and Callarco Mathew, eds., *Animal Philosophy: Ethics and identity*, New York, London: Continuum.

Moser, Benjamin (2009), *Why This World? A Biography of Clarice Lispector*, Oxford: Oxford University Press.

Noys, Benjamin (2000), *Georges Bataille: A Critical Introduction*, London, Sterling, Virginia: Pluto Press.

Oliver, Kelly (2001), *Witnessing: Beyond Recognition*, Minneapolis: University of Minnesota Press.

Parker, Richard Guy (2009), *Bodies, Pleasures and Passions: Sexual Culture in Contemporary Brazil*, Nashville: Vanderbilt University Press.

Peixoto, Marta (1994), *Gender Narrative and Violence in Clarice Lispector*, Minneapolis: University of Minnesota.

Phillips, W. P., John (2011), 'The Poetic Thing (On Poetry and Deconstruction)', *The Oxford Literary Review* 33:2, 231–243.

Piers, Armstrong (1999), *Third World Literary Fortunes-Brazilian Culture and Its International Reception*, London, Ontario: Associated University Presses.

Regier, Willis Goth (2004), *Book of the Sphinx*, Lincoln, NE: Bison Books.

Ross, Stephen David (2004), 'The Writing of the Birds in My Language.' In Peter Atterton and Callarco Mathew, eds., *Animal Philosophy: Ethics and Identity*, New York, London: Continuum.

Chapter 8

Agamben, Giorgio (2004), *The Open: Man and Animal*, trans. Kevin Attell, Stanford: Stanford University Press.

Blake, William (1997), 'Milton: A Poem.' In Erdman, David, Harold Bloom and William Golding, eds., *The Complete Poetry and Prose of William Blake*, Flushing, MI: Anchor.

———— (1997), 'Urizen.' In Erdman, David, Harold Bloom and William Golding, eds., *The Complete Poetry and Prose of William Blake*, Flushing, MI: Anchor.

Deleuze, Gilles (2000), *Proust and Signs*, trans. Richard Howard, Minneapolis: University of Minnesota Press.

———— (2005), *Francis Bacon: The Logic of Sensation*, trans. Daniel W. Smith, London: Continuum.

Derrida, Jacques (1995), *Geschlecht*, Vienna: Passagen Verlag Ges.M.B.H.

———— (2002), *Without Alibi*, ed., trans., and with an introduction by Peggy Kamuf, Stanford: Stanford University Press.

Deleuze, Gilles and Félix Guattari (1987), *A Thousand Plateaus: Capitalism and Schizophrenia*, trans. Brian Massumi, London: The Althone Press.

Lawlor, Len (2007), '"Animals Have No Hand": An Essay on Animality in Derrida', *CR: The New Centennial Review* 7:2, 43–69.

Chapter 9

Agamben, Giorgio (1998), *Homo Sacer: Sovereign Power and Bare Life*, Stanford, CA: Stanford University Press.

———— (2004), *The Open: Man and Animal*, Stanford, CA: Stanford University Press.

Ansell Pearson, Keith (1999), *Germinal Life*, London, UK: Routledge.

Aoki, Tetsuo (2005), *Curriculum in a New Key: The Collected Works of Ted T. Aoki*, Mahwah, NJ: Lawrence Erlbaum Associates, Publishers.

Braidotti, Rosi (2011), 'The Politics of "life itself" and New ways of Dying.' In Diane Coole and Frost Samantha, eds., *New Materialisms: Ontology, Agency, and Politics*, Durham, NC: Duke University Press.

Colebrook, Claire (2010), *Deleuze and the Meaning of Life*, New York: Continuum.

———— (2011), 'Time and Autopoeisis: The Organism Has No Future.' In Laura Giallaume and Hughes Joe, eds., *Deleuze and the Body*, Edinburgh: Edinburgh University Press.

Cubberly, E (1916/1929), *Public School Administration*, Cambridge, MA: Riverside Press.

Deleuze, Gilles (1994), *Difference and Repetition*, trans. Paul Patton, New York, NY: Columbia University Press.

——— (2000), *Proust and Signs*, trans. Richard Howard, Minneapolis: University of Minnesota Press.

Deleuze, Gilles and Claire Parnet, Gilles Deleuze's ABC Primer, dir. Pierre-Andre Boutang, accessed December 13, 2010, http://www.langlab.wayne.edu/Cstivale/D-G/ABC1.html.

Deleuze, Gilles and Félix Guattari. (1986), *Kafka: Toward a Minor Literature*, trans. Dana Polan, Minneapolis: University of Minnesota Press

———(1987), *A Thousand Plateaus*, trans. Brian Massumi, Minneapolis, MN: University of Minnesota Press.

———.(1994), *What Is Philosophy?*, trans. Hugh Tomlinson and Graham Burchell, New York: Columbia University Press.

Deleuze, Gilles and Claire Parnet, *Gilles Deleuze's ABC Primer*, dir. Pierre-Andre Boutang, accessed 13 December 2010, http://www.langlab.wayne.edu/Cstivale/D-G/ABC1.html.

Dosse, Francois (2010), *Gilles Deleuze & Felix Guattari: Intersecting Lives*, New York: Columbia University Press.

Genosko, Gary. (2002), *Felix Guattari: An Aberrant Introduction*, New York: Continuum.

Gough, Noel (2004), 'RhizomANTically Becoming-cyborg: Performing Posthuman Pedagogies', *Educational Philosophy and Practice* 36: 253–265.

Guattari, Felix., (1972), *Psychanalyse et transversalité*, Paris: Maspero/La Decouvertéé.

——— (2009), *Chaosophy: Texts and Interviews 1972–1977*, trans. David L. Sweet, Jarred Becker and Taylor Adkins, New York: Semiotext(e).

——— (2000), *The Three Ecologies*, trans. Ian Pindar and Paul Sutton, New Brunswick, NJ: Althone Press.

Guattari, Félix and Suely Rolnik (2008), *Molecular Revolution in Brazil*, trans. Karel Clapshow and Brian Holmes, New York: Semiotext(e).

Hardt, Michael and Antonio Negri (2001), *Empire*, Cambridge, MA: Harvard University Press.

Harman, Graham (2009), *Towards Speculative Realism: Essays and Lectures*, Washington, DC: Zero Books.

Holland, Eugene (2012), *Nomad Citizenship: Free-market Communism and the Slow-motion General Strike*, Minneapolis: University of Minnesota Press.

Hroch, Petra (2013), 'Becoming-Ecological: Dwelling withlin the "Animal Kingdom"', *Journal of Curriculum and Pedagogy* 10: 18–20.

Lambert, Gregg (2005), 'What the Earth Thinks.' In Ian Buchanan and Lambert Gregg, eds., *Deleuze and Space*, Toronto, ON: University of Toronto Press.

Levine, Jonathan. [Director],(2013),*Warm bodies* (Motion Picture), USA: Summit Entertainment.

Lewis, T. and R. Khan (2010), *Education out of Bounds: Reimagining Cultural Studies for a Posthuman Age*, New York, NY: Palgrave Macmillan.

MacCormack, Patricia (2004), 'The Probe-head and the Faces of Australia: From Australia Post to Pluto', *Journal of Australian Studies* 28:81, 135–143.

——— (2012), *Posthuman Ethics*, Farnham: Ashgate.

——— (2013), 'Gracious Pedagogy', *Journal of Curriculum and Pedagogy* 10:1, 13–17.

Morton, Timothy (2007), *Ecology without Nature: Rethinking Environmental Aesthetics*, Cambridge, MA: Harvard University Press.

——— (2010), *The Ecological Thought*, Cambridge, MA: Harvard University Press.

Nietzsche, Friedrich (2000), *On the Genealogy of Morals*, trans. Walter Kaufman, New York: Random House.

Reynolds, Brian (2002), *Becoming-criminal: Transversal Performance and Cultural Dissidence in Early Modern England*, Baltimore: The Johns Hopkins University Press.

Rousseau, Jean-Jacques (1979). *Emile or on Education*, trans. A. Bloom, New York: Basic Books.

Spinoza, Baruch (1985), *The Collected Writings of Spinoza vol. 1*, trans. Edwin Curley, Princeton: Princeton University Press.

Steel, Keith (2012), 'With the World, or Bound to Face the Sky: The Postures of the Wolf-child Hesse.' In J.J. Cohened., *Animal Vegetable, Mineral: Ethics and Objects*, Washington, DC: Oliphant Books.

Thacker, Eugene (2011), *In the Dust of this Planet: Horror of Philosophy vol.1*, Washington, DC: Zero Books.

Uexküll, Jakob von (2010), *A Foray into the Worlds of Animals and Humans: A Theory of Meaning*, trans. Joseph D. O' Neill, Minneapolis: University of Minnesota Press.

Chapter 10

Babiker, Gloria and Lois Arnold (1997), *The Language of Injury: Comprehending Self-Mutilation*, Leicester: The British Psychology Society.

Brickman, Barbara Jane (2004), '"Delicate" Cutters: Gendered Self-Mutilation and Attractive Flesh in Medical Discourse', *Body and Society* 10:4, 87–111.

Butler, Judith (2004), *Precarious Life: The Powers of Mourning and Violence*, London: Verso.

Favazza, Armando R. (1996), *Bodies Under Siege: Self-Mutilation and Body Modification in Culture and Psychiatry*, Baltimore: The Johns Hopkins University Press.

Freud, Sigmund (1961), 'The Economic Problem of Masochism.' In ed. and trans. James Strachey, *The Standard Edition of the Complete Psychological Works of Sigmund Freud, Volume XIX*, London: Hogarth Press and the Institute of Psychoanalysis.

Grosz, Elizabeth (1994), *Volatile Bodies: Towards a Corporeal Feminism*, Bloomington, IN: Indiana University Press.

Kafka, Franz (2000), 'The Hunger Artist.' In Kafka, Franz, *The Metamorphosis, In the Penal Colony, and Other Stories*, trans. and ed. Joachim Neugroschel, New York: Scribner Paperback Fiction.

Kaplan, Louise J (2000), *Female Perversions*, London: Penguin.

Kristeva, Julia (1982), *Powers of Horror: An Essay on Abjection*, trans. Leon S. Roudiez, New York: Columbia University Press.

——— (1984), *Revolution in Poetic Language*, trans. Margaret Waller, New York: Columbia University Press.

Lyotard, Jean-François (1993), *The Inhuman*, trans. Geoffrey Bennington and Rachel Bowlby, Cambridge: Polity Press.
MacCormack, Patricia (2012), *Posthuman Ethics*, Farnham: Ashgate.
Scarry, Elaine (1985), *The Body in Pain*, New York: Oxford University Press.
Sontag, Susan (2003), *Regarding the Pain of Others*, London: Penguin.
Strong, Marilee (2000), *A Bright Red Scream: Self-Mutilation and the Language of Pain*, London: Virago Press.

Chapter 11

Blanchot Maurice., (1995), *The Writing of the Disaster* trans. Anne Smock, Lincoln: University of Nebraska Press.
Baofu, Peter (2007), *Future of Complexity: Conceiving a Better Way to Understand Order and Chaos*, River Edge, NJ: World Scientific.
Bataille, Georges (1992), *Theory of Religion*, trans. Robert Hurley, New York: Zone Books.
Braidotti, Rosi (2006), *Transpositions*, Cambridge: Polity.
Cocks, Doug (2003), *Deep Futures: Our Prospects for Survival*, Montreal: McGill-Queen's University Press.
Colombat, André (1996), 'Deleuze's Death as an Event', *Man and World* 29:3, 235–249.
Deleuze, Gilles (1994), *Difference and Repetition*, trans. Paul Patton, New York: Columbia University Press.
Deleuze, Gilles and Félix Guattari (1987), *A Thousand Plateaus: Capitalism and Schizophrenia*, trans. Brian Massumi, London: The Althone Press.
Gatens, Moira and Genevieve Lloyd (1999), *Collective Imaginings: Spinoza Past and Present*, London: Routledge.
Guattari, Félix (2000), *The Three Ecologies*, trans. Ian Pindar and Paul Sutton, London: Athlone.
—— (2011), *The Machinic Unconscious*, trans. Taylor Adkins, New York: Semiotext(e).
Leslie, John (1998), *End of the World: The Science and Ethics of Human Extinction*, London: Routledge.
McKee, Jeffrey Kevin (2003), *Sparing Nature: The Conflict Between Human Population Growth and Earth's Biodiversity*, New Brunswick, NJ: Rutgers University Press.
Nancy, Jean-Luc (2000), *Being Singular Plural*, trans. Robert D. Richardson and Anne E. O'Byrne, Stanford: Stanford University Press.
Serres, Michel (2000), *The Birth of Physics*, trans. Jack Hawkes, Manchester: Clinamen.
—— (2002), *The Natural Contract*, trans. Elizabeth MacArthur and William Paulson, Ann Arbor: The University of Michigan Press.
Spinoza, Baruch (1957), *The Road to Inner Freedom*, trans. Dagobert D. Runes, New York: Philosophical Library.
—— (1994), *Ethics*, trans. Edwin Curley, London: Penguin.
Weinstone, Ann (2004), *Avatar Bodies: A Tantra for Posthumanism*, Minneapolis: University of Minnesota Press.

INDEX